Spiritual Gems

The Mystical Qur'ān Commentary
Ascribed to Ja'far al-Ṣādiq
as contained in
Sulamī's *Ḥaqā'iq al-Tafsīr*
from the text of Paul Nwyia

Translated and Annotated
Farhana Mayer

FONS VITAE

First published in 2011 by
Fons Vitae
49 Mockingbird Valley Drive
Louisville, KY 40207
http://www.fonsvitae.com
Email: fonsvitaeky@aol.com

Library of Congress Control Number: 2009933709

ISBN 9781891785306

Printed in Canada

Set in Adobe Minion Pro 10.5/13.5

The Fons Vitae Qurʾānic Commentary Series
Directly available from Fons Vitae

Tafsīr al-Jalālayn by Jalāl al-Dīn al-Suyūṭī
and Jalāl al-Dīn al-Maḥallī

Tafsīr Ibn ʿAbbās by Ibn ʿAbbās (attrib.)
and Muḥammad ibn Yaʿqūb al-Fīrūzābādī (attrib.)

al-Wāḥidī's *Asbāb al-Nuzūl* by ʿAli Aḥmad ibn al-Wāḥidī

Tafsīr al-Tustarī by Sahl b. ʿAbd Allāh al-Tustarī

The Immense Ocean (*al-Baḥr al-Madīd*) by Aḥmad ibn ʿAjība A Thirteenth Century Quranic Commentary on the Chapters of the All-Merciful, the Event, and Iron

Spiritual Gems: The Mystical Qurʾān Commentary
by Jaʿfar al-Ṣādiq (ascribed)

Table of Contents

Foreword

My first introduction to the Qur'ānic commentary attributed to Imām Jaʿfar al-Ṣādiq was from a brief mention of it in Annemarie Schimmel's 1975 work, *Mystical Dimensions of Islam*. This brief "taste" (to use a Sufi term) of Shīʿī and Sufi hermeneutics whetted my appetite for more and, in fact, led me to begin my studies of the Arabic language. Like mystical commentary itself, Farhana Mayer's translation, notes, and analysis address many layers of meaning and different kinds of readers. For scholars of Islamic texts, she has provided invaluable notes on how specific Arabic terms are used and their relationship to other areas of Islamic thought. For those interested in the Qur'ān, she has given us a very readable but accurate translation of a highly influential and early mystical commentary. The accompanying analysis of its themes and methodologies skillfully illuminates the coherency of what might otherwise seem atomistic. For those who read works such as this one for their ongoing power to inspire, the subtlety and richness of Jaʿfar al-Ṣādiq's comments are fully on display here. In short, Farhana Mayer has provided an exquisite "setting" for these beautiful gems. Her efforts are our good fortune.

Kristin Zahra Sands
Professor of Islamic Studies, Sarah Lawrence College

بِسْمِ ٱللَّهِ ٱلرَّحْمَٰنِ ٱلرَّحِيمِ

Acknowledgements

أَفَلَا يَتَدَبَّرُونَ ٱلْقُرْءَانَ أَمْ عَلَىٰ قُلُوبٍ أَقْفَالُهَآ ﴿٢٤﴾

Will they not ponder the Qurʾān or have [their] hearts their locks upon them?

My heartfelt thanks to Virginia Gray Henry and Neville Blakemore for their loving embrace of this work, for working with patience over long distance, under pressure, and thank you, Paul Carney and Elena Lloyd-Sidle. Particular thanks to Reza Shah Kazemi for putting forward the idea of this translation and for checking the script. My respectful and fond thanks to K. R., an inspiring lady, full of understanding support and gentle encourgement. Jamil Javaheri, I thank for his kind and generous help with computer matters. I am grateful to Toby Mayer for the support he gave and for reading most of the script—his comments were most useful. My special thanks also to Feras Hamza for his invaluable review of the translation. Needless to say, all errors and oddities are mine. I thank the Institute of Ismaili Studies, London, Maha Sharba, Fiona Ward, Mustafa Shah and Omar Alí-de-Unzaga for his support.

I would also like to acknowledge my daughter, Nadia Mariam, whose birth marked the advent of this other treasure-trove in my life, and who then was accomodating and understanding as I laboured to give birth to this book.

God reward them all.

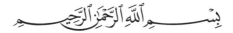

Spiritual Gems has been written as a work of engaged scholarship. As well as containing the translation, it is an exposition of the commentary. This book should be read on a spiritual register. Though it is clothed in Muslim garments, the wisdom is universal. The truths appearing here in Qurʾānic and Islamic form are to be found in all traditions within their diverse forms.

This wisdom and these truths are shared with all readers, in this book and in its companion volumes. Among the readers will be some who will smile with quiet recognition; some who are overwhelmed, at least initially, but who persevere; some who will baulk heavily and who should perhaps set this aside. And there will also be those who immediately taste the dew upon their lips, maybe not for the first time, and who respond to the gentle, beckoning caress, the soft, silent swirl of the holy mist of God's peace and set forth, walking with God, towards the unimaginably beautiful and peaceful, the indescribably loving and lovable.

وَٱلْحَمْدُ لِلَّهِ رَبِّ ٱلْعَـٰلَمِينَ وَبِهِ نَسْتَعِينُ

بِسۡمِ ٱللَّهِ ٱلرَّحۡمَٰنِ ٱلرَّحِيمِ

Translator's Introduction

THE IMĀM JAʿFAR AL-ṢĀDIQ

Islamic history suffers from no dearth of luminaries, be they mystics, philosophers, theologians, physicians, or grammarians. A star among these is Abū ʿAbd Allāh Jaʿfar al-Ṣādiq b. Muḥammad al-Bāqir b. ʿAlī Zayn al-ʿĀbidīn b. Ḥusayn b. ʿAlī, the fifth generation grandson of the Prophet of Islam. He was born in Medina in the year 83/702, and although he travelled outside Medina, it was there that he lived and then died, in the year 148/765.

Jaʿfar al-Ṣādiq is a meeting point for diverse Muslims. Through his parentage Jaʿfar brought together in his person, the Prophet's familial line and that of the paramount Sunnī Companion, Abū Bakr, from whom his mother, Umm Farwah bint Qāsim b. Muḥammad b. Abī Bakr al-Ṣiddīq, was descended. Within the Shīʿī world, he is the last imam common to both the Ithnā ʿasharīyah, or Twelvers, and the Ismāʿīlīyah, or Seveners (some of whom who hold him to be the fifth imam).[1] Among the Sufis he is venerated as a spiritual 'pole' (*quṭb*) and is to be found in the lineages (*silsilahs*) of most Sufi orders (*ṭuruq*). The Sunnīs have a deep reverence for him, holding him next only to his forefather ʿAlī b. Abī Ṭālib (d. 40/661) for his combination of holiness and knowledge.[2]

By all accounts, Jaʿfar's profoundly God-aware ethics of truthfulness, justice, tolerance, and peaceability, were exemplary indeed. Reports in

---

1 See M. G. Hodgson, *The Venture of Islam*, vol. 1 (Chicago: University of Chicago Press, 1974), p. 261; Ibn ʿInabah, *ʿUmdat al-ṭālib* (Najaf: Manshūrāt al-Maṭbaʿah al-Ḥaydarīyah, 1961), pp. 195–96.

2 See Victor Danner, 'The Early Development of Sufism', in *Islamic Spirituality: Foundations* (London: SCM Press Ltd., 1989), p. 246: 'the early Shīʿite Imams of the first century or so of Islam were also authorities in Sunnism and in Sufism.'

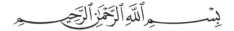

Muslim sources,[3] not least this commentary, reveal his ontological role towards God and creature: when he faced creation he was a divine ambassador, manifesting God's constant and patient availability, transmitting the divine qualities, guiding to that wise proximity to God that comes through living in a godly manner, in harmony with the divine; when he faced God, he was an intercessor for creation.

It was at the age of thirty-four years that Jaʿfar succeeded his father Muḥammad al-Bāqir (d. 117/736), as the imam of the Shīʿah. In the midst of the unstable and violent contemporary political situation, Jaʿfar maintained an attitude of quietism. Rather than engage in rebellions or pursue political power, he chose to focus on developing spirituality and the various branches of knowledge, even when undergoing periods of imprisonment due to Umayyad and ʿAbbāsid suspicions of the Alid imam. Distancing himself from power struggles, he concentrated his energy and formidable intellect on the religious and spiritual dimensions of the imamate, resulting in his extraordinary, extensive impact on the Islamic world.[4]

For his community directly, he was their imam, their religious and spiritual guide. Shīʿī jurisprudence received its definitive form at the hands of Jaʿfar al-Ṣādiq, who was responsible for the codification of Shīʿī religious law—called the Jaʿfariyya *madhhab*. The majority of Shīʿī *ḥadīth*s and traditions are reported on the authority of the Imām al-Ṣādiq and his father, Muḥammad al-Bāqir.[5]

Yet for non-Shīʿah too, he provided such guidance appropriately, as is evident in his preeminent position among the Sufis. He was a plenary

---

3 See, for example, the works of Furāt al-Kūfī, Muḥammad b. Yaʿqūb al-Kulaynī, Qāḍī Nuʿmān al-Tamīmī, ʿAbd al-Karīm al-Shahrastānī.

4 See Y. Richard, *Shi'ite Islam*, trans. A. Nevill (Oxford, UK: Blackwell, 1995), pp. 36–37; M. S. Hodgson, 'Dja'far al-Ṣādik', *EI²*, pp. 374–75; al-Shahrastānī, *Kitāb al-milal wa'l-nihal*, trans. A. K. Kazi, J. G. Flynn, *Muslim Sects and Divisions* (London: Kegan Paul International, 1984), p. 142 of *Muslim Sects*; F. Daftary, *Ismāʿīlīs in Medieval Muslim Societies* (London: I.B.Tauris and the Institute of Ismaili Studies, 2005), p. 20.

5 See S. M. Ḥ. Ṭabāṭabāʾī, *Shi'ite Islam*, trans. Seyyed Hossein Nasr (Albany: State University of New Press, 1977), p. 204, where it is reported that 'the number of traditions preserved from the fifth and sixth Imams is more than all the hadith that have been recorded from the Prophet and the other ten Imams combined'.

teacher and had among his students more than one early 'father' of the Islamic sciences. For instance, eminent Sunnī theologians and foundational traditionists such as Abū Ḥanīfah (d. 150/767), Mālik b. Anas (d. 180/796), and Sufyān al-Thawrī (d. 161/788) studied with al-Ṣādiq.[6] His study circles are said to have produced some four thousand scholars in *ḥadīth* studies and other fields of learning.[7] The alchemist Jābir b. Ḥayyān (d. 199/815)—one of the first people to be known as 'Sufi'[8] and to whom the esoteric science of *jafr* is also ascribed—was taught by Jaʿfar al-Ṣādiq, as was Wāṣil b. ʿAṭāʾ (d. 131/748), founder of the Muʿtazilah, to name but a few.[9] The impact of Jaʿfar was thus widely felt, in varying degrees, within the Muslim community and in numerous fields of Islamic learning, including law and jurisprudence (*fiqh*), *ḥadīth*, theology, alchemy, and Qurʾān interpretation (*tafsīr/taʾwīl*). Such an impact was outstanding, even among the imams who are held to receive, in succession, divinely inspired knowledge vouchsafed to the line of filial heirs of the Prophet.[10]

In the Shīʿī doctrine of the imam's knowledge, the imam is the 'speaking Qurʾān' (*Qurʾān nāṭiq*) while the Qurʾān is the 'silent imam' (*imām ṣāmit*). That is, the imam is considered the true interpreter of the Book. There are numerous comments of Qurʾānic exegesis ascribed to Jaʿfar. These are cited in various books of Shīʿī scholarship, including the commentaries of Muḥammad al-Ayyāshī (d. 320/932) and ʿAlī al-Qummī (d. 350/961). In addition to Shīʿī works, a Sufi collection

---

6 See M. Momen, *An Introduction to Shiʿi Islam* (Oxford: George Ronald Publishers, 1985), p. 38; Richard, *Shi'ite Islam*, pp. 36–7.

7 See Muḥammad b. Yaʿqūb al-Kulaynī, *al-Uṣūl min al-kāfī* (Tehran: Dār al-Kutub al-Islāmīyah, 1968), vol. 1, p. 472.

8 See Danner, 'Early Development', pp. 249 and 251 where '. . .already in the middle of the 2nd/8th century, we hear of the word [Sufi] in conjunction with certain individuals, e.g., Ibn Ḥayyān, disciple of Jaʿfar al-Ṣādiq and Abū Hāshim al-Kūfī al-Ṣūfī.'

9 Hodgson, 'Djaʿfar al-Ṣādik', pp. 374–75; Arzina Lalani, 'Jaʿfar al-Sadiq,' in *Medieval Islamic Civilisation*, ed. J. Meri (New York: Routledge, 2006), pp. 409–11.

10 Shīʿī doctrine holds that the knowledge of all past and present events and the correct interpretation of *all* monotheistic scriptures is included in the imam's *ʿilm*. See D. Crow's unpublished thesis: *The Teaching of Jaʿfar al-Ṣādiq, with reference to his place in early Shīʿism;* Daftary, *Ismāʿīlī*, pp. 20–21.

of Jaʿfar's exegetical comments can be found in the compendium of Qurʾānic commentary compiled by Muḥammad al-Sulamī (d. 412/1021). This Sufi collection of Jaʿfarī commentary is the subject of this study.

As mentioned, a central aspect of the Shīʿī imam's divinely conferred knowledge (*ʿilm*) is the correct interpretation of the Qurʾān. The Sufi recension of Jaʿfar al-Ṣādiq's exegesis of the Qurʾān propounds a spiritual and mystical interpretation—the commentary is fully permeated with the profoundest wisdom. Certain comments are particularly saturated, containing a depth of, and intimacy with, spiritual and mystical experience (*dhawq*) that is breathtaking; indeed, it is transporting. The wisdom (*ḥikmah*) is revelatory with the pure scent of authentic *ʿilm ladunī*.[11] In the exegesis, we find central tenets of spiritual and mystical doctrines such as the sole reality of God; His absolute and total oneness and uniqueness (*aḥadīyah, wāḥidīyah*); the vision of God (*ruʾyat Allāh*); the assembly of the witnessing (*mashhad al-mushāhadah*); effacement and continuity (*fanāʾ* and *baqāʾ*); the remembrance/invocation of God (*dhikr Allāh*); the divine secret (*sirr*) embedded in humankind; mankind's absolute neediness unto God (*iftiqār*); and the love and knowledge of God (*maḥabbat Allāh, maʿrifat Allāh*). These tenets are discussed more fully below, under 'Themes,' being of paramount relevance to this work.

The *tafsīr Jaʿfar* also contains technical terms and concepts which may or may not be regarded as possible precursory elements, in particular, in the fields of *tafsīr*, Sufism, and Islamic philosophy. These are discussed below under 'Language.'

After Jaʿfar, the Shīʿah divided into groups, the two main groups being the Ismāʿīlīyah (Seveners), who upheld the imamate of Ismāʿīl; and the Ithnā ʿasharīyah (Twelvers), who upheld Mūsā al-Kāẓim's imamate. Ismāʿīl, who predeceased his father, was the son of Jaʿfar's first wife, Fāṭimah, descended, according to the *Sharḥ al-akhbār* of Qāḍī Nuʿmān (d. 363/974), from Ḥasan b. Ḥasan b. ʿAlī. Qāḍī Nuʿmān notes that Jaʿfar took no other wife or concubine while

11 *ʿIlm ladunī* refers to 'knowledge from God/from God's Presence' (*ʿilm ladun Allāh*). It is knowledge that is imparted to a soul directly from God.

Fāṭimah lived.[12] Muḥammad b. ʿAbd al-Karīm al-Shahrastānī (d. 548/1153) notes the same in his *Kitāb al-milal wa-l-nihal* but cites Ḥusayn b. Ḥasan b. ʿAlī as her father.[13] Mūsā al-Kāẓim's mother was a Berber slave named Ḥamīdah, acquired by Jaʿfar after Fāṭimah's demise. Jaʿfar's description of her, 'as purified as a gold ingot'[14] and her agnomen '*al-muṣaffāt*' (from the verbal root *ṣ-f-w*, meaning 'the purified woman'), are reminiscent of alchemy.

The controversies regarding the heir to the imamate after Jaʿfar, and relevant dynastic developments down to the present day, are treated in numerous works of political history. They are not of concern in this *tafsīr*. Rather, the focus is on Jaʿfar's universal spiritual teachings, which remain, to this day, a point of unity for diverse Muslims, a guide and a light, a 'philosophers' stone'. Qāḍī Nuʿmān reports: 'One day Sufyān al-Thawrī came to [Jaʿfar] and heard from Jaʿfar a statement that pleased him, whereupon he said: "By God, O son of the Messenger of God, [that is] a gem!" And Jaʿfar b. Muḥammad ﷺ, said to him: "Nay, this is better than a gem. For is a gem aught but a stone?"'[15]

THE COMMENTARY

Textual Source: The *Ḥaqāʾiq al-Tafsīr* of Abū ʿAbd al-Raḥmān al-Sulamī (d. 412/1021)

The Arabic text used for this translation of Imām Jaʿfar al-Ṣādiq's commentary from the *Ḥaqāʾiq* is Paul Nwyia's edition, which is based on a study of three manuscripts of the *Ḥaqāʾiq* and was published as '*Le Tafsīr Mystique attribué à Gaʿfar Ṣādiq, Edition critique*' in *Melanges de l'Université Saint-Joseph*, vol. 43 (Beirut: Imprimerie Catholique, 1968).[16] Note that Nwyia's text does not include all the passages related to Jaʿfar al-Ṣādiq that were recorded by Sulamī in his commentaries, rather it

12 al-Nuʿmān, *Sharḥ al-akhbār fī faḍāʾil al-aʾimma al-athār* (Qum: Muʾassasat al-Nashr al-Islāmī, n. d.), p. 309.

13 al-Shahrastānī, trans. Kazi and Flynn, *Muslim Sects*, p. 163.

14 al-Kulaynī, *al-Uṣūl*, vol. 1, p. 477

15 al-Nuʿmān, *Sharḥ*, p. 299, entry no. 1204.

16 This corpus has not been translated into English in full; Michael Sells has published some passages of Jaʿfar's comments from the *Ḥaqāʾiq* in his volume *Early Islamic Mysticism* (New York: Paulist Press, 1996).

is a portion of the Jaʿfarī commentary in Sulamī's *Ḥaqāʾiq al-tafsīr*.

The *Ḥaqāʾiq al-tafsīr* is a compendium of early Sufi comments on the Qurʾān; it was compiled by Abū ʿAbd al-Raḥmān M. b. al-Ḥusayn al-Sulamī. The *Ḥaqāʾiq*, thought by scholars to have been completed by 370/980,[17] contains a collection of interpretive comments on Qurʾānic phrases by a number of early Muslim mystics such as Abū Yazīd al-Bisṭāmī (d. 261/784–5), Sahl al-Tustarī (d. 283/896), and Abū Bakr al-Wāsiṭī (d. 320/932) among others. It is also the source for the Sufi recension of Jaʿfar al-Ṣādiq's Qurʾān commentary, which contains 309 comments by the Imam, making him one of the most frequently quoted authorities in the compendium. Sulamī states in his introduction that he reproduced the recension of Jaʿfarī comments established by Ibn ʿAṭāʾ al-Adamī (d. 309/ 921 or 311/923–4).[18] This corpus of exegetical comments ascribed to Jaʿfar al-Ṣādiq may, arguably, constitute the earliest extant mystical commentary on the Qurʾān.

The Style of the *Tafsīr*

Unlike later Qurʾān commentaries that systematically address the whole of the Book, in the Sufi recension of the *tafsīr Jaʿfar* corpus only select Qurʾānic verses, words, or phrases are discussed. This selectivity is typical of mystical commentaries universally and reflects the multifaceted nature of heavenly communication, whereby a phrase or word that is immediately pertinent to one thing, perhaps of general import, is at the same time intelligibly and legitimately applied to other matters, perhaps of personal import, at a later time, in isolation from the historical relevance of the initial matter and from any textual context. This type of interpretation is ultimately rooted in the living, personal relationship of a soul with heaven, with words or phrases acting as indications or allusions to matters that the soul and heaven know of (if it is a personal understanding) or as references to what heaven wishes to disclose to the soul.

The comments in the *tafsīr* often include the actual Qurʾānic words that they pertain to. Or the comment may follow the Qurʾānic phrase

---

17 See Gerhard Böwering, *The Minor Qurʾān Commentary of Abū ʿAbd ar-Raḥmān Muḥammad b. al-Ḥusayn as-Sulamī (d. 412/1021)* (Beirut: Dār al-Mashriq, 1997), p. 18.

18 As Paul Nwyia notes in his study of the Sulamī recension.

as the second half of a sentence follows the first, e.g., 3:150. A third way in which the comments are presented is through an interpretive paraphrase of the Qurʾānic words, so that the comment is spoken 'in the voice of God'; for example in 4:64, 4:80, 22:34, 27:21.

Typically, a Qurʾānic verse or phrase is cited, followed by a comment that is introduced by 'qāla Jaʿfar' [Jaʿfar said] or 'qāla Jaʿfar b. Muḥammad' [Jaʿfar b. Muḥammad said] or 'qāla Jaʿfar al-Ṣādiq' [Jaʿfar al-Ṣādiq said]. More than one comment on a phrase or word may be recorded, in which case the second and following comments may be introduced simply by 'wa qāla' [and he said] or 'wa qāla ayḍan' [and he also said] or 'wa qāla Jaʿfar' [and Jaʿfar said]. This method of citing or providing as many possible interpretations of the text is part and parcel of the hermeneutical ethic. This principle seeks to explore the meanings of the text from different angles. Exoteric and esoteric commentators alike do this, especially the compilers. However, unlike his exoteric counterpart, Ṭabarī, Sulamī does not provide his own opinion or preferred interpretation.

In the selection of the Qurʾānic phrases hardly any minatory (*waʿīd*) verses are chosen for comment. The instances of severity are few, for example, at 27:21, 38:78, 82:13–14, 104:6–7. Yet even with such instances, the preponderance in the commentary is on the positive, as at 104:6–7, where the verse is from a *sūrah* that deals solely with the fate of slanderers and materialistic, acquisitive people, yet the commentary discusses the fires of love and gnosis more than the fire of hell.[19]

THE TRANSLATION

Approach

This work presents a translation of this *tafsīr* ascribed to the Imām al-Ṣādiq as it stands and, approaching the text from within, attempts to understand and explore the fuller implications and meanings of the comments and the Qurʾānic phrases to which they pertain. As discussed below, an investigation of whether or not the text is correctly attributed

19 This 'positivity' goes hand in hand with an adamantine rigour in the spiritual dimension, for example concerning the purity of *dhikr* (at 51:55), total detachment from all other than God (at 3:35, 102, 138, 159; 6:79; 6:153) etc.

to the Imam is not within the purview of this study. Consequently, I only offer an introductory discussion of the historicity of the comments; without drawing attention to this question in the annotation to the translation. Notes are supplied to help understand the comments or to offer possible alternative renderings of the Arabic, or to convey the broader connotations of a single Arabic word. It is hoped that the course struck through the translation is one that will be of interest and use to scholars and lay people, Muslims and non-Muslims. However, it is in the nature of the subject that a familiarity with the text of the Qurʾān itself is a must. The reader should be able to read the translation as it stands on its own, but they may well wish to have a copy of the Qurʾān at hand for reference.

Notes on Style

Variants between the Qurʾānic citations in the text of Nwyia's edition and the standard Ḥafṣ reading of the *muṣḥaf* are found and noted at: 3:110, 8:53, 4:128, 12:31, 38:25, 40:51, 43:71, and 52:48. The variants, which might be no more than mistakes in copying, are minor and do not vitally affect the meaning; the translation follows Nwyia's edition, always noting the wording of the standard *muṣḥaf* in the notes.

If Arabic words or technical terms are given in transliteration in the body text of the translation, they are in round brackets ( ) and italicised. Round brackets ( ) are also used for a slight difference of wording, but not meaning, between the English and Arabic texts, e.g., '(God's) words' for 'His words'. Again this liberty is taken to facilitate the flow of the English text. Hard brackets [ ] are used for my additions, given for easier understanding of the English text. Taking the cue from Arabic, capitalisation has been kept to a minimum in the English translation. This should not be misunderstood as a lack of respect. Transliterated divine names are not italicised, but do appear in capitals. Where the word 'Truth' has an initial capital letter, it renders the divine name al-Ḥaqq.

The comments are often expressed through interpretive paraphrase such that a comment may consist simply of a paraphrase of the Qurʾānic words, e.g., 26:80. In phrases such as *man āmana, man ʿarafa, man ḥāmada*, the Arabic perfect tense is rendered in the English continuous as it is felt that this conveys the meaning more accurately despite the tense shift.

While seeking to stay close to the literal text, the translation at the same time seeks to convey the subtler flavour of this highly mystical text, a flavour that is sometimes implicit. This, together with the need for the English text to read smoothly, has meant that, in places, the translation reads more loosely than a rigidly literal rendering would. In such cases, the literal translation is given in the notes. Moreover, absolute consistency in the rendering of terms has not been applied, although the translation of a single term is restricted to a limited selection of options. Thus, for example, *maʿrifah* appears mostly as 'gnosis' or 'spiritual knowledge', and a few times as 'realisatory knowledge'; likewise *sirr* is rendered as 'inmost self' or 'inmost secret'; and *nafs* is rendered as 'lower soul' or 'ego', but at other times as 'soul' or 'self'. This flexibility allows for the exigencies of context and textual emphasis, and enables the English text to flow more smoothly. The terms are discussed in the notes.

Due to the polysemous nature of Arabic words, on occasion two English words are needed to render a single Arabic word, e.g., 'pure, exclusive' for '*khāliṣan*' (in *ʿabdan khāliṣan* at 3:35). This is in order to convey more fully the meaning and implication of the single Arabic word.

In the Introduction, comments are cited from the text, bringing them together according to thematic continuity. This should not be dismissed as the imposition of an arbitrary arrangement. The arrangement of the Arabic text, following the order of the Qurʾān, is most likely the work of the compiler and not the original author, as discussed below.

HISTORICAL QUESTIONS

Ascription

Students of history question the ascription of this corpus of Qurʾānic commentary to the Imam. The question of authorship and the composition of the text still needs to be researched and studied to the satisfaction of academia; it relates to a number of matters. First, the different extant recensions and manuscripts of the corpus must be systematically and comparatively studied in order to establish what might be termed 'the original body'.[20] Such a process would assist in identifying and dating any 'accretions' to the original corpus. In addition, there is the question of dating the original corpus and ascertaining, as far as possible, whether or not it could be said to stem from one person. Finally, there is the question of who the author/s might have been.

These matters do not fall within the purview of the present work, which aims to produce an annotated translation of the Sulamī recension. This research contributes to the discussion of the *substance* of hermeneutical thought as documented in this corpus and offers insights that result from an interaction with the content of the work.

Prominent among these insights, I note that, on the whole, the thematic content of the Sulamī text itself displays a coherence and consistency of thought, moral attitude, and spiritual perspective (e.g., the concepts of the soul and the heart; of *walāyah* and *nubūwah;* the *laṭāʾif* and the *ḥaqāʾiq*); this supports the view that much of the corpus may well have emanated as a unity. The threads of thematic cohesion can be noted in comments that are not found side by side, but pertain to non-consecutive verses of the Qurʾān. The colours of the different thematic threads surface here and there in the text as laid out by Sulamī, who followed the Qurʾānic order of the verses. It may well be, however, that in oral teaching or in the earlier sources from which the Ibn ʿAṭāʾ recension was compiled, the verses were presented differently, according to a thematic order rather than the scriptural order; bringing together the different pertinent verses of the Book when expounding a specific subject was not uncommon. However, when compiling a book with the specific intention of presenting a documentation of mystical *tafsīr* (Sulamī's stated intention in compiling the *Ḥaqāʾiq*), the Qurʾānic order of verses would be followed. It would be up to the reader to note the colours and link up the relevant verses according to theme—and so come full circle.

Language

The issue of dating a text is closely related to the terms and vocabulary used in the text. The language may be taken as an indicator of the text's

20 It is hoped that a comparative study with the Imam's exegetical corpus as preserved in Shīʿī circles will be forthcoming in the near future.

historical period; or the ascribed date of the text may be understood as indicating the period to which the language belongs.

There are a number of terms used in the text which became part of the technical terminology of different Islamic disciplines. Some of these terms appeared as early heralds of later fully-fledged terms, the seeds of future terms and doctrines. For example, the more antiquated word *māʾīyah* (for quiddity/quintessence) occurs in the *tafsīr*, at 1:1 and 53:37. Without fixing the date of the text, this indicates that, broadly speaking, it predates al-Farābī's time (late ninth/early tenth century), by which time the later philosophical term *māhīyah* was well-established for quiddity.[21] Another indicator of the early nature of the text lies in a certain fluidity of terminology when referring to concepts which in later history acquired specific and rather more rigid referents; for instance the concept of 'qualities' or 'attributes' is indicated by any of the following terms: *awṣāf*, *ṣifāt*, *maʿānī*, and *naʿt*, all of which are used in the text to refer to the qualities of God and man. Later theologians and philosophers settled on the words *ṣifah*/*ṣifāt* as the reference to attributes and qualities in the given sense.

In the *tafsīr* the negative connotations of passionate love (*ʿishq*), with regard to Zulaykha's love of Joseph, also bespeaks an early period because in later Sufism, when *ʿishq* became part and parcel of Sufi common vocabulary, it is used positively with reference to the deep love of God.

The word *walāyah* (sanctity, divine friendship) presents an interesting case. On the basis that it involves a far broader application than the Shīʿī use of the term, some readers might be tempted to take the discussion of *walāyah* in the text as presenting an exclusively Sufi view of sanctity, which would set the dating to a later period. However, though *walāyah* was, and remains, for the Shīʿah, particularly related to the imams, nevertheless, there is more than one type of *walāyah* even in Shīʿism. There is the *walāyah* that is located restrictively in the

---

21 *Māʾīyah*, from the root *m-w-h*, literally means 'sap, juice'. Here, at 1:1 and 53:37, it is used to mean 'quiddity, quintessence': 'the God of creation, His quiddity far transcends being attained to (*ilāhu'l-khalqi munazzahun ʿan kulli darakin māʾīyatuhu*)' (1:1); 'the quintessence of sincerity (*māʾīyatu'l-ṣidqi*)' (53:37). It is possible that the use of this word is simply a scribal error for *māhīyah*, but it is easy to see how *māʾīyah* might be used, at a time before technical terms were fixed, to mean quiddity/quintessence.

imāmah, and there is another, more universal, type called *al-walāyah al-muktasibah*, 'acquirable' sanctity. The former is the birthright of the imams, while the latter is open to the rest of humanity. Thus, for example, at 12:100 we read, with regard to the phrase *verily my Lord is kind unto whom He wills*—'unto His slaves to whom care and friendship (*walāyah*) from Him have already been granted.' And at 55:11, with regard to the variously endowed palm tree mentioned in the Qurʾānic phrase, we read: 'Everyone harvests from it a type in keeping with the scope of his effort and (according to) the manifestations of mystical knowledge and the effects of divine friendship (*walāyah*) that are unveiled for them.' Thus the use of *walāyah* in our text could well be indicative of its Shīʿī and even Jaʿfarī origin; while the universal application of the term does not preclude a Shīʿī interpretation of it.

The use of al-Ḥaqq as *the* reference to God is definitely Sufi—but it is also known that Jaʿfar al-Ṣādiq bequeathed this usage to the Sufis.[22]

However, other terms used in the *tafsīr* are well-established Sufi technical vocabulary, e.g., *haybah* (awe), *uns* (intimacy), *khawf* (fear), *rajāʾ* (hope), *maʿrifah* (gnosis or spiritual/mystical knowledge), *maḥabbah* (love), *maqām* (station), *tajallī* (theophany), *sirr* (secret/inmost self), *ḥayrah* (bewilderment), *baqāʾ* (subsistence) *mushāhadah* (witnessing), *maḥall* (locus), the use of the verb *faniya* (to be effaced), and the more philosophical term *ḥadath* (incepted thing). Furthermore, comments like those on the stellar mansions (25:61), the twelve springs of the Children of Israel (7:160), and the light verse (24:35) have the quality of being lists of mystical states and stations: the *aḥwāl* (states) and *maqāmāt* (stations) of the Sufis. These could seem to indicate the state not of seed but of flower or even of back-pollination from those flowers. In other words, the use of these terms in our text may be taken as an indication of the later date of the relevant comments. Thus, historians may argue that some of the comments are clearly back dated from a later period because they display ideas associated with that later period; but other scholars may be inclined to think that such comments are not a case of back-pollination from later flowers but are the actual seeds of those flowers, being the early usage of terms which later became well established within Sufi technical vocabulary.

---

22 See L. Massignon, *Essai sur les origines du lexique technique de la mystique musulmane* (Paris: Vrin, 1954), p. 203.

The distinction between the universal mercy of *al-Raḥmān* and the more specific mercy of *al-Raḥīm* provides another interesting point as regards dating. At 1:1, on the *basmalah*, we read: 'Allāh is the God of everything, the Gracious (*al-Raḥmān*) to all of His creation, the Merciful (*al-Raḥīm*) to believers in particular (*al-Raḥmān li-jamīʿi khalqihi, al-Raḥīm bi-l-muʾminīna khāṣṣatan*).' This is a concept which, though Qurʾānic in origin, was made famous by Ibn ʿArabī. Thus, the presence of this concept in this *tafsīr* could indicate any period of time for the relevant comments, ranging from before Jaʿfar al-Ṣādiq's time right through to Ibn ʿArabī's time.

I believe it is almost impossible to ascertain beyond academic doubt the period/s to which this text and its different parts may be datable. From the academic point of view, the best that can be done is to compare all the extant texts attributed to the author and, working on the assumption that some of these ascriptions are authentic, work towards identifying or not, a common corpus.

Needless to say, it is important to know the lineage of a text, especially when its origin is pertinent in establishing its legal legitimacy and authority, particularly with regard to matters pertaining to the *sharīʿah*, and also for students of history. Nevertheless, for a text such as ours, which is above all a spiritual and mystical scriptural exegesis, it is in the *content* that the actual value resides for students of the Qurʾān and Qurʾān commentary, in other words, for those who wish to understand better the text and its explanations *per se,* and the oceans behind the ink of the letters. Moreover, spiritual and mystical realities are not bound to the historical and denominational categories in which they manifest in particular form. With this in mind some of the prominent themes of this text are discussed later in this introduction.

Shīʿism and Sufism

As noted above, another historical question that this text highlights is the relationship between Sufism and Shīʿism; this is shown in the possible connections between the Sufi recension of the *tafsīr Jaʿfar* and the Shīʿī corpus of the Imam's exegetical teachings. Do both branches stem from Jaʿfar al-Ṣādiq? Did the Imam present two distinct types of

Qurʾān commentary, one for the early 'proto-Sufis'[23] who learnt from him, and one for the Shīʿah? This subject will require a whole study itself, including a thorough comparative analysis of both exegetical bodies and their chains of transmission,[24] and this falls beyond the confines of this work. Here a brief presentation of the discussion to date, including some insights afforded by this study, shall have to suffice.

First, it should be noted that early Shīʿī *tafsīr* takes the form of reported sayings (*akhbār;* sing. *khabar*) from the imams. These *akhbār* are understood to transmit knowledge that the imams inherited from the Prophet himself. As noted above, the fifth and sixth imams have a predominant role in *ḥadīth*-transmission.

Concerning the comments attributed to Jaʿfar al-Ṣādiq by the Sufis, Louis Massignon offered the following tradition of transmission for the Imam's exegetical comments contained in Sulamī's *Ḥaqāʾiq*. In the century after the Imam's death, individual interpretive *aḥādīth* attributed to Jaʿfar al-Ṣādiq were circulated in the Sufi circles of Kūfah and Baghdad. In the following century (fourth century AH), these *aḥādīth* constituted a '*musnad min ṭarīqi ahli'l-bayt*';[25] which indicates an independent collection, by the Sufis, of Jaʿfarī exegetical comments—but this is not to say that the comments did not originate in Shīʿī circles.

Paul Nwyia has compared Sulamī's Sufi recension in the *Ḥaqāʾiq* with Muḥammad b. Ibrāhīm al-Nuʿmānī's (d. 360/971) Shīʿī recension of the *tafsīr Jaʿfar*. Nuʿmānī was a student of Kulaynī (d. 329/940), one of the primary sources for the Shīʿī transmission of Jaʿfar al-Ṣādiq's exegetical comments. Nwyia is of the opinion that in addition to identical doctrinal elements between the two recensions 'we are in the presence of the same work, having the same inspiration, the same style and the same spiritual content. Moreover, in places we find sentences

23 In the sense of those who were among the earliest to be *called* Sufis—for the Sufis, as cited in Hujwīrī's *Kashf al-maḥjūb* from al-Fushanjī, said that at the beginning of Islam, Sufism was a reality without a name.

24 This is brought up by Nwyia, in the introduction to his edition of the Sulamī recension '. . . it would be necessary to establish the proof of the mutual independence of the two traditions. For if the *ḥadīths* which gave rise to the sixth imam's commentary on the Qurʾān were preserved within Shīʿī milieux independently of Sunni Sufi circles, the contrary is by no means self-evident.' See Nwyia, p. 182.

25 See Massignon, *Essai sur les origines*, pp. 201–13.

which are literally the same, containing, however, important variants which indicate two different sources of transmission.'[26] Nwyia went as far as to state that the Sufis may well have acquired their recension from a Shīʿī source—in other words, that the Sulamī recension was derived from the Nuʿmānī recension.[27]

Gerhard Böwering, who notes that 'one fourth of the [Jaʿfarī] material is cited consistently by Sulamī under a specific Shīʿī *isnād* of Manṣūr b. ʿAbd Allāh—Abū l-Qāsim al-Iskandarī—Abū Jaʿfar al-Malaṭī who links up with the chain of the Shīʿite imams ascending from ʿAlī al-Riḍā' (d. 203/818) through Mūsā al-Kāẓim (d. 183/799) to Jaʿfar al-Ṣādiq',[28] nevertheless disputes Nwyia's claim arguing that even within Shīʿī sources the exegetical comments ascribed to al-Ṣādiq are not uniform, Nuʿmānī's *tafsīr Jaʿfar* being quite distinct from the Jaʿfarī exegesis cited by ʿAlī b. Ibrāhīm al-Qummī (d. 350/961) and Muḥammad b. Masʿūd al-ʿAyyāshī (d. 320/932).[29]

My own limited reading of Qummī's and ʿAyyāshī's commentaries, and for that matter, Jaʿfar b. Manṣūr al-Yaman's (d. before 346/957) *tafsīr*, does indeed reveal a Jaʿfarī corpus of a different tenor from that of Sulamī's recension, and this confirms the distinction noted by Böwering.

Given the breadth of Jaʿfar al-Ṣādiq's influence, it may be that both traditions—the posited Sulamī-Nuʿmānī recension and the Qummī-ʿAyyāshī-Yaman corpus—do stem from him as independent bodies or that both stem as selections from a single Jaʿfarī corpus. In the latter case, it might be that the different transmitters of the single

---

26 This is the Bankipore ms 1460. See Nwyia's introduction to his edition of the Sufi recension: '*Le Tafsīr Mystique*, attribué à Gaʿfar Ṣādiq,' in *Mélanges de l'Université Saint-Joseph* 43 (Beirut: Imprimerie Catholique, 1968), vol. 43.

27 In his discussion of the *tafsīr Jaʿfar* in *Exégèse coranique et langage mystique* (Beirut: Librairie Orientale, 1970), pp. 158–59, in addition to the Bankipore ms, Nwyia mentions another ms—Istanbul, Nafiz Pasa ms 65—which coincides in places with the Sulamī recension but has explicit Shīʿī comments too. Furthermore, there is an ms of the Sulamī recension of the *tafsīr Jaʿfar*—Yeni Cami ms 43—which also has a Shīʿī *tafsīr*.

28 See Gerhard Böwering, 'The Qurʾān commentary of al-Sulamī', in *Islamic Studies presented to Charles J. Adams* (Leiden: Brill, 1991), p. 53.

29 Ibid., pp. 53–4.

corpus from Jaᶜfar either left out or modified the aspects that they found problematic in that corpus. Thus, to pick up on *walāyah*, the Sufis would have concentrated on the universal aspect of sanctity in their recension. Böwering feels that 'one may be on firm ground by arguing that the items included in the *Ḥaqāʾiq* on Jaᶜfar al-Ṣādiq's authority may be understood as reflecting 3rd/9th and 4th/10th century Sufi terms and ideas that echo certain fundamental notions of Jaᶜfar al-Ṣādiq yet are stripped of any specifically Shīᶜite colouring'.[30]

In the possible case of the two traditions stemming independently from the Imam, it is conceivable that Jaᶜfar taught what was suitable to those for whom it was suited. He served as a spiritual master not just for those who were 'of the Shīᶜah' but also for those outside this sphere. As noted earlier in this introduction, the Imām al-Ṣādiq had several types of disciples and students. It may be that sometimes he presented the same basic information to more than one circle but with modifications tailored to the audience. Or he may have presented quite different teachings to different groups. This should not be misunderstood; a great teacher of profound depth and breadth of knowledge may present information selectively and appropriately to the large diversity of souls that come to learn from him. In such cases, it should hardly be surprising that, at times, there was something of an overlap, or difference, in what was given to different circles of students.

Within the body text (*matn*) of the Sufi recension, there is one instance in which the Shīᶜī-Sufi attitudes seem to come together in a revealing manner. The comment on 57:10 mentions 'the greatest sincere one, God's pleasure be upon him' (*al-ṣiddīq al-akbar, riḍwānu'llāhi ᶜalayhi*). Now although the title *al-ṣiddīq al-akbar* is used by the Shīᶜah, but not the Sunnīs, for ᶜAlī b. Abī Ṭālib, the blessing *riḍwānu'llāhi ᶜalayhi* is a Sunnī eulogy for all four caliphs; the Shīᶜī eulogy for the Imām ᶜAlī is *ᶜalayhi al-salām*. This implies that the comment was cited by a non-Shīᶜī Sufi, but came from a Shīᶜī source—serving to support the idea of a link between the Sulamī-Nuᶜmānī recensions.

However, a detailed and direct comparative study between the two texts is needed to substantiate this possible connection between the Sulamī and Nuᶜmānī recensions. Likewise, the Nuᶜmānī recension must

30 Ibid., p. 55.

be studied and compared with the ʿAyyāshī-Qummī-Yaman traditions.[31]

Shīʿī and Sunnī Tones in the Commentary

Confining ourselves to the text of the Sufi recension, it is noteworthy that while the vast majority of the 309 comments within our text are of a universal spirituality (bearing in mind earlier notes on *al-walāyah al-muktasibah*), there are only two instances that reveal explicitly Sunnī attitudes, whereas there are several instances of comments containing strong, if not explicit, Shīʿī implications. In the comments on Q. 24:35, the Sunnī stance vis-à-vis the first caliphs seems explicitly condoned twice. At 24:35 the commentary states: 'He has illumined the paths unto God with the light of Abū Bakr, ʿUmar, ʿUthmān, and ʿAlī ﷺ—it is for this reason that the Prophet ﷺ said: My companions are like the stars—whomever of them you choose to follow, you shall be rightly-guided.' Further on, concerning this same verse, it is stated: 'He illumined the earth through Abū Bakr, ʿUmar, ʿUthmān, and ʿAlī ﷺ.'

Such an evident Sunnī perspective might be taken by some as evidence that this whole text, or parts of it, was the work of later Sufis; or it may be seen as a non-Jaʿfarī interpolation into a predominantly Jaʿfarī corpus. If taken as actually coming from the Imam, it may be understood as dissimulation (*taqīyah*) or as evidence of intra-Muslim tolerance: that though the way of ʿAlī and his progeny is the best for the Shīʿah, the other Islamic paths are also 'rightly-guided'.

At the same time there are a number of comments which may be interpreted as presenting aspects of Shīʿī doctrine. To give a few examples, in the comment on 1:1 we read: 'the secret of prophethood which the Prophet confided to the elite of his community'; the 'elite' can be taken as an allusion to the Shīʿī imams, the progeny of ʿAlī who would have received the secret of prophecy; while by the Sufis it would be understood with more general reference. The Shīʿī doctrine that only the imam understands the Qurʾān correctly is clearly implied in

31 The most likely scenario may be that the Sufi recension does contain a corpus of broader applicability stemming from Jaʿfar. The original corpus of the Sufi stemma would be that which Massignon described as circulating among the Sufis of Kūfah and Baghdad, and would most likely not have contained any explicitly Shīʿī comments but only those of a more universal reference.

the comment on 3:138: 'only he perceives it [the Qurʾān] clearly who is supported by Him with the light of certainty and purity of inmost self'; yet this may be taken, as it must have been by the Sufis, as of general reference, that is, anyone whom God chooses may be supported with the light of certainty and purity of inmost self. At 2:128, the *ahl baytī* are mentioned, with obvious Shīʿī connotations: 'Jaʿfar said . . . protect me and my household (literally 'the people of my house') . . .' The comment on 3:31 is of an anti-*ghulūw* nature, which is in keeping with what is known of Imām Jaʿfar al-Ṣādiq's attitude concerning such matters.[32] Likewise, 12:76 could be understood in Shīʿī terms, namely as a reference to the imams.

Then there are the more explicit references. On 22:26, the comment interprets *al-rukkaʿiʾl-sujūd* as reference to 'the foremost imams, who return to the beginning from the utmost end'. At 41:44 it is stated in the comment that 'the Qurʾān is a healing for him who is in the shade of impeccability (*ʿiṣmah*) while it is inscrutable for him who is in the darkness of being abandoned'. In this there are references to two Shīʿī doctrines: (1) the infallibility or impeccability of the imams—their *ʿiṣmah*; and (2) the true understanding of the Qurʾān which only the imams have as part of their divinely conferred *ʿilm* (as mentioned earlier in this Introduction).

To conclude this discussion, if the text is read through a Shīʿī lens there are numerous allusions susceptible of an imamological interpretation. If the text is read with a Sufi lens, the very same comments may be understood with broader reference. Moreover, ultimately, on the spiritual register, the two readings of the *tafsīr* as a whole, can coincide, because, setting aside political and jurisprudential affiliations, how much of a difference is there between the two routes to sanctity? And sanctity *is* the meeting point. As mentioned earlier, in Shīʿism there is a specific *walāyah* that is reserved for the imams, but there is also the universal sanctity in which the common man participates to the extent that he is effaced in the imam. The imam

32 See Momen, *An Introduction to Shīʿī Islām*, pp. 65–68; Hodgson, 'Djaʿfar al-Ṣādik', p. 375: 'Djaʿfar made a point of keeping them [i.e., Shīʿī ideas] within bounds'; A. A. Sachedina, 'The Significance of Kāshī's *Rijāl*', in *Logos Islamikos* (Toronto: Pontifical Institute of Mediaeval Studies, 1984), especially pp. 196–97.

is both macrocosmic and microcosmic. The microcosmic imam is the inner continuity of the prophetic reality just as the macrocosmic imam is the continuity of the Prophet in the world. Effacement in the inner imam is realised through an ontological actualisation of the prophetic reality. Likewise, in Sufism, sanctity is realised through an ontological effacement in the inner *nabī*, the microcosmic extension of the prophetic reality.

LEVELS AND METHODS OF INTERPRETATION

In the opening citation of the *tafsīr*, the following is related from Jaʿfar al-Ṣādiq: 'The Book of God has four things: literal expression (*ʿibārah*), allusion (*ishārah*), subtleties (*laṭāʾif*), and the deepest realities (*ḥaqāʾiq*). The literal expression is for the commonalty (*ʿawāmm*), the allusion is for the elite (*khawāṣṣ*), the subtleties are for the friends (of God) (*awliyāʾ*), and the deepest realities are for the prophets (*anbiyāʾ*).' Allusion (*ishārah*), subtlety (*laṭīfah*), and reality (*ḥaqīqah*) define the different levels of interpretive comments contained in the *tafsīr Jaʿfar*, and place the reading of this commentary on the spiritual register.

Allusion (*ishārah*)

Ishārah can refer to more than one style of allusive interpretation.

Principle of Correspondence (*taṭbīq*)

First, *taṭbīq* is the principle of correspondence whereby macrocosmic entities are interpreted with reference to man as a microcosm; it is a system that involves analogues. Thus external or physical things like mountains, rivers, and stars are explained as corresponding to inner spiritual elements within the human being. For instance, at 14:35, where Abraham prays to God to make the valley of Mecca safe, saying *make this land safe*, 'land' is taken as a reference to the hearts of sages, 'make them sanctuaries of Your secret and safe from being cut off from You'; at 2:158, the hills of Ṣafā and Marwah are interpreted as symbols of the spirit and the soul respectively; at 27:61 the earth is understood as 'the hearts of His friends', the rivers are 'increase from His beneficence' and the mountains are 'trusting reliance upon God', the two seas are the heart and the soul, and the barrier between them consists of God-given success and the intellect.

Thus, through the principle of micro-macrocosmic correspondence (*taṭbīq*), symbolic allusion acts as a key to the less explicitly stated spiritual dimension of certain Qurʾānic words and phrases which *prima facie* pertain to external entities that are interiorised and understood as elements of the spiritual landscape.[33] This technique was used systematically by later Sufis such as ʿAbd al-Razzāq al-Qāshānī (d. 736/1336), whose *tafsīr* is an example of the highly refined and systematic use of *taṭbīq*.

Interpretation (*taʾwīl*)

Second, *taʾwīl* is the literal aspect that is used as a springboard for disclosing a deeper meaning of a word. In such cases, the very letters of the relevant words are used for an interpretation on the basis of their associated meanings; that is to say, the interpreter 'goes back' (*awwala*—from which we get the word *taʾwīl*, meaning interpretation) to the verbal root of the word and links it to other meanings derived from the root letters. It is a form of paronomasia, 'a play on words' whereby the commentator arrives at broader interpretations based on the associated verbal meanings.

The most prominent example of this is the interpretation of Ṣafā as the spirit (*rūḥ*), and Marwah as the heroic soul (*nafs*) in the comment on the Qurʾānic phrase, *Verily, Ṣafā and Marwah are among the rites of God* (2:158): 'Ṣafā is the spirit (*rūḥ*) because of its being pure of the dirt of oppositions (to God), and Marwah is the soul (*nafs*) because of its use of the heroic virtues in the performance of service(s) (for) its Master.' The word Ṣafā is related to the word for purity—*ṣafāʾ*, both being derived from the verbal root *ṣ-f-w*, meaning 'to be pure'; and the word Marwah, containing the letters *m-r-w* is related to *murūwah* (heroic virtues; chivalry also contains those three letters although *murūwah* is derived from the verbal root, *m-r-ʾ*, meaning 'to be healthy, manly'). Thus, while both Ṣafā and Marwah mean 'rock' or 'stone' they are here interpreted on the basis of their broader meanings drawn from

33 That is, such elements are substantially different to the physical counterparts yet are literal aspects of the subtle landscape.

letter associations, to reveal a compelling image of the spiritual life: with the *rūḥ* being a pure continuity of the flow of the divine spirit; and the soul being heroic in striving to ensure that the pure radiance of the spirit's light shining upon it may continue to extend through the soul.

Knowledge of the Occult (*jafr*)

The third form of *ishārah* in the *tafsīr* is *jafr*. The *jafr* in this commentary pertains to the esoteric significances of letters (*ʿilm al-ḥurūf*). This involves taking the individual letters of a given word and interpreting them as indicators of whole concepts. *Jafr* as a science of esoteric knowledge is said to have originated with ʿAlī b. Abī Ṭālib, who was taught it by the Prophet himself; it was thereafter passed to the imams as the heirs and successors of ʿAlī and the Prophet. Knowledge of the esoteric properties of the letters of the alphabet and of the divine names is part of *jafr* and is used in the spiritual and mystical interpretation of the Qurʾān. The general Shīʿī view is that this dimension of *jafr* passed from imam to imam; however, according to some sources, it is said to have passed from ʿAlī through his uncle Zayd b. ʿAlī to Jaʿfar al-Ṣādiq.[34]

Jafr occurs the least of the three types of *ishārah*, coming mainly at the beginning, on the divine names in the *Fātiḥah*, on the detached letters at the start of *sūrah*s 3 and 68, and at the end on the Names 'al-Ṣamad' and 'al-Aḥad' and the pronoun 'huwa' in *Sūrat al-Ikhlāṣ*. This *jafr* is profound and potent, yet it is very straightforward, quite unlike later highly refined expressions of *ʿilm al-ḥurūf*, for example the totally systematic application to the Ismāʿīlī hierarchy of the letters of the alphabet, down to the dots, as contained in the *tafsīr* by Jaʿfar b. Manṣūr al-Yaman (d. before 346/957). *Jafr* is the most obscure aspect of *ishārah* in our text.

To give an example of *jafr*: concerning the word *bism* from the phrase بِسْمِ ٱللَّهِ ٱلرَّحْمَٰنِ ٱلرَّحِيمِ, meaning: *In the name of God, the Gracious, the Merciful*, different interpretations of the three letters of the word are given. The comment on 1:1 says: '[The word] *bism* has three letters: *bāʾ*, *sīn*, and *mīm*. The *bāʾ* is the gate (*bāb*) of prophethood, the *sīn* is the secret (*sirr*) of prophethood that the Prophet confided to the elite of his community, and the *mīm* is the kingdom (*mamlakah*) of faith

34 See Hodgson, 'Djaʿfar al-Ṣādik', *EI*^{2}.

that embraces the white and the black.'[35] Immediately following this, a different interpretation is offered, namely that the *bāʾ* pertains to the divine brilliance (*bahāʾ*), the *sīn* to God's resplendence (*sanāʾ*) and the *mīm* to His glory (*majd*). Clearly the interpretations pertain to different levels; however, the foundations on which these interpretations are erected lie in the *ghayb*, for they are not immediately evident.

On a different note, it is not without significance that in the first comment cited above, the secret of prophethood (*sirr al-nubūwah*) is confided to the *khawāṣṣ*, to whom the aspect of *ishārah* was specifically related in the opening quote from the Imām al-Ṣādiq. This indicates that *ishārah* is related also to *ḥaqīqah*, which pertains to *nubūwwah*. This connection is borne out at a profound level, in the concepts of the heart and soul contained in the *tafsīr*.

Subtlety (*laṭīfah*) and Reality (*ḥaqīqah*)

The link between *ishārah* and *ḥaqīqah* passes through *laṭīfah*, the interpretive level of subtlety. *Laṭīfah* pertains to the interface of sanctified soul and ensouled spirit, while *ḥaqīqah* pertains to the heart (*qalb*), and more specifically to the holy content of the heart, as we shall see in the next section in the discussion on *walāyah* and the concept of the *qalb*. In the portrait of the human microcosm that this *tafsīr* depicts, the heart is that element within the human being that is the locus which receives the direct inflow from heaven, namely the *nabī* that receives the holy and radiant *rūḥ*;[36] while the sanctified soul is the theophanic soul of the *walī* whose Marwah has, with God's help and by His grace, uprooted from the soul all base and 'wretched'[37] qualities so that the light of the spirit may radiate through it unobstructed.

With *laṭīfah* and *ḥaqīqah* we enter the realm of subtle facts (*laṭāʾif* and *ḥaqāʾiq*), leaving the symbolic realm behind.[38] For *laṭīfah* and

---

35 There are different possible explanations of the meaning of this comment, among them, that it may be a reference to ʿAlī as the gate to the city of knowledge referred to in the prophetic saying: 'I am the city of knowledge and ʿAlī is its gate'.

36 See notes on 76:21 for the complete microcosmic portrait.

37 The word 'wretched' is used in the *tafsīr* to describe the lower soul's own qualities at 19:93.

38 It can be said that we are in the realm of *al-ḥaqāʾiq al-laṭīfah*. The rendition

ḥaqīqah are not about symbolism; they are to be taken literally—but not understood in a dense material manner. Rather, the literality of subtleties and deepest realities is situated in the subtle realms of which divine light, and not dense physical matter, is the substance.

These *laṭāʾif* and *ḥaqāʾiq* are exemplified in the comments that pertain to the soul, the spiritual heart and the matter of qualities—all of which constitute prominent themes and shall be discussed at length under that heading. At this juncture only three examples shall be cited.

Commenting on *that you may bring forth mankind from the darknesses into light* (14:1), Jaʿfar offers the following as one of the interpretations of this phrase: '[that you may bring them forth] from the darknesses of the [lower] soul into the lights of the heart'.

In the commentary on the Qurʾānic phrase (27:61): *and He (God) placed between the two seas a barrier*, we read: '[He placed a barrier] between the heart and the lower soul lest the lower soul should overwhelm the heart with its darknesses and thus oppress it. So (God) placed God-given success (*tawfīq*) and the intellect (*ʿaql*) as the barrier between the two.'

Then, in the comment on the Qurʾānic phrase: *and the likeness of a harmful word is as a harmful tree* (14:26), when explaining the harmful tree referred to, the lower soul (*nafs*) is named as the soil of the harmful tree. The harmful tree is explained as an allusion to the carnal appetites.[39]

Thus it is clear that whether it is an application of macrocosmic references to the subtle dimension of the microcosm that man constitutes (*taṭbīq*), or the very letters of Qurʾānic words and phrases that are used as springboards into the subtle and deepest realms (*taʾwīl* and *jafr*), the role of allusion (*ishārah*) in the *tafsīr Jaʿfar* is to open doors to the *laṭāʾif* and *ḥaqāʾiq* for a disclosure of the inner, specifically

---

'fact' is deliberately used here for *ḥaqīqah*, in order to try to convey something of the broader meaning of the Arabic word, which would have been in the minds of the early readers/listeners: truths are factual realities.

39 Needless to say, the harmful tree of the carnal appetites is not the only harmful tree that sprouts forth from the soil of the lower soul, for the lower soul, the soul that commands wrong (*al-nafs al-ammārah biʾl-sūʾ*), contains the vices that would destroy the heart and the higher aspects of the soul.

spiritual and mystical content of the Book and to show how man himself is full of the signs of God. *Ishārah* thus acts as a gateway to the innermost reaches of holy text and holy man.

PROMINENT THEMES IN THE COMMENTARY

As mentioned above, the concepts of the soul and the heart and the status of the human being are among the foremost themes in the *tafsīr Jaʿfar*. These are interwoven with the tiered structure of the correlation between *walī*, *nabī*, and *malak* that is presented in the commentary. Connecting these—sanctified soul, the heart and its holy content, saint, prophet, angel, and the interpretive levels of *ishārah*, *laṭīfah*, and *ḥaqīqah*—is the matter of qualities which runs through the important themes as a tent pole holds up a tent. At the apex of the pole, lying beyond the tent, comes the point where, as we are told in the comment on 112:3: 'Majestic is our Lord (beyond) that delusive imaginations, intelligences, or sciences should perceive Him. Rather He is as He described Himself and the modality of His description is not intellectually perceivable. Glory to Him (beyond) that understandings or intelligences should attain unto His modality! *everything is perishing save for His Face* (28:88)';[40] and in the comment on 57:3, 'Jaʿfar said: He is the one who makes first the first and makes last the last, who manifests the manifest and conceals the hidden. Then these concepts fall away and there remains [only] He.'

The tent pole of qualities has two key pegs: *mawāfaqah bi'llāh* (harmony and consistency with God) and its antithesis, *mukhālafatu'llāh* (opposition or contrast to God). These two terms are applied, as appropriate, to the states of the soul and the spirit, demarcating the absence or presence of light.[41]

---

40 *Wajh*, also means 'essence' and 'identity'. Both essence and face pertain to the identity of a person. A person is identified by their face; likewise their true identity, their deepest reality, is revealed in their essence. With regard to the Qurʾānic verse, it means that everything apart from God's own identity perishes. This is pertinent to the discussion of qualities.

41 As this discussion unfolds, bear in mind the comments on 35:32, namely: 'The lower soul is wrongful; the heart is moderate, and the spirit is foremost.' 'Who looks with his soul to the world is wrongful; who looks with his heart to the hereafter is moderate; who looks with his spirit to

Soul (*nafs*) and Spirit (*rūḥ*)

To begin with the soul, the Qurʾānic anatomy of the soul presents three types of *nafs*: 1. *al-nafs al-ammārah bi'l-sūʾ* (12:53), i.e., the soul that incites to wrongdoing, which is the realm of darkness and sin; this aspect of the *nafs* is rendered by the phrase 'lower soul' in the translation. 2. *al-nafs al-lawwāmah* (75:2), i.e., the soul that censures and rebukes itself; this is the 'heroic soul'—symbolised by Marwah—that sees the darknesses within itself and strives to combat them; and 3. *al-nafs al-muṭmaʾinnah* (89:27), i.e., the soul at peace, the soul appeased—this is the theophanic soul that is peacefully conjoined and at one with its pure self and its individuated, differentiated holy spirit.

The interpretation of Ṣafā, already cited above, as the spirit (*rūḥ*)[42] because of its purity and freedom from the dirt of oppositions (to God) (*daran al-mukhālafāt*), and of Marwah as the soul because it uses the heroic virtues in performing services for its Lord (cited above as an example of both *taṭbīq* and *taʾwīl*), introduces the term *daran al-mukhālafah.* This term is explained, and its antithesis introduced, in the comment on the phrase from 53:44: *and that it is He who deadens and enlivens,* where we read, 'He deadens souls through opposition (*mukhālafah*) (to Him) and He enlivens hearts with the lights of harmony (*muwāfaqah*) (with Him).' Thus harmony with God (*muwāfaqah bi'llāh*) is life; contrast or oppositon to God is spiritual death—which, in this case, is not non-existence, but a deformed, darkened inner state of being. *Muwāfaqah bi'llāh* is enlivenment in that through this consistency with God, the lights of the divine qualities

the Truth is foremost.'

42 Ultimately there is only one spirit: the Spirit of God. The realm of the undifferentiated Spirit of God lies beyond the realm of being. Within the undifferentiated Spirit of God, God forms/shapes individuations. These individuated spirits are as etchings demarkated within the substance of the one divine Spirit. They are individual consciousnesses; they are the archetypes of differentiated beings. Differentiation takes place when God places an individuated spirit into a soul within the realm of being. The realm beyond being is undifferentiated existence, uncontaminated spirit (see at 76:21). However, beyond beyond-being, there is the unindividuated core of the divine essence: the *kunh*, totally and purely unindividuated and One, absolute and infinite divine oneness (the *tafrīd al-tawḥīd* in 18:46); the *huwīyah* (see at 57:3).

are allowed to permeate the soul and continue to extend through the creature; while *mukhālafah* is *daran* (dirt) that darkens the soul of the creature and thereby impedes the extension of the divine light [the divine being and qualities; the radiation of the divine spirit] in the locus of the soul.

The equation that lights are equal to qualities is made in the commentary on the *āyat al-nūr*, where thirty-seven qualities are listed for the different lights. First we are given qualities that pertain either to God in His relationship with the soul (protection, generosity, compassion, grace to name some of them) or to states of soul that open the soul to the divine influx (fear, hope, shame, surrender). But the last fourteen qualities pertain to God in Himself (His majesty, eternity, singularity, totality (*kullīyah*) and His Self-identity/ipseity (*huwīyah*). In other words, the initial qualities pertain to *muwāfaqah* inasmuch as those states of the soul are harmonious with divine qualities and allow passage to the latter; and the second list speaks of non-relational divine qualities. The summation that is given in the *tafsīr* states that the lights are all from the lights of al-Ḥaqq which God has mentioned in His words *God is the light of the heavens and the earth* (24:35). Al-Ḥaqq is the divine name that is used consistently throughout the *tafsīr* as *the* reference to God; even more so than the *ism al-mufrad*, Allāh; and here there is a clear equation between al-Ḥaqq and Allāh.[43] So with God the Truth, with al-Ḥaqq, come the lights divine. This shall be encountered again later at the deepest level of the heart.

Returning to the pivotal terms, with regard to the heroic soul, in the comment at 42:9, the *murūwah* of Marwah is defined for we are told how it is that the soul serves God. Regarding the phrase *wa huwa yuḥyī'l-mawtā; and He enlivens the dead*, we read: 'He (God) enlivens the souls (*nufūs*) of the believers through service to Him (*khidmatihi*) and He deadens the souls of the hypocrites through opposition to Him (*mukhālafatihi*).' So, as we saw above, God enlivens hearts with lights; while the soul is enlivened through *khidmah*. *Khidmah* here is given as the opposite of *mukhālafah*, in other words *khidmah* is *muwāfaqah*: consistency with and conformity to the divine. So the service (*khidmah*)

43 As mentioned earlier, Jaʿfar al-Ṣādiq's use of al-Ḥaqq in this way as practically a synonym for the *ism al-mufrad*, and the prominence of the divine name al-Ḥaqq are part of his legacy to Sufism.

of the soul lies in harmonising itself with the divine spirit; in other words the *murūwah* of Marwah lies in striving to become like Ṣafā: by eliminating, from the soul, the dirt of contrast to God.[44]

This process of eliminating dirt, of cleansing the soul, is directly related to the birth of the sanctified soul of the saint, the friend of God (*walīyu'llāh*). Thus the symbolic interpretation of Ṣafā and Marwah feeds directly into the subtle level of the *laṭāʾif* of the Book. That the interpretive level of *laṭīfah* pertains to sanctity (*walāyah*) is made clear at the very beginning of the *tafsīr* in the initial quote from the Imam, the quote that relates the subtleties (*laṭāʾif*) of the Book to the friends of God (the *awliyāʾ*).[45]

Subtlety (*laṭīfah*) and Friendship (*walāyah*)

Walāyah then, is the station of friendship with God. This entails the norm or convention of the *awliyāʾ*, which, we are told in the comment on 4:59, is to uphold/fulfil the pledge and to be patient in times of suffering and distress. With regard to upholding/fulfilling the pledge, at 3:76 on the phrase *rather the one who fulfils his pledge and is God-aware; for verily God loves the God-aware*,[46] we read that Jaʿfar said: 'The fulfilment of the pledge is being with (God) by excising that which is other than Him.' This excision of what is other than Him is the elimination of the *daran al-mukhālafah*; it is the work accomplished

44 So, for example, the heroic soul strives to allow the divine qualities of mercy, peace, love, patience, forgiveness, tolerance, wisdom, beauty, and compassion to manifest in the soul, even in the face of the opposite. The heroic soul, Marwah, to use the symbolism of the *tafsīr*, strives to overcome the greed, selfishness, and self-centredness within it so that the divine generosity and altruism may prevail; it strives to uproot the ugliness and darkness within it lest that cast a dust-shadow over the radiant beauty of the individuated spirit, of Ṣafā. In this striving to harmonise itself with the spirit lies the heroism of the soul.

45 The terms *walī/walīyu'llāh* and *walāyah,* which literally mean 'friend (of God') and 'friendship (with God),' are used as an equivalent for 'saint' and 'sainthood' respectively, although there is a case to be made for using 'friend' rather than 'saint', since the term 'friend' is susceptible of a broader application.

46 At 3:102, Jaʿfar defines *taqwā* (God-awareness) as follows: '*(Taqwā)* is that you see nothing in your heart other than Him.'

at the stage of Marwah. The resultant soul, the soul in which there is nothing that is other than Him, is in perfect harmony with Him. This soul is the theophanic soul, *al-nafs al-muṭmaʾinnah*, the soul at peace with and in God. This is the state of the highest soul which is a clear conduit for the divine lights (qualities). And that is the state of the friend of God.

As is made clear in the citations immediately below, it is to be noted that the *source* of the divine friendship is always God: it is *God* who is always the Friend (al-Walī), it is *God* who elevates the believers to the rank of friendship, just as it is *God* who took Abraham for friend (*khalīl*). When God befriends a soul, *He* makes it into a friend of His, a *walīyuʾllāh*. It is God who sanctifies a soul by befriending it. Friendship with God requires of the soul 'only' that it be receptive and allow God free passage in and through it. This is the reason for the *murūwah* and the spiritual battles.

God's hand is always extended, open in friendship, for He says: *God is the Friend of those who believe* (2:257). On the phrase *and God is the Friend of the believers* in 3:68, Jaʿfar says: '*and God is the Friend of the believers* in elevating them to reach the station of "the friend" (*al-khalīl*) 🌸 because proximity to (God) is a rank of love'. 'The friend' (*al-khalīl*) and 'the friend of God' (*khalīluʾllāh*) are epithets of the Prophet Abraham, based on the Qurʾānic phrase *and God took Abraham as a friend* (4:125).

Thus through their meaning, the epithets for Abraham are connected in the commentary with the other term for 'friend', namely, *walī*. The Prophet Abraham, friend of God, thus serves as the interface between *walāyah* and *nubūwah*, between *laṭīfah* and *ḥaqīqah*; in other words, between *walī* and *nabī*. From what follows below, it will be seen that the *tafsīr* presents the following correlation—the *nabī* is perfect *walī*.

It is said of Abraham in the Qurʾān that he 'rendered fully'. The Qurʾānic phrase is: *And Abraham who rendered fully* (53:37).[47] On this, Jaʿfar comments: 'the quintessence of sincerity is (faithful) fulfilment

---

47 The Qurʾānic verse is a comprehensive statement. Elsewhere in the Qurʾān it is stated that people do not esteem Him as it is His right to be esteemed (39:67); and the believers are exhorted to be aware of God as is His due (3:102). Full rendition to God is no less than total sanctity.

in every state and in every deed.'[48] *Waffā*, being the second form of the verbal root *w-f-y*, means to render fully a due or a right; to pay fully what is owed. This is why Abraham is no less than the high and intimate Friend of God, *khalīlu'llāh*, because to give God His due right is to be a faithful friend of God, a perfect saint, who in every state and action faithfully fulfils what is due to God. Reading this in the light of the above discussion of the fulfilment of the pledge, the Abrahamic fulfilment would be to allow God's qualities to shine through him in every state and deed.

However, the saints or friends of God are faithful friends of His not because *they* are friends to Him, for it is impossible for a creature to render fully to God His due, but because *He* is a friend to them. Only God can render fully to Himself His due. Sanctity is divine friendship—from God to God through the form of the saint-friend;[49] just as the divine speech is from God to God through the form of the creaturely locus, as seen in the last part of the comment on 20:12, where God tells another prophet, Moses: 'None bears My oration other than Me, nor answers Me except Me—I am the speaker and the one spoken to, while you are in the middle, a corporeal form in whom lies the locus of the oration.'

Through the theophanic sanctified soul of the *walī* and the perfect sanctity (*walāyah*) of the *nabī*, the above citation takes us beyond the connective interface between *laṭīfah* and *ḥaqīqah,* and brings us to the interface between prophet (*nabī*) and angel (*malak*). This latter interface is entirely on the level of the *ḥaqāʾiq*. The *tafsīr* may be said to present this interface most strongly in the passages on the Prophet Moses who, like his forefather, constitutes an example of how the *nabī*

---

48 This comment provides the equation of *wafāʾ* (the being faithful to a promise or trust) with *ṣidq* (sincerity, faithfulness, trustworthiness). Moreover, the implication, the dynamic of which is familiar from other comments, is that sincerity (towards God) is, quintessentially, faithfulness to Him and such faithfulness (the full rendering of what is due) is friendship with Him and this friendship is sanctity, sanctity is holiness and all holiness belongs to God the Holy, al-Quddūs and to Him alone.

49 See Q. 18:44, *thus it is, friendship/sanctity belongs to God the Truth; He is best in recompense and best in final consequence.*

is a perfect *walī* through allowing the divine qualities that abide in the spiritual heart to extend through the soul.

Reality (*ḥaqīqah*) and Prophethood (*nubūwah*)

If, through the sanctified soul, the level of *laṭīfah* pertains to sanctity, the level of *ḥaqīqah* pertains to the inner *sanctum sanctorum*, the spiritual heart, as we shall now see in the concept of the heart (*qalb*) presented in this commentary.

At 14:32 it is stated explicitly that '(God) has made the heart of the believer of service to His love and His knowledge. God's share of the slaves is their hearts and nothing else, because the heart is the receptacle of (God's) gaze and the repository of His trust and of the knowledge of His secrets.' This is why it was said above that in the *tafsīr* the heart is the element within the human being that is the locus which receives the direct influx from heaven.

To look at some details in the following comments concerning the heart, at 6:59 we read 'through hearts (God) unlocks guidance'—thus divine guidance is opened to a person through their spiritual heart.

At 6:79 Jaʿfar says of God '[He who] is totally and perfectly able to protect my heart from blameworthy thoughts and harmful whisperings which are not suited to al-Ḥaqq (the Truth, the Real)'—from which we understand that the human heart contains the divine truth and reality. Moreover, it is to be remembered that the divine name al-Ḥaqq is used consistently throughout the *tafsīr* as *the* reference to God. This implies that the heart is a receptacle for the divine presence. The heart is the inner 'holy of holies.'

At 9:111 the heart is referred to as being the conduit of love whereby God enlivens people with the means for attachment to Himself—which means that divine love flows to a person through their spiritual heart and thus provides them with the means of becoming attached to God, in which attachment lies their enlivenment, i.e., divine love begets attachment to God which equals life.

Thus, divine guidance (*hidāyah*), divine truth and the divine presence (al-Ḥaqq), divine love (*maḥabbah*) and life all flow to the human being through the subtle or spiritual heart. The heart thus receives and conducts the divine qualities. It seems incontrovertible that the divine qualities—which is tantamount to saying the divine lights, which is tantamount to saying the divine spirit—are the trust which is deposited in the heart as stated in the *tafsīr*, and that the gaze of God both conveys these qualities to the heart and nurtures them to fruition.

This trust—which is the *ḥaqīqah* of *insān*; the deepest reality of the human being, the holy content of the heart—consists then of a theophany (*tajallī*) of the divine qualities: God's mercy, love, beauty, wisdom, compassion, courteousness, His loving kindness, His truth, to name some. This theophany in turn, may then shine through the soul, to the extent that the soul is free of the *daran al-mukhālafāt* or the darkness of sins and ungodliness. For to the degree that the soul is in harmony with the divine, to that extent it is sanctified and to that extent the soul participates in and is a prolongation of the theophanic state of the heart, which in turn is a prolongation of the divine *ḥaqīqah* within the heart.

It is related from Jaʿfar that he said, commenting on the phrase *there is none in the heavens nor the earth but comes unto the Gracious as a slave*: (19:93) 'There is none but comes to the Gracious as a slave, either poor and wretched through his own qualities (*awṣāf*) or noble through (and) corroborating the qualities (*awṣāf*) of al-Ḥaqq.'

This is illustrated graphically in the comments on Moses at the burning bush where, through the profoundest *taʾwīl*, we are shown that the praiseworthy qualities in man are, in their *ḥaqāʾiq*, literally divine. We read at 7:142–3 on the phrase: *And when Moses came unto Our appointed tryst and his Lord spoke to him*: 'God . . . spoke to him through his inner disposition and his slavehood (*ʿubūdīyah*)—and Moses disappeared from his soul and was effaced from his qualities; then his Lord spoke to him through the deepest realities of his (praiseworthy) good qualities; and Moses heard, from his Lord, the description of Moses. *ʿUbūdīyah*, slavehood, means possessing nothing of your own; here it means that everything in the slave (*ʿabd*) is from the Lord (*Rabb*). With the qualities that pertain to the creature out of the way, God spoke in that creature through the roots (the deepest realities) of the praiseworthy qualities in the creature. That these are God's own qualities is made clear in the comment on 20:11–12, *then when he came to it (the fire) he was called 'O Moses! Verily I am I your Lord . . . so put off your two sandals.'* where we read that at the point of effacement Moses said to God:

'Moses has no standing with You nor has he the courage to speak unless You allow him to subsist through Your eternal subsistence and *(unless) You qualify him with Your character* so that You are wholly the orator and the one addressed.' Then He said: 'None bears My oration other than Me, nor answers Me except Me—I am the speaker and the one spoken to, while you are in the middle, a corporeal form[50] in whom lies the locus of the oration (*maḥallu'l-khiṭāb*)'. Nothing can sustain the divine except the divine. To bear the divine speech, Moses had to be qualified with the divine character.

The *nabī* then, the one who receives the divine speech, is the one qualified with the divine character. As in the case of Moses, and Abraham too, all non-divine qualities have been effaced from the souls of the *anbiyā*ʾ to make room for the divine replacement (*ʿiwaḍ*); and even as the souls of the *awliyā*ʾ have had excised from them all that is other than God; neither *nabī* nor *walī* contains any *daran* that obscures the gold of the *ḥaqīqah* within them. Here then is the ontological continuity between the *walī* and the *nabī*, between *laṭīfah* and *ḥaqīqah*—for both saint and prophet may be described as theophanic souls: ontological messages of God—like angels.

This equation with angels is made explicit in the comment at 28:29, '[Moses] saw a fire—an indication of the [divine] lights, for he saw light in the form of the fire. When he drew near to it, the lights of holiness pervaded him and the robes of intimacy encompassed him. Then he (Moses) was addressed with the subtlest oration and the most beautiful response was called for from him. *Through that he became a noble angel brought close to God.*' With the passage of the divine speech through him, Moses became a noble angelic being, i.e., a pure soul manifesting a perfect continuity of the divine spirit—like Ṣafā.

And so a circle is completed here, rejoining Ṣafā and Marwah, the allusive (*ishārī*) interpretation of which was the *madkhal*, the point of entry, into the other two categories of interpretation found in the commentary. This time, however, the approach to Ṣafā and Marwah is from within, through the *ḥaqīqah* for which they are the gateway. The examples from the text show how the deep current of the concepts of the soul and heart flow rapidly in the river of allusion (*ishārah*),

---

50 Or bodily form: *shabḥun*. See E. W. Lane, *Arabic-English Lexicon* (Cambridge, UK: Islamic Texts Society, 1984), at *sh-b-ḥ*.

through the waters of subtlety (*laṭīfah*), and end up in the ocean of the deepest realities, the *ḥaqāʾiq*: the essences of things, their reality or true nature. It has also been seen that qualities provide the continuing link between *ishārah*, *laṭīfah*, and *ḥaqīqah,* not just in the text but in the sacred human being who is made 'in the best image',[51] who is a friend of God in his soul, and is a messenger and message of God in his deepest reality.

We shall show them Our signs, upon the horizons and in themselves (41:53).

Prophet (*nabī*) and Angel (*malak*)

Returning to the discussion of the hierarchical relationship between saint, prophet, and angel as documented in this *tafsīr*, the account of Abraham presents the continuity between *walī* and *nabī* and shows how the *nabī* is the perfect *walī*. The account of Moses also shows that the *nabī* is the perfect *walī*, but goes a step further to reveal that that perfect *nabī* is *malak* (angel). This correlation is also presented in the commentary on the Joseph verses. On the phrase from 12:19, *here is a slave boy, and they concealed him for merchandise*, the commentary states:

'Jaʿfar said: God, most high, had a secret in Joseph. He hid the situation[52] of His secret from them, for had He disclosed to them the reality (*ḥaqīqah*) of what He had deposited in (Joseph), they would have died. Do you not see how they said "*Here is a slave boy*"? Had they known the traces of the [divine] power in him they would have said "Here is a prophet and a truthful one." Indeed, when part of the matter was disclosed to the women they said: *this is no human, this is naught but a noble angel*.' (12:31)

On the phrase, *then when they saw him and they extolled him*, from 12:31, 'Jaʿfar said: The awe of prophethood [that fell] upon them overlaid the situation of their desire for him, then they extolled him.' In other words, when the women (unlike the merchants who drew Joseph out of the well) perceived Joseph's prophetic status, their love for his

---

51 To use the words of the *tafsīr* on 95:4, *We have surely created mankind in the best form*. Jaʿfar said: 'In the best image.' That is to say: in the image of God.

52 Or 'rank', 'position', 'location', all of which are the meanings of *mawḍiʿ*.

external beauty was transformed into reverence for the manifestation of the divine beauty that they recognised in him.

Furthermore, Joseph receives the collective blessings of his blessed forefathers: 'Ja'far said [at 12:76]: "Thus We manifested in Joseph the collective blessings of his sincere/truthful forefathers inasmuch as We protected him ('aṣimnāhu) through (the divine contrivance) in the time of affliction."' The use of the verb 'a-ṣ-m, implies the protection of his innocence, his 'iṣmah.[53]

For the next step, which is an ascent from within the completed circle of ishārah, laṭīfah, and ḥaqīqah, we return to Abraham's account. As noted in the earlier discussion of 'Abraham who rendered fully' (Ibrāhīma'lladhī waffā), Abraham is presented as the perfect saint through being the faithful friend of God. The depth of the high rank of Abraham, prophet and faithful friend of God, is made graphically clear in the comment on the phrase the honoured guests of Abraham in 51:24. Concerning this phrase, Ja'far commented that the visiting angels were 'honoured inasmuch as they were given hospitality by the noblest of creatures, the most manifest of them in chivalry, the most distinguished of them in soul, the most exalted of them in fervour, [namely] the friend (al-Khalīl) [of God] 🕮'. In other words, the angelic visitors of Abraham are understood as being 'his honoured guests' not just because they were honourable in themselves or because he showed them much respect and honour but because he was the one receiving them. It was an honour to the three holy archangels Michael, Raphael, and Gabriel to be received by the Prophet Abraham, Faithful Friend of God.

The Moses and Joseph verses, where the perfect nabī is seen to be

---

53   The term 'iṣmah, innocence, is akin to chastity on the spiritual register. They both denote a pure receptivity towards God. This is what is meant by the Qur'ānic phrase ḥūr, 'chaste-eyed'. The word ḥūr is the plural of both aḥwar (masculine) and ḥawrā' (feminine). The chastity of the eye signifies the absence of anything that presents a contrast to the lights of the divine qualities/Spirit. The word 'ayn means eye, spring, and essence or core. The word wajh (as noted elsewhere) means both face and essential identity. The eye is the essential aspect of a face: the 'ayn is the essential aspect of the wajh. In the spiritual realm, the eyes of the angels literally manifest the divine light/s, in other words the divine quality/ies, that are flowing through their essences at that moment.

an angel, provide the interface between *nubūwah* and *malakīyah*. Now, with Abraham, the *tafsīr* takes us to the higher end of the interface between prophet and angel—where the perfect prophet and saint is higher than the archangels. Abraham's high detachment is manifest at 14:35 in the comment on the phrase *and preserve me and my sons from worshipping idols,* which provides the following paraphrase: 'Jaʿfar said: 'Do not take me back to my witnessing the friendship [that I have with You], nor take my offspring back to witnessing the prophethood.' In other words, Abraham regarded the awareness of sanctity or prophethood as 'idols' to the extent that they distract from God-awareness; i.e., when the awareness of the elevated status is an intrusion of ego-consciousness.

However, there is another element to Abraham's exalted station—namely, that Abraham, who was prepared to sacrifice his much beloved son, manifests partially, and by analogy, that divine aspect which sent the divine Word to be sacrificed to save the world.

At this juncture, the reader should perhaps recall that the *tafsīr*'s discussion of the *anbiyāʾ* is at the level of the deepest realities, the *ḥaqāʾiq*. In addition, as we move on to the comments on the Prophet Muḥammad, the reader is advised to keep in mind the literal meaning of his name: 'praised', and to bear in mind the application of these comments to the microcosm at the level of the *ḥaqāʾiq*. Furthermore, the reader should be aware that the *tafsīr* contains a dynamic interplay between the macrocosmic and microcosmic roles of a prophet, which manifests in the roles of the prophets vis-à-vis each other.

The comments on the Prophet Muḥammad are also situated on the higher interface of the prophetic rank that is superior to the archangels. Thus at *sūrah* 17 we read: 'It is said that a man came to Jaʿfar b. Muḥammad and said: Describe for me the ascent (*miʿrāj*). He replied: How should I describe for you a station which even Gabriel, with all the magnitude of his rank, was not able [nor permitted] to enter.' And at 53:8 'Jaʿfar said: . . . Do you not see that God, most high, veiled Gabriel from (the Prophet's) nearness [to God] and from his Lord's nearness to him (the Prophet).' At 3:31, on the phrase *say, if you love God, then follow me,* Jaʿfar said: 'The inmost selves (*asrār*) of the truthful have been bound to following Muḥammad ﷺ, in order that they know that although their states are exalted and their ranks are elevated, they are unable to exceed him or [even] touch him.'

It is also related from Jaʿfar b. Muḥammad (at 53:2), that he said: 'He [the Prophet] has not strayed from His nearness for even the twinkling of an eye.' At 53:18, on the phrase *truly he saw some of the greatest signs of his Lord*, we read, 'Jaʿfar said: He witnessed such indications of love as are too great to be related.'

The perfection of the Prophet and his exalted station is further explained at 48:2 in the comment on *and to complete His blessing upon you* 'Jaʿfar said, Part of the perfection of the blessing upon His Prophet ﷺ is that He made him His beloved; . . . and [that] He made him ascend unto the place of closest proximity and protected him in the ascent (*miʿrāj*), such that (*his gaze*) *did not waver, nor did it overstep the bounds* (53:17) . . . and [that] He made him an intercessor [with God] whose intercession is accepted; and He made him the lord of the progeny of Adam; and [that] He has joined his remembrance with His remembrance, and his satisfaction with His satisfaction; and [that] He has made him one of the two pillars of monotheism. This and the like thereof are among the perfection of the blessing upon the Prophet ﷺ and, through him and his rank, upon his community.'

Echoes of Abraham's intimate friendship with God are found at 53:11, on *the heart belied not what it saw*, in the commentary on the Prophet's *miʿrāj*. 'Jaʿfar said: No one knows what he saw, except He who showed and he who saw. The Beloved came close to the beloved, a confidant for him (*najīyan lahu*), an intimate friend with him (*anīsan bihī*). God, most high, has said: *We raise [by] degrees whom We will*' (6:83).

The ontological continuity between perfect *ʿabd* and *Rabb* is stated clearly at 9:128. Jaʿfar al-Ṣādiq said, God knows the weakness of His creatures in obeying Him and He informs them of that so that they know that they cannot attain purity (*ṣafw*)[54] through [their] service of Him. So He has established between Himself and them a creature of their own kind in form. Thus He says: *there has come unto you a messenger from among yourselves for whom what they have (of distress) is hard to bear.*(9:128) Thus [said Jaʿfar], He clothed him from His quality of pity and mercy and sent him forth unto creation as a faithful ambassador (*safīr ṣādiq*). And He made obedience to him obedience to

54 *Ṣafw* is from *ṣ-f-w* like Ṣafā and Muṣṭafā.

Him and conformity to him conformity to Him[55] for He says: *whoever obeys the messenger, verily he has obeyed God* (4:80).'[56] This continuity is implied also in the comment at 94:4, on the phrase *and* (*have not*) *We raised high your mention* where we read that whenever the Prophet is mentioned as messenger, God is mentioned as Lord.

Thus the *nabī* who is higher than the archangels is God's *safīrun ṣādiqun ilā'l-khalq*, the faithful ambassador of God unto creation. It is amply clear from the above comment that the ambassadorship is ontological; it pertains to the Prophet being clothed with the divine qualities—even as Moses was qualified by the divine character in order to receive and transmit the divine speech to creation.

The Faithful Ambassador of God

As faithful ambassador of God (*safīru'llāh al-ṣādiq*),[57] the Prophet Muḥammad conveys God's qualities to the world. On the phrase *as for the blessing of your Lord, speak [of it]*, from 93:11, Jaᶜfar said: 'Inform creation of that with which I have blessed them through you and your position.' The presence of the praised Prophet in the world imparts the divine qualities to the rest of creation.

The divine ambassador is also the way to approach the One who sent him. On 4:64, Jaᶜfar said, 'Whoever aims not for Us according to your way and customs and guidance (O Muḥammad), has gone astray and is misguided.' Elsewhere, we read: 'There is no way to the love of God except in following His beloved; nor is access to the Beloved sought with anything better than pledging allegiance to (His) beloved.'[58] The way to Him is through the 'praised' personification and beloved

---

55 Corresponding to Marwah's realised, theophanic conformity to Ṣafā.

56 See also 48:17, 33:71, 4:13, 3:32.

57 In addition to 'faithful', *ṣādiq* also means 'truthful, sincere'. *Ṣidq* and its associated words are, in this book, usually rendered as 'sincerity,' etc. However, in the phrase *ṣafīru'llāh al-ṣādiq*, 'faithful' is the rendition that best conveys the significance of the ambassador of God who fulfils his function of being existentially loyal to God, of conveying God's lights/qualities in and to the world.

58 This is a comment on 3:31, but it is located within the comment at 4:125. Clearly for the Muslim commentators, their Prophet is the best way to God, just as for the Christians it is Christ, and for the Hindus it is the *ishta-devta*.

manifestation of the divine qualities in the earthly realm.

And again on the phrase *this day I have perfected for you your religion*, (5:3) we read, 'Jaʿfar b. Muḥammad said, *This day* is a reference to the day that Muḥammad the Messenger of God ﷺ was sent, and the day of his prophetic message.' Religion and faith are perfected when the perfect *safīr* of the divine qualities, the praised one, the ontological message of God, arrives in the world, be it the microcosm or the macrocosm.

Then at 4:125 (*and God took Abraham as friend*), it is related 'from Jaʿfar b. Muḥammad, [that] he said: (God) proclaimed the title of friendship for Abraham, for the friend is obvious in meaning. But He kept hidden the title of love for Muḥammad ﷺ because of the perfection of his state.' Abraham, elsewhere the prophet who bestows honour upon the archangels through his presence, here represents the *walī* while the Prophet Muḥammad represents the *nabī ḥabīb*, and is called, further on in the comment, *ṣafiyihi*, 'His pure, bosom friend'.[59]

Thus the *tafsīr* states the superiority of the Prophet Muḥammad over the archangels and all other creatures. And again the question arises: since the other prophets and the archangels are pure, loving conduits of the divine spirit and qualities—in what lies this superiority? The answer is given in the commentary on the *āyat al-nūr* (24:35) which, as mentioned above, interprets the lights as qualities and lists qualities both human and divine. The commentary says, 'Each one of these lights has its people; it has its state and its locus. All (the lights) are from the lights of the Truth, which God, most high, has mentioned in His words: *God is the light of the heavens and the earth*. Each one of His slaves has a drinking place at one of these lights; and it might be that (a slave) has an apportioned lot from two lights or three. These lights are never perfected[60] except for *al-muṣṭafā*, the Chosen One,[61] ﷺ—for he stands

59 *Ṣafiy* means both 'bosom friend' and 'pure'—hence the double rendition above; it has also the connotation of being a specially chosen one (see Lane at *ṣafiy* and *ṣāfin*). This comment shows the flux between the roles of the prophets as contained in the *tafsīr*.

60 The Arabic verb *tamma* means 'to complete, perfect, to finish, to accomplish'. Thus the phrase '*lan tatimm li...*' could have been translated as: 'These lights are never accomplished (or attained) except by the Chosen One' because they are *given* to the chosen one by God.

61 Or, 'the Elect One'. *Iṣṭifāʾīyah* (pre-election) pertains to the chosen elect.

with God, through the condition of having perfected[62] slavehood and love. For He is Light, and he from his Lord is in possession of light.'[63]

The superiority of the Prophet Muḥammad then lies in the *comprehensive* perfection of his loving *ʿubūdīyah*, his slavehood, his receptivity towards his Lord. Where there is perfect and comprehensive loving *ʿubūdīyah* there the lights of the Lordship (*rubūbīyah*) may extend unimpeded, unadulterated. The comprehensive, perfect, loving *ʿabd* is *safīru'llāh al-ṣādiq*, the *nabī* that is higher than the archangels.

At 7:143 the commentary reads, 'Moses disappeared from his soul and was effaced from his qualities; then his Lord spoke to him through the deepest realities of his praiseworthy qualities and Moses heard, from his Lord, the description of Moses. Muḥammad ﷺ heard, from his Lord, the description of his Lord, for he was the most praised of the praiseworthy, in the sight of his Lord. Hence, the station of Muḥammad ﷺ was the lote tree at the utmost limit while the station of Moses was the mountain. Since God spoke to Moses on the mountain, He effaced its quality and never shall there appear thereon any vegetation or human settlement.'

The comment on 7:143 emphasises the point that Moses in himself is nothing, his quality is nothing—that is why he heard from his Lord that Moses is naught but a form in whom the locus of the divine speech is located—and that is why the mountain of Moses is bare. The mountain is cognate with Moses' soul—it had to be rendered bare, stripped of all its own qualities so that the divine speech could descend upon it, as discussed above. Moses here represents the soul empty for God; while Muḥammad, the most praised of the praiseworthy, represents the heart replete with only divine qualities, for only what is God's is most praiseworthy.[64]

Muṣṭafā, Ṣafā, *iṣṭifāʾīyah*, *ṣafīy* are all from the same verbal root: *ṣ-f-w*.

62 *Taṣḥīḥ* is the verbal noun from the second form of the root *ṣ-ḥ-ḥ*, meaning to render healthy, sound, free from any imperfection or defect. See Lane. Cf. Qurʾān 26:89 'Only he who comes to God with a sound heart (*qalbin salīmin*).'

63 The choice of words here recalls the Qurʾānic phrase: *and so he is in possession of a light from his Lord* (39:22). *ʿAlā* has 'in possession of' as one of its usages. See Hans Wehr, *A Dictionary of Modern Written Arabic*, ed. J. Milton Cowan (Beirut: Librairie du Liban, 1980), at *ʿa-l-y*.

64 The hierarchical prophetic map of the macrocosm presented in the

Likewise, on *and be patient—and your patience can only be through God*, in 16:127, 'Jaʿfar said, God enjoined patience upon His prophets; and He appointed the highest portion (of patience) for the Prophet [Muḥammad] ﷺ, inasmuch as He commanded him to be patient through God, not through himself.' In other words, He commanded him to be patient through the divine quality not through the human quality. Again, as long as the quality is through God it is 'praised', *muḥammad.*

Mary, Mother of Jesus

There remains one more rank to mention, that of Mary, Mother of Jesus. Of her, the commentary states (at 3:37) on the phrase, *her Lord accepted her*, 'Jaʿfar said, He accepted her so much so that the prophets, despite their exalted ranks, marvel at the magnitude of her rank with God. Do you not see that Zakarīyā said to her: *whence have you this? She said: It is from God*, that is, "it is from the one who accepted me."'

The acceptance mentioned pertains to the prayer of Mary's own mother. When she was pregnant with Mary, she said to God: *verily, I have dedicated unto You that which is in my womb, (as) consecrated (unto You)* (3:35). The *tafsīr* explains the word *muḥarraran* (*consecrated*) as follows: 'Free from bondage to the world and its inhabitants', and 'a pure/exclusive slave of Yours, who is not enslaved by anything among beings'. In other words, Mary was consecrated to be a pure *ʿabd*, which is to say, with absolute receptivity towards God, signified on the physical level by her chastity.

As mother of Jesus Christ, the historical Holy Virgin bore a historical manifestation of the redemptive divine Logos. Thus she was a perfectly pure manifestation on earth and of corporeality, of the divine aspect that contains and brings forth the salvific and self-sacrificing divine Logos—that is an aspect of the actual *ḥaqīqah* of Mary's inner 'rank with God', the magnitude of which causes the prophets to marvel (3:37).

To conclude this discussion, a tiered, yet interfaced, ascent of *nubūwah* is presented. Abraham and Moses exemplify the *nabī* who is perfect *walī*. Moses and Joseph show that the perfect *nabī* is an

---

commentary is to be understood on the microcosmic level too.

angel. Abraham, a *nabī-walī,* is higher than the archangels because he partially manifests the sacrificial divine aspect. Muḥammad as prophet-ambassador (*nabī-safīr*) and pure, bosom-beloved (*ṣafīy-ḥabīb*) is higher than the archangels and all creatures, through his comprehensive perfection of *ʿubūdīyah*; and Mary, Mother of Jesus, manifests on earth, the 'womb' *in divinis* that contains and brings forth the salvific *nabī-kalimah* or prophet-logos.

However, on closer inspection we see that this interfaced-hierarchy is still more intimately interwoven. Mary, chaste bearer of the divine Word, is an absolute *ʿabd Allāh*, a totally pure and chaste recipient of the divine; her chastity is perfect *ʿubūdīyah.* Moses, bearer of the divine speech, is purged of anything related to himself, his bare soul is chaste unto the Lord. Both Mary and Moses, as bearers of the divine Word, are empty for God, and are qualified with the divine character, in other words, both are '*muḥammad*' ('praised'). Muḥammad, bearer of the divine Word, is '*muḥammad*' and *safīru'llāh* through being clothed with the divine qualities. Joseph's prophetic *ḥaqīqah* evoked praise and thus was '*muḥammad*', his innocence (read *ʿubudīyah*) was safeguarded by God Himself; he manifested the collective blessings of his holy forefathers. Abraham, the prophet who bestows honour on the archangels through his presence, the most distinguished *walī,* the noblest of creatures, has naught but the divine qualities in his soul—his soul is *muḥammad,* it is totally free of any *daran al-mukhālafah,* totally in harmony with Ṣafā.[65]

And we are back with the centripetal, spiraling circles of *ishārah, laṭīfah, and ḥaqīqah* from the centre-point of which this divine display of God's lights in *nubūwah* erupts in a powerfully whirling vortex: Mary, Muḥammad, Abraham, Moses, Joseph, all '*muḥammad*', perfect

65 The broad nature of prophethood is underlined in the following phrase from 46:9 and the comment on it. *I (the Prophet Muḥammad) am not a new thing among the messengers.* Concerning this verse, Jaʿfar said [in explanatory paraphrase of these words and speaking in the voice of the Prophet]: 'There is nothing to do with me in my prophethood. It is purely something which I was given, not because of me but rather by grace from God when He made me suitable for His message and described me in the earlier Books of the prophets, God's blessings upon them all.'

ʿ*ubūdīyah*, reascending to the *rubūbīyah* whence they poured down.[66] Jaʿfar said: 'as he (Muḥammad) came down, lights radiated from him'.[67]

Divine pre-election (*iṣṭifāʾīyah*), Grace (*faḍl*), and Faithfulness (*ikhlāṣ*)

Having brought us to the heights of this holy vortex, the *tafsīr* has one more word. This is to indicate the extent of the reach downwards of the ascending vortex, that is to say, to show how far the dynamic pull of the vortex reaches into creation. At the apex you have the *nabī-safīr* who is *muḥammad* and who, as the chosen one, al-Muṣṭafā, is the comprehensive and perfect recipient of the divine influx by virtue of the divine pre-election, or *iṣṭifāʾīyah*, to partake of all the lights. The following citation shows the importance of that key term, *ikhlāṣ*, which means faithfulness, sincerity, truthfulness. Furthermore, the citation shows the all-encompassing nature of God's grace.

Qurʾān 35:32 reads: *Then We made those of Our slaves whom We elected, to inherit the Book; among them is he who wrongs his own soul and among them is he who is moderate and among them is he who is foremost through good deeds; that is the great grace.*

'Jaʿfar said: God, most high, distinguished [in the Book] three categories of believers. First, He called them *muʾminīn* (*believers*) then He called them ʿ*ibādinā* (*Our slaves*), thus attaching them to Himself as a grace and generosity from Himself; then He said, *(whom) We chose*—He made them all [specially chosen] bosom friends (*aṣfiyāʾ*)[68] knowing their different stations. Then, at the end of the verse, He put them all together, at the entry into paradise, for He said, *gardens of Eden which they enter* (35:33). Moreover, He commenced with those who wrong their souls, by way of informing us that He shall not be drawn close to except purely by His generosity. For wrongfulness (*ẓulm*) has

66 As the commentary has at 1:1: 'He (is) the foremost in praising Himself, before His creation; and by this precedence of His praise [of Himself], [His] benefaction settled upon His creation and they then (acquired) the ability to praise Him.'

67 Comment on 53:1, with reference to the descent of the star (*najm*).

68 *Aṣfiyāʾ* is the plural of *ṣafīy*, the title of the Prophet. In this comment, the *aṣfiyāʾ* are being included in the divine pre-election (*iṣṭifāʾīyah*)—they are among the ones whom God chose.

no effect on [divine] pre-election (*iṣṭifāʾīyah*). Then He (mentions) next the moderate, for they are between fear and hope. Then He sets the seal with the foremost lest anyone feel safe from His plot. All of them are in paradise because of the sanctity of one word, that is, the word faithfulness (*ikhlāṣ*).'[69]

The chosen elect: faithful ambassador, faithful friend, faithful believer, and unfaithful but chosen one. Clearly, the holy faithfulness which guarantees entry into paradise is *God's* faithfulness.

At first sight the comment seems counter-intuitive—why should the sinner (*ẓālim*) enter paradise—indeed how can they; how can darkness enter the realms of light? First, it should be understood that *ẓālim* may be taken as referring to someone who is, technically, a disbeliever or to an unfaithful believer. Indeed, it is not disbelief but wrongdoing that is mentioned; unfaithfulness refers to the all too common existential insincerity of the believer who generates *daran* in his soul, thereby wronging it.[70] The believing *ẓālimun li-nafsihi*, the one who darkens his soul by sins, who oppresses it (*aẓlama*),[71] is unfaithful because though he believes in God, his acts produce darkness (*ẓulm*)—both within the microcosm of his soul and in the macrocosm of the external *dunyā*. Such unfaithfulness, though not technically disbelief amounts to existential *kufr* because this darkness obscures or veils the divine light. The verb *kafara*, from which come the words *kāfir* and *kāfirīn*, means 'to disbelieve (in God) or to deny (God)'; it also means 'to veil or obscure or cover'. When a person behaves in a way that is not in conformity with the divine qualities, that person veils, obscures and covers up God's light—in other words that person performs an act that existentially denies God because it blocks the flow of the divine qualities

69 *Ikhlāṣ* is more commonly translated by others as 'sincerity' or 'purity', but 'faithfulness' is one of its primary meanings.

70 As ʿAbd al-Razzāq al-Qāshānī stated, centuries later, in his commentary on Q. 59:7–9: '*They are the truthful*, possessing well-established faith, their actions testifying to their beliefs. For the mark of inner certitude lies in its effect on the person's behaviour—so that their every movement is in conformity with the testimony of their knowledge.' In other words, 'behaviour is the gauge of our sincerity.'

71 The verbal root *ẓ-l-m* from which *ẓulm* and *ẓālim* are derived, comprises the meanings to darken, to oppress, to tyrannise, to treat unjustly, to wrong, to sin. All these need to be kept in mind.

through that soul. Yet such a fallen one is brought into paradise.

However, the unfaithful sinner does not enter paradise in the state of *ẓulm*.[72] Rather, the grace of God ensures that such a fallen chosen one is pulled up by a vortex of the holy, and is brought into a state of heavenly harmony. In short, the sinning chosen one (*muṣṭafā*) undergoes purgation either on earth or in the earlier stages of the afterlife, in order to become fully *qualified* to re-enter paradise. In the commentary, no less than Adam (at 20:121–2) and especially the prophet-king David provide an example of this.

To focus on David, at 38:25, on the phrase, *and David guessed that We had tried him, so he begged forgiveness of his Lord*, 'Jaʿfar said: Part of that is what God, most high, mentions about His trying David and his trial and test, and what was brought forth for him in the way of immense renunciation, remorse, continual weeping, sorrow and immense fear, such that he clung close to his Lord. Thus, although the occasioning sin therein was extensive, its final outcome was immense, glorious and exalted—because through it, God gave (David) intimate closeness and the favoured state of being beloved.' Let it be noted that the repentance, *tawbah,* was 'brought forth for him', it was given to him by God to purify him; and it entailed clinging to God, which is part of 'the intimate closeness'. When grace touches the fallen *muṣṭafā*, it picks him up and places him 'between the shirt and the skin'.

Then in 34:10 God states: *and indeed We gave unto David grace from Us.* 'Jaʿfar said: *Grace*—confidence in God and trusting reliance upon Him.' Thus this high chosen one, redeemed from his unfaithfulness, re-infused with God-awareness, relied on God and was carried by God to the place always destined for him. 'Jaʿfar said: The God-aware [person] is he who is wary of everything other than God; and the God-aware is he who is wary of following his desires. Whoever is characterised [qualified] thus is carried by God, flanked by light, to the Presence of witnessing so that the people at the assembly might

72 God's mercy forgives all wrongs (*verily God forgives all sins*). However, this is not to say that the spiritual realm is illogical or contains illogical leaps. Quite the contrary. Logic, as we know it, exists because of God's logic. Muddy water cannot subsist in the airy heights unless the mud is shed and the water becomes vapour; in that transformation lies the magic of the divine mercy.

know his place among them.'[73]

At the other end of the scale from the rophet-king David is the common fallen *muṣṭafā,* who, in the face of his own tests and trials, fails. He too (along with all those between him and royal David), is taken up and held close to the divine breast[74] and taken through his divinely-tailored purgation.[75] Allowing for differences of degree, intensity and appropriateness (*munāsabah*), the treatment meted out by grace to God's fallen elect is the same.[76] Grace activates, or re-activates, and strengthens, the Marwah of such a person; and grace carries this Marwah through the 're-sitting' of the spiritual journey, overlooking weaknesses and faults, forgiving and redeeming time and time again, sustaining and strengthening Marwah to *khidmah* and *murūwah*; and it is grace that brings this utterly fallible heroic soul into Ṣafā's divine holiness.[77]

That is the grace of God, He gives it to whom He will, and God is the possessor of tremendous grace (57:21).

Further Themes

The above is not an exhaustive treatment of the subject of prophets, angels and saints in the *tafsīr*—but it brings to light some of the deepest aspects and correlations. As the reader goes through the commentary

73 Comment on *the day We gather the God-aware;* from 19:85.

74 As cited above, God makes them all *aṣfiyāʾ* (pure, bosom friends).

75 Adam himself underwent this process. On the phrase: *and Adam disobeyed his Lord and thus went astray* (20:121), Jaʿfar said: 'He viewed paradise and its bliss with his eye and so it was proclaimed against him, until the day of judgement: *and Adam disobeyed his Lord.* Had he looked at it with his heart, a complete abandonment would have been proclaimed against him for all eternity. But then God had compassion on him and was merciful to him, (as seen) in His words: *then his Lord chose him and relented towards him and guided (him)'* (20:122).

76 Even Abraham prayed: *and when I am ill He heals me* (26:80). This is glossed in the *tafsīr* as follows: 'And when I am sickened by the sight of my deeds and my states, He heals me with the reminder of (His) grace and generosity.'

77 As stated at 27:61, God placed God-given success (*tawfīq*) and the intellect as the barrier between the lower soul with its darknesses and the heart. Grace protects Ṣafā, and grace brings Marwah successfully into union with Ṣafā.

he or she will come across other dimensions of the spiritual life, such as the virtues—particularly *tawakkul* (trusting reliance upon God), *iftiqār* (neediness unto God), *inqiṭāʿah* (detachment), among others. He will meet with the highest explanations of the remembrance of God, *dhikru'llāh* (at 18:24; 51:55). At 51:55, the commentary provides a most rigorous standard for authentic remembrance of God: 'Whoever remembers God but then forgets His remembrance, was untouched by His remembrance.' The *tafsīr* then immediately proceeds to define 'His remembrance': 'The remembrance of God . . . is His oneness, His prior eternity, His will, His power, and His knowledge—never does any forgetfulness or unawareness befall Him for they are among human qualities. Whoever, then, remembers God, most high, remembers Him through His remembrance of Him.' There it is again: 'His remembrance of Him' is through His qualities. This is existential, or ontological, *dhikr*.

At this point, I would draw the reader's attention to the principle of 'potency in subtlety' which permeates the whole matter of the divine interaction with the human. Faced with the divine light, whether the advent of the divine qualities be through the passage of the divine speech or in the vision of God, the absolute power of the subtle light of God is inescapable and it obliterates. The lights, which are so utterly subtle, are, concomitantly, totally potent. This exemplifies, at the highest levels, the spiritual principle of 'potency in subtlety'.[78] For God is the very most Subtle and He is the very most Powerful; indeed He *is* subtlety and He *is* power.

In general, the lights divine purge. 'Jaʿfar said: . . . when gnosis

78 Which is found even in something like homoeopathy. An aspect of this potency is the element of indubitability. Ultimately, the Presence of the Subtlest One is the most irrefutable. This may seem paradoxical initially but it is not. Within the physical realm we have the analogy of the sun and sunlight for God and His qualities (an analogy much loved by mystics of all traditions). The creatures who abide in the muddy depths of a riverbed will not understand much other than muddy earth and dark water; the fish who swim in clearer waters will know something about light. But, for example, a bird such as an eagle, who not only flies in the air but soars above the clouds, circling higher and higher, will know the indisputable presence of light, which he cannot touch but which he sees all around him and the heat of which permeates his whole body.

enters hearts, it removes from them all demands and all desires—so that there is no place in the heart for anything other than God, most high'.[79] The light is a fire that burns away all that is unlike it. 'Jaʿfar said: He (Moses) saw a fire—an indication of the [divine] lights, for he saw light in the form of the fire. When he drew near to it, the lights of holiness pervaded him and the robes of intimacy encompassed him'.[80] The ignited fires of love and gnosis in the hearts of the monotheists and the believers, 'burn up every eagerness for (what is) other than God, and every remembrance other than His remembrance'.[81]

The unveiled lights eradicate all else; but inasmuch as they are divine, they are the most exquisite bliss. In the same instant that they burn away the ugly *daran al-mukhālafāt*, they replace it with their own indescribable beauty and purity. When Moses approached the burning bush, holiness permeated him, intimacy embraced him; he was effaced and replaced at once. Even so David was purged and replenished at once. The negation (*nafī*) and the affirmation (*ithbāt*) occur in one breath.[82] As the *tafsīr* states at 8:17, when God 'has effaced them from their souls, He Himself is the replacement of their souls for them'.

Seeing God

Other preeminent mystical matters, such as man's secret inmost self (*sirr*) and the spiritual ascent (*miʿrāj*) are also included in the *tafsīr*. These are all discussed in the notes at the relevant places. Here, the subject of the vision of God will be considered. This subject is presented in the commentary through different terms: *mushāhadah*, *ruʾyah*, and *naẓar*. Initially, there seems to be a distinction entailed by the different terms. However, on closer inspection of the meanings, we begin to feel again the now familiar circular dynamic, as yet again we find that these terms overlap and interpenetrate. All three terms have been used in the

79 Comment on: *verily, kings, when they enter a town, destroy it* (27:34).

80 Comment on: *he perceived, on the side of the mountain, a fire* (28:29).

81 Comment on: *The kindled fire of God. Which rises up, overwhelming hearts* (104:6–7).

82 *Lā ilāha illā'llāh*. After that, the 'praised' is the messenger of God, *muḥammadun rasūl Allāh*, which, with the holy, is a permanently stable inner state, while lesser souls experience it with varying fluctuations as an ongoing organic process of spiritual growth.

text in a way that bespeaks that intriguing weave of the single thread of reality, which in places emerges on the external side (*ẓāhir*) of the garment of existence, in other places showing on the inner side; sometimes at a higher level, sometimes at a lower level—all at the same time.

Mushāhadah (witnessing) pertains to a beholding by being present. In other words, *mushāhadah* refers to witnessing by seeing or by experiencing or through presence. At 25:20 we are told that the inmost selves of the prophets are never disengaged from the witnessing, and on 26:62, we read 'who is [engaged] in witnessing (God) and is in [the divine] Presence, how should he be affected by that which proceeds from him or redounds to him'. These comments indicate, firstly, that *mushāhadah* is located at the level of the deepest reality, that of the inmost self, the *sirr*, which is the *ḥaqīqah;* but secondly, at the same time, there is a duality, for the creature is engaged in things that proceed from him or redound to him while the inmost self is ceaselessly witnessing, present in the divine Presence without any interruption.

Ruʾyah (seeing) pertains to the unveiled vision of God with the eye. The eye to eye seeing of God (*ruʾyati'llāh muʿāyanatan*) is discussed in the Mosaic verses (7:143) even more powerfully than the speech of God was. In the speech of God, a tantalising blend of duality/non-duality is retained: God told Moses that God is the speaker and the One spoken to. But the unveiled vision of God would be such an obliteration, such a complete annihilation of the creature, that Moses is not granted his request to see God 'eye to eye'. The key to understanding this is the term 'eye to eye'. The eye is the core of the face; the face is the part of the body that identifies a person; it is our identity. In Arabic the word for eye (*ʿayn*) means also 'essence, core, source'. So the eye of the face is the essence, the source, the core of the identity. Thus, the term 'eye to eye' means 'deepest essence to deepest essence'. That would have entailed Moses' corporeal death, the shedding of his soul, the evaporation of his decontaminated, differentiated divine spirit into the pure, undifferentiated divine spirit, and the complete re-absorption of his individuated divine spirit into the unindividuated divine spirit, into the core essence of the divine identity, the eye (*ʿayn*) of the divine face (*wajh*). The *ruʾyah*, then, entails the absolute effacement of the creature and the re-absorption of the spirit into its full self beyond being, in other words, a comprehensive *fanāʾ fī'llāh.*

Naẓar (gazing) pertains to looking at God. The gazing at God (*naẓar ilā'llāh*) is described as the highest rapture in the hereafter, in the comment on *and therein is that which the souls desire and enraptures the eye* (at 43:71): 'Jaʿfar said: What a difference between what the souls desire and that which enraptures the eye. For all the blessings, desirable things and delights of paradise are, in comparison with the rapture of the eye, as a finger dipped in the ocean—because the desirable things of paradise have a limit and an end, for they are created. But in the ever-abiding abode the eye is enraptured only in gazing upon the Ever-abiding [Himself] ﷻ, and that has no limit, nor description, nor end'—because it pertains to the realm beyond creation, beyond being and entails a passing beyond any duality, as with the *ruʾyah* and the ceaseless *mushāhadah*.

Yet the looking, or 'gazing', at God (*naẓar ilā'llāh*), seems also to have a manifestation with duality. Concerning *in the seat of sincerity* (54:55), 'Jaʿfar said: . . . none but the sincere ones are seated therein. It is the seat wherein God fulfils the promises [made to] His friends, in that they are permitted to look (*naẓara*) at His august face.' But at 61:13, the gloss describes the seeing of God in the 'Assembly of Truth' as the *ruʾyah* of God—with all that *ruʾyah* denotes in the way of the annihilation of the creature. The conclusion is that the *naẓar ilā'llah* takes place at different levels with varying degrees of intensity, like *mushāhadah*.

The three commentarial terms for the vision of God are thus seen to pertain to overlapping and interpenetrating yet ascending levels—like the levels of being. Different degrees of intensity at different levels experienced either consecutively or simultaneously. An ascending spiral that increasingly narrows until it coincides with the infinite divine eye, while remaining extended right down into density. *Then He/he drew near, reaching down He/he drew nearer* (53:8). As is noted in the comment, the word *tadallā* is remarkably evocative, meaning 'to hang down, draw near, descend'—but crucially *tadallā* is understood to denote a coming down *without leaving* the highest place.

Individual Predestination (*qadar*)

Readers will also encounter an adamantine predestinarian attitude. At 8:44, absolute predetermination is affirmed: 'That which He has decreed in pre-eternity, He manifests in moment after moment and instant after instant.' On the phrase *and with Him is the Archetype of the Book* (*wa ʿindahu ummu'l-kitāb*), (at 13:39), the following gloss is given: 'The Book in which distress and felicity are ordained. Nothing is added to it nor is anything subtracted from it. *The Word with Me is not altered* (50:29). Deeds are signs. Then he for whom felicity (*saʿādah*) was ordained will have felicity at the end, while he for whom distress (*shaqāwah*) was ordained will have distress at the end.'

At 53:32 on *He knows you best*, 'Jaʿfar said: He knows you best because He created you and ordained for you [whatever] distress and felicity [is to come to you] even before your birth in being. Yet you are agitated by that which has been settled upon you preveniently, of the appointed time (of death), sustenance, felicity, and distress. Works of obedience do not procure felicity nor do deeds of opposition (to God) procure distress. Rather the prevenient ordinance is what sets the seal to that which was begun.' The positive prevenient ordinance would seem to correspond to *iṣṭifāʾīyah*, and the negative one would then be the absence of pre-election.[83]

The issue of why some souls are elected and some not, is not addressed by the *tafsīr*, beyond stating that God's plot is more hidden than the crawling of an ant on a black rock on a pitch-black night (at 27:50). However, we begin to get indications of what direction the commentary might take on this matter, in the emphasis on God's foreknowledge—He knows everything about every soul before they are brought into being—and in the universal interpretation of the divine patronage expressed in *rather God is your protecting patron* (3:150)—'Jaʿfar said: [He is] in charge of all your affairs, from the beginning unto the end.' Nonetheless, the subtle difference between God's absolute foreknowledge and predetermination is not expressed in the commentary. So this question shall be set aside for the present, perhaps to be returned to in another work.

---

83 From the Islamic point of view, most souls on earth do not know what happens before the scenario of the present earth is enacted 'on stage'; nor is it commonly known what will happen with a given soul after the present scenario on earth is over, though some are granted some knowledge, as God wills. The prior existence and post-corporeal states of a soul are part of the knowledge of the unseen (*ʿilm al-ghayb*)—and God is the knower of the unseen, that which is absent from us, and of the seen, that which is present with us.

Intercession (*shafāʿah*)

The matter of intercession (*shafāʿah*) is brought up briefly in the comments on 108:1, 48:2, and 53:10. The commentary refers to the intercession granted to the Prophet. *Kawthar* (abundance), at 108:1, is interpreted as 'intercession for your community.' However, intercession is not restricted to the *anbiyāʾ*, for at 22:34 we read that the nature of the *glad tidings* in the phrase *give glad tidings to the humble* is: 'Authority in intercession.' In other words, the humble are to be given the glad tidings of receiving the authority to intercede.

A distinction is drawn between intercession *per se* and intercession that is accepted. The latter is part of the perfect blessing upon the Prophet: 'Jaʿfar said: Part of the perfection of the blessing upon His Prophet ﷺ is that He made him . . . an intercessor [with God] whose intercession is accepted' (at 48:2).

States (*aḥwāl*) and Stations (*maqāmāt*)

The spiritual states (*aḥwāl*) and stations (*maqāmāt*) of the Sufis are mentioned in the comment on the phrase *O you people* (4:1). 'Jaʿfar said: That means, be among those people who are truly human and do not be forgetful of God. For whoever has recognised that he is from that human being whose nature (God) endowed with that with which He endowed it, his fervour becomes too great [for him to] seek [only] the lower (spiritual) stations, and his rank is raised until the Truth [Himself] is his final ending: *to your Lord is the final end* (53:42). The eminence of his fervour comes through the privileges of communication and inspiration with which he has been favoured.'

Maqāmāt are specified and named in 7:160 and in 25:61 during the *ishārī* interpretation of the twelve springs of the Banī Isrāʾīl and the stellar mansions (*burūj*) respectively, and in the light verse (24:35). With regard to the springs, it is related: 'From gnosis there gush forth twelve springs. All people drink from one of those springs, in a [given] rank, at a [given] station, according to their scope.' There then proceeds a listing of spiritual stations, in a way that is reminiscent of the *āyat al-nūr* comment. Just as the lights all proceed from the light of al-Ḥaqq, the springs all gush from the one spring of intimacy and aloneness with God: 'this is the very spring of gnosis.' However, the light verse listing is longer and fuller whereas the twelve stations named for the springs and the twelve stellar mansions are much more compact lists. This might seem to indicate that the light verse comment is from a later date, when the Sufi schema of stations was more developed. Then again, it may simply be that with the springs and stellar mansions, the number was limited—but in the light verse no number is indicated, therefore the commentator was able to provide a more extensive list, especially since the concept of lights is conducive to that. As the commentary on the light verse has already been discussed above, the focus here shall be on the other two verses.

Though the qualities given in each list are not identical, there is an overlap, sometimes explicitly in the terms, sometimes implicitly in the meaning. There is no overlap in the order of placement. In the verse of the springs (7:160) the list is as follows.

1. (professing) God's unity (*tawḥīd*);
2. slavehood (*ʿubūdīyah*) and joy (*surūr*) in it;
3. faithfulness (*ikhlāṣ*);
4. sincerity (*ṣidq*);
5. humility (*tawāḍuʿ*);
6. contentment (*riḍāʾ*) and entrustment to God (*tafwīḍ*);
7. the Peace (of the Divine Presence) (*al-sakīnah*) and dignity (*waqār*);
8. liberality (*sakhāʾ*) and confidence in God (*thiqqah biʾllāh*);
9. certainty (*yaqīn*);
10. intellect (*ʿaql*);
11. love (*maḥabbah*); and
12. intimacy (*uns*), aloneness (with God), (*khalwah*), and gnosis (*maʿrifah*).

In the mansions verse (25:61) the list is:

1. faith (*īmān*);
2. gnosis (*maʿrifah*);
3. intellect (*ʿaql*);
4. certainty (*yaqīn*);
5. submission (*islām*);[84]

84 *Islām* (submission to God) is to be understood as a willing receptivity of the influx of the divine qualities, a willing submission of the soul (be it hard-won or otherwise!) to this influx.

6. goodness (*iḥsān*);[85]
7. trusting reliance upon God (*tawakkul*);
8. fear (*khawf*);
9. hope (*rajāʾ*);
10. love (*maḥabbah*);
11. yearning (*shawq*); and
12. rapture (*walah*).

Both lists contain an ascension. However, the dynamics of the ascent are described differently. The ascent in the springs list seems linear: 'Whosever drinks from one of these springs finds its sweetness and strives hopefully for the spring which is higher than it—from spring to spring until he attains unto the origin. When he reaches the origin he realises the Truth.' Whereas the mansions of the heart orbit within the spiritual heart, radiating their qualities and thus sustaining the health of the heart. 'The mansions of the sky are the orbits of the sun and moon . . . There are mansions in the heart too . . .' The mansions of the heart are dimensions of faith and gnosis, through which the heart ascends: 'Now the heart is a sky because through faith and gnosis it rises (*yasmū*) without limit or end. Just as the one known has no limit to Him, even so knowledge of Him has no limit to it.' Thus the spiritual heart rises endlessly in the sky of the Endless One, in a spiralling ascent through the orbiting dimensions of faith and the infinite knowledge of the Infinite One; while in the other list, the *sālik* (the 'journeyman' of the alchemists)[86] ascends an axis that springs from and feeds back into the Truth Himself, drinking from the springs until he comes to, and drowns in the Original Ocean. In both cases, yet once again the *tafsīr* has retraced ontological oneness through qualities.

Some of the prominent seams in this *tafsīr* have been discussed above at some length, while others have been touched on briefly. It is hoped that this provides a platform from which the reader shall continue to

85 *Iḥsān* also denotes sincerity of *islām* and *īmān*; cf. the saying of the Prophet '*iḥsān* is that you worship God as though you see Him. . .'

86 That this commentary contains spiritual alchemy should be self-evident by now; it is not so much a matter of turning dirt/dust (*daran*) into gold, but of eliminating the *daran* to reveal the Gold within.

mine these strata and all the others, extracting the numerous gems contained in this collection of exegetical comments ascribed to the Imām Jaʿfar al-Ṣādiq.

NOTE ON THE ARABIC TEXT

The Arabic text of Paul Nwyia's edition has been reproduced in appendix 1 which, being based strictly on manuscripts, contains absences such as hamzas and the vocalisation of the Qurʾānic citations. In this translation, the Arabic text of the Qurʾān follows the Ḥafṣ recitation as per the Medina printing of the Qurʾān, which has been transliterated in the *tafsīr*.

At the beginning of his edition, Nwyia has the following quotation from Sulamī's introduction to the *Ḥaqāʾiq al-tafsīr*. This citation indicates that it was part of Sulamī's aim, as compiler, to arrange the comments that he collected in their codical order.

> None of them occupied himself with bringing together the understanding of His oration, according to the language of the people of reality, except for some scattered verses, not in order, ascribed to Abīʾl-ʿAbbās b. ʿAṭāʾ and some verses mentioned (as being) from Jaʿfar b. Muḥammad al-Ṣādiq ﷺ.
>
> *Ḥaqāʾiq al-tafsīr liʾl-Sulamī*

Spiritual Gems

Spiritual Gems from Jaʿfar al-Ṣādiq

Bismi'llāhi'l-Raḥmāni'l-Raḥīm

In the Name of God, the Gracious, the Merciful

It is related from Jaʿfar b. Muḥammad that he said: The Book of God has four things: literal expression (*ʿibārah*), allusion (*ishārah*), subtleties (*laṭāʾif*) and the deepest realities (*ḥaqāʾiq*).[1] The literal expression is for the commonalty (*ʿawāmm*), the allusion is for the elite (*khawāṣṣ*), the subtleties are for the friends [of God] (*awliyāʾ*),[2] and the deepest realities are for the prophets (*anbiyāʾ*).

1 *Ḥaqāʾiq*, singular *ḥaqīqah*, signifies the essence, or reality or true nature of something; it also means a factual truth. See Lane, at *ḥaqīqah* under *ḥ-q-q*.

2 *Awliyāʾ Allāh*, 'the friends of God', is the Muslim term for saints.

1

سُورَةُ الفَاتِحَةِ

al-Fātiḥah (The Opening)

1:1 بِسۡمِ ٱللَّهِ ٱلرَّحۡمَٰنِ ٱلرَّحِيمِ ١

Bismi'llāhi'l-Raḥmāni'l-Raḥīm[3]

In the Name of God, the Gracious, the Merciful.

[Concerning the word] *bism*, Jaʿfar b. Muḥammad said: The [letter] *bāʾ* is His eternal subsistence (*baqāʾuhu*); the *sīn* is for His names (*asmāʾuhu*) and the *mīm* is His sovereignty (*mulkuhu*).[4] The faith of

3 It is almost impossible to translate these divine names with single words in a way that even comes close to conveying their fuller significances. The verbal root of these two divine names, *r-ḥ-m*, comprises the meanings of graciousness, mercy, and compassion. These meanings show, respectively, that God is gracious in Himself, merciful to those other than Him, and thirdly, fully empathetic—because compassion can only arise from empathy. This last indicates the oneness of being, because unless you share something with the other you cannot experience empathy. Empathy is ontologically impossible in the absence of a common factor. The one thing that all beings share in common is being. This is not to fall into pantheism. An analogy is the mother who totally transcends the baby in her womb: the baby is not the mother, but the mother is all around the baby and within the baby in such a profound manner that were it not the case, the baby would not exist. Moreover, while the baby is in the womb, it is totally dependent on the mother. The whole of being is to God as the unborn baby is to the mother. This analogy is well suited to these names, since the words for womb (*raḥim/riḥm*) also derive from the root letters *r-ḥ-m*.

4 Knowledge of the occult properties of the letters of the alphabet (*ʿilm al-ḥurūf*) and of the divine names is part of the science of '*jafr*'. In origin, *jafr* is said to be 'esoteric knowledge of an apocalyptic nature reserved

the believer is his recollection of His eternal subsistence, and the service of the [spiritual] seeker is his recollection of His names, while the extinction[5] of the sage from the kingdom is through its King.

He also said: [The word] *bism* [has] three letters: *bāʾ*, *sīn*, and *mīm*. The *bāʾ* is the gate (*bāb*) of prophethood, the *sīn* is the secret (*sirr*) of prophethood which the Prophet confided[6] to the elite of his community,[7] and the *mīm* is the kingdom (*mamlakah*) of faith which

---

for the imāms . . . heirs and successors of ʿAlī' (Hodgson, 'Djafr al-Ṣādik', *EI*²). ʿAlī b. Abī Ṭālib is said to have been taught this knowledge by the Prophet posthumously. *Jafr* then became 'assimilated to a divinatory technique accessible to the wise whatever their origin, particularly the mystics' (Hodgson, 'Djafr al-Ṣādik', *EI*²). The science of *jafr* grew to cover knowledge of what is ordained (*jafr wa jāmiʿ* as expressions of *qaḍāʾ wa qadar*); gematria and isopsephy (*ḥisāb al-jummal*); transposition and substitution of letters one by another (*atabash*, and other methods used in Qabbalah); and astrological knowledge (of Indian origin). Most importantly for our purposes, *jafr* is used in spiritual and mystical interpretations of the Qurʾān. This dimension of *jafr* is attributed by Ibn Saʿd to ʿAlī b. Abī Ṭālib from whom it is said to have passed to Jaʿfar al-Ṣādiq through his uncle Zayd b. ʿAlī. It is said that Jaʿfar had a book that contained this esoteric teaching. On his authority, this book was copied by Hārūn al-Ijlī, and came to be called *kitāb al-jafr* because of the skin upon which it had been written (*jafr* also means a lamb or kid). The *kitāb al-jafr* contained statements on the authority of the Imām Jaʿfar about the interpretation of the Holy Book and its inner meaning. It is not extant as a whole book but fragments of it are known.

5 *Fanāʾ* (extinction, annihilation, effacement) and *baqāʾ* (eternal subsistence), with which it is usually paired, are important terms in Islamic spirituality, referring to the eternal subsistence of God and the effacement of all else, and specifically to the effacement of the spiritual seeker, in Him. In Qurʾān 55: 26–27, the verbs from which these terms are derived are used to state that everything is always in a state of transience, perishing (*fānin*) while His Face/Identity/Self (*wajh*) is that which alone remains (*yabqā*). The influence and use of these terms in Sufism is traced back to Imām al-Ṣādiq's use of them in his *tafsīr*. See Carl Ernst, *Words of Ecstasy in Sufism* (Albany: State University of New York Press, 1985), p. 10.

6 'Confided' (*asarra*, which also means 'to make happy, to gladden').

7 For the Shīʿīs, this would be a reference to the imams as inheritors of the mantle of the Prophet; while for the Sufis this would be a reference to the imams but also to whoever attains the high rank of *fanāʾ fī'l-nabī* (extinction in the Prophet).

embraces the white and the black.

[It is related] from Jaʿfar b. Muḥammad that he was asked about *bismi'llāhi'l-Raḥmāni'l-Raḥīm; in the Name of God, the Gracious, the Merciful.* He said: The *bāʾ* is the brilliance (*bahāʾ*) of God; the *sīn* is His resplendence (*sanāʾ*), and the *mīm* is His glory (*majd*). Allāh is the God of everything, the Gracious (al-Raḥmān) to all of His creation, the Merciful (al-Raḥīm) to believers in particular.[8]

[It is further related] from Jaʿfar that he said, about God's word *Allāh*, that it is a perfect name, for it has four letters: the *alif*, which is the pillar of the oneness of God (*tawḥīd*),[9] while the first *lām* is the tablet (*lawḥ*) of understanding and the second *lām* is the tablet of prophethood (*nubūwah*), and the *hāʾ* is the ultimate allusion.

The name Allāh is the unique, incomparable name. It is not ascribed to anything, rather all things are ascribed to it. The meaning (of the word Allāh) is the Worshipped One who is the God of creation; His quiddity[10] far transcends being attained to [by any understanding] and His nature (far transcends) comprehension; He is the one hidden from sight and imagination,[11] the Self-veiled—by His majesty—from perception.

[It is related from] al-Riḍāʾ [reporting] from his father [who reported] from his grandfather, about God's words *al-Raḥmāni'l-Raḥīm; the Gracious, the Merciful*, [that] he said: It (the phrase) concerns those who aspire and those who are desired.[12] Thus the name al-Raḥmān is for the desired ones [i.e., those desired by God] because of their

---

8 The mercy of *al-Raḥmān* (*al-raḥmah al-raḥmānīyah* to use Muḥyī 'l-Dīn b. al-ʿArabī's later phrase) is all-encompassing and indiscriminate, while that of *al-Raḥīm* is discriminating, singling out those who believe in God and do good which merits a reward.

9 *Tawḥīd* is variously rendered by translators, including myself, as 'the divine unity/God's unity' or 'the divine oneness/God's oneness'. Literally, it also denotes the declaration or affirmation of God's oneness and belief in it.

10 *Māʾīyah*; perhaps the precursor of the later philosophical term *māhīyah*, which was well established by Fārābī's time (late ninth/early tenth century).

11 Literally, 'He is the one hidden from eyes and imaginations'.

12 *Murīdīn* and *murādīn*: those who aspire to God and those whom God desires, respectively. *Murīd* is also a specific Sufi term referring to novices or aspirants to the spiritual life.

being immersed in the [divine] lights and truths, while al-Raḥīm is for those who aspire, because of their remaining with themselves and their occupation with making good outward matters.[13] Al-Raḥmān, the Gracious, through His munificence[14] leads ultimately to that which has no limit, for He has already bestowed His mercy in pre-eternity, and that is the extreme limit of munificence and its ultimate degree,[15] at the beginning and at the end.

Al-Raḥīm, the Merciful, bestows His mercy through the *yāʾ* and the *mīm*; it is to Him (this name) that the mercy (pertaining to) the world, good health, and sustenance is attached.

1:2 ٱلْحَمْدُ لِلَّهِ رَبِّ ٱلْعَٰلَمِينَ ٢

al-ḥamdu li'llāhi Rabbi'l-ʿālamīn

Praise be to God, Lord of the worlds.

It is cited from Jaʿfar al-Ṣādiq, concerning (God's) words *al-ḥamdu*

---

13 *Ẓawāhir*, here rendered 'outward matters' could be understood as a reference specifically to the literal meanings of the Qurʾān and the Sunnah, in which case the distinction being made here would be between those who are preoccupied with upholding the letter of the law and those who are immersed in the inward depths of the spiritual realm (which, while not being preoccupied with the law to the detriment of the spiritual dimension, does not presume a neglect of it). However, *ẓawāhir* also refers, self-evidently, to matters of the world as opposed to spiritual and religious matters.

14 *Karāmah* indicates munificence, favour, or mark of honour. The plural, *karāmāt*, is used specifically for miracles that are vouchsafed to saints.

15 The Arabic text contains a play on the word *ghāyah*, which means both 'limit' and also 'extreme limit, utmost degree, objective, goal'; and on the verb *intahā* from which the words *al-muntahī ilā* ('leads ultimately to') and *muntahāhu* ('its ultimate degree') are derived. There is a possible alternative interpretation of the second half of this sentence, namely, 'and *He* is the goal of the noble generosity and its utmost degree, at the beginning and at the final end', whereby the meaning would be that the Gracious leads to that which has no limit (the infinite One Himself), and He (the infinite Gracious One Himself) is the ultimate goal to which His generosity leads. This comment is in keeping with the predestinarian stance manifest throughout the *tafsīr*.

li'llāh; praise be to God, that he said: The one who praises God through His qualities, even as He has described Himself, has truly praised Him. For praise *(ḥamd)* is a *ḥā'*, a *mīm*, and a *dāl*. The *ḥā'* is from *waḥdānīyah*, [God's] onliness;[16] the *mīm* is from *mulk*, [God's] sovereignty; the *dāl* is from *daymūmīyah*, [God's] permanence. Whoever knows Him through [His] onliness, sovereignty, and permanence (truly) knows Him.

Jaʿfar b. Muḥammad was asked about [God's] words *praise be to God, Lord of the worlds*, and he said: The meaning of (the verse) is 'thanks be to God, He being the Bestower (*al-Munʿim*) of all His graces upon His creation and [for] the goodness of His handiwork and [for] the favours (in) His trials'.

The *alif* in *al-ḥamd* is from *ālā'uhu*,[17] 'His favours', He being the Only (al-Wāḥid). Through His favours He delivered the people who have realisatory knowledge[18] of Him, from His displeasure and from the misfortunes of His decree.[19] The *lām* is from *luṭfuhu*, 'His kindness', He being the Only (al-Wāḥid). In His kindness, He gave them to taste the sweetness of His compassion and gave them to drink the cup of His beneficence. The *ḥā'* is from *ḥamduhu*, 'His praise', He being the foremost in praising Himself, before His creation; and by this precedence of His praise [of Himself], [His] benefaction settled upon His creation and they then (acquired) the ability to praise Him. The *mīm* is from *majduhu*, 'His glory'; through the majesty of His glory He adorned them with the light of His holiness. The *dāl* is from *dīnuhu*, 'His religion', *al-islām*;[20] for He is Peace (al-Salām) and His religion is

---

16 Linguistically, *waḥdānīyah* denotes an incomparable one and onliness, an inassociable solitariness, whereas *aḥadīyah* denotes an indivisible unity.

17 The words transliterated in the nominative case in this passage occur in the genitive form in the Arabic text.

18 'Realisatory knowledge' renders the important word *maʿrifah*, which for the Muslim mystics meant a cognitive, experiential, realisatory, spiritual knowledge of God bestowed by God, not just acquired by learning.

19 In other words, from divinely decreed tribulations.

20 The word *islām*, meaning submission (to God), also means 'to commit oneself (to God)', and is from the same verbal root as the divine name al-Salām, which means Peace. This literal connection between the two words extends at a profound level to the connection in meaning. In keeping with the spiritual tenor of this *tafsīr*, what the submission to God involves in real terms for the individual person, the microcosm, is to submit the soul to the influx of divine qualities. If the soul is thought

submission and His abode is peace and their greeting[21] therein is 'peace to the people of submission, in the abode of peace'.

1:3 ٱلرَّحۡمَٰنِ ٱلرَّحِيمِ ٣

al-Raḥmāni'l-Raḥīm

the Gracious, the Merciful.

[It is related] from Jaʿfar b. Muḥammad al-Ṣādiq [that] he said: *The Gracious*[22] [is He] who provides for and bestows upon creatures in both the outer and the inner [dimensions]. The provision of the outer [dimension] is food, drink, and good health while the provision of the inner [dimension] is the intellect, gnosis,[23] and understanding and the

---

of as a pane of glass, this submission, this *islām*, is tantamount, in the first place, to uncovering the soul so that it is exposed to the lights of God's qualities; and further, the submission applies to receiving the divine influx as fully as the soul is able to. The person who has submitted their soul to being exposed to the divine lights (the *muslim*, in other words) is ultimately going to be at Peace and a person of Peace. The opposite of this willing exposure and receptivity, of this *islām*, is called *kufr* (infidelity).

21 That is to say, the greeting of/for the inhabitants of God's abode of Peace, is peace. God's abode of Peace incorporates not just the paradisical hereafter, but also the state of peace and peaceability even within the physical and corporeal realm. These words of the commentary have been carried down through the centuries and brought to us today, when again they need to be voiced loud and clear for all to hear: God is Peace. . .

22 Gracious: thus the *raḥmah al-raḥīmīyah* is comprised within the *raḥmah al-raḥmānīyah*; in other words, the specific mercy of *al-Raḥīm* is part of the comprehensive mercy of *al-Raḥmān*.

23 In the English text, *maʿrifah* is translated, for the most part, as either 'gnosis' (knowledge of spiritual mysteries), 'realisatory knowledge' or 'spiritual knowledge'. These renditions, it is felt, convey the connotations of the word. *Maʿrifah* denotes knowledge associated with intellection, cognition, realisation, perception, experience; but it also refers to learning, lore, information, and experience. Thus the word *maʿrifah* is very close to the word *ʿilm* in meaning. In Lane, at *maʿrifah* under *ʿa-r-f*, the distinction between the two is given: '*Maʿrifah* is the perceiving a thing by reflection, and by consideration of the effect thereof [upon the mind or sense] so that it has a more special meaning than *ʿilm*, and its contrary is *inkār*.' *Inkār* means 'denial', while the opposite of *ʿilm* is *jahl*, meaning 'ignorance'.

types of wonders contained in (man) such as [the faculties of] hearing, sight, smell, taste, touch, thought, and fervour.

1:7 صِرَٰطَ ٱلَّذِينَ أَنْعَمْتَ عَلَيْهِمْ

ṣirāṭa'lladhīna anʿamta ʿalayhim

the way of those You have blessed.

[Concerning the above verse] Jaʿfar b. Muḥammad al-Ṣādiq said: *The way of those You have blessed* through knowledge (*ʿilm*) of You and understanding of You.

Jaʿfar said [concerning the word] *āmīn*: that is, those aiming directly towards You; You are too generous to disappoint one who aims (for You).[24]

Hence *maʿrifah* is an affirmative knowledge, whereas *ʿilm* is simply knowledge that one has, irrespective of one's agreement with what one knows, or with the affirmation or denial of it.

24 The *āmīn* is said at the end of the *Fātiḥah* as at the end of a prayer. This interpretation of *āmīn* as *qāṣidīn* is based on a reading of the word with *tashdīd* of the *mīm*, i.e., *āmmīn* (from *āmma*), which is synonymous with *qāṣidīn*: 'aiming at; endeavouring to reach; directing one's course towards'. See Lane at *āmīn* and *a-m-m*.

﴾2﴿

سُورَةُ البَقَرَةِ

al-Baqarah (The Cow)

2:32 سُبۡحَٰنَكَ لَا عِلۡمَ لَنَآ

subḥānaka, lā ʿilma lanā

glory to You we have no knowledge.

Jaʿfar said: When they boasted of their deeds, their praise [of God] and their dedication, He struck them all with ignorance until they said *we have no knowledge.*[25]

2:125 وَإِذۡ جَعَلۡنَا ٱلۡبَيۡتَ مَثَابَةً لِّلنَّاسِ

wa idh jaʿalnā'l-bayta mathābatan li'l-nās

and when We appointed the House as a place to which people return time after time.

[It is related] from Jaʿfar b. Muḥammad [that] he said: In this place, the House is Muḥammad ﷺ, so whoever believes (*amana*) in him and affirms his message enters the domains of safety (*amn*) and protection (*amān*).

25 In the immediate Qurʾānic context, these words are spoken by the angels. In the comment they are applied universally.

2:125 مَّقَامِ إِبْرَٰهِـۧمَ

maqāmi Ibrāhīm

the station of Abraham.

The station[26] of the *qiblah*. (God) has made your heart the station of gnosis and your tongue the station of the testimony and your body the station of obedience. Whoever safeguards them is indeed one whose prayer is definitely answered.

2:128 رَبَّنَا وَٱجْعَلْنَا مُسْلِمَيْنِ لَكَ

Rabbanā wa'j'alnā muslimīna laka

Our Lord, and make us submissive to You.

Said Jaʿfar: *Make us submissive to You*, that is, protect me and my household[27] so that we surrender ourselves and our hearts to You and do not choose save that which You have chosen for us.

He also said: Make us (people) who stand with You for You.

2:158 ۞إِنَّ ٱلصَّفَا وَٱلْمَرْوَةَ مِن شَعَآئِرِ ٱللَّهِ ۖ

inna'l-ṣafā wa'l-marwata min shaʿā'iri'llāh

verily, Ṣafā and Marwah are among the signs of God.[28]

[It is related] from Jaʿfar b. Muḥammad (that) he said: Ṣafā is the spirit

26 *Maqām*—in Sufi technical terminology it refers to an enduring spiritual station. Alternative translations of the word are 'place', or 'standing'. The *qiblah* is, of course, the direction which Muslims face during the canonical prayers, namely, the direction of the Holy Kaʿbah.

27 *Ahl baytī*, literally, 'the members of my house'. This phrase has clear Shīʿī overtones, being a reference to the line of the Prophet's familial descendents. The method of repeating the basic formulation of the Qur'ān text but with different elucidatory words—as in the second sentence of this comment—became commonplace among later commentators.

28 In his translation of the Qur'ān, Muhammad Asad has '. . . are symbols set

because of its being pure (*ṣafāʾ*) of the dirt of opposition (to God); and Marwah is the soul because of its use of the heroic virtues (*murūwah*) in the performance of service(s) (for) its Master.[29]

He [also] said: Ṣafā is the purity of gnosis; and Marwah is the heroic valor of the sage (*ʿārif*).

2:201 رَبَّنَآ ءَاتِنَا فِى ٱلدُّنْيَا حَسَنَةً

Rabbanā ātinā fī'l-dunyā ḥasanatan

Our Lord, grant us good in the world.

Jaʿfar said [explaining the word *ḥasanah, good*]: [It is] the companionship of those who are righteous.

---

up by God', with the more literal '... God's symbols' in a note. Muhammad Asad, *The Message of the Qurʾān* (Gibralter: Dar al-Andalus, 1984).

29 Another instance of paronomasia. Literally, both Ṣafā and Marwah mean 'stone' or 'rock' but Ṣafā derives form the verbal root *ṣ-f-w* meaning 'to be pure', while Marwah is derived from the verbal root *m-r-ʾ* meaning 'to be healthy, manly'. Thus these are interpreted on the broader basis of their associated verbal meanings to reveal a compelling image of the spiritual life: with the spirit being a pure continuity of the divine because it is in perfect harmony with God containing nothing that constitutes a contrast or opposition to the divine; and the soul being heroic in striving to serve God. The concept of *murūwah*—chivalry, valor, manliness—gained great currency among later Sufis, being espoused especially by Abū Ḥafṣ ʿUmar al-Suhrawardī (d. 632/1234), who founded the *futūwah* guilds. The definition of Ṣafā given here (being free of the *daran al-mukhālafah*; the dirt of opposition to God) contains one of the pivotal terms for the concept of qualitative continuum as contained in the *tafsīr,* namely, *mukhālafah,* opposition/contrast. The other, antithetical pivotal term is *muwāfaqah*, meaning harmony, consistency/conformity as in *muwāfaqah bi'llāh.*

2:210 هَلْ يَنظُرُونَ إِلَّآ أَن يَأْتِيَهُمُ ٱللَّهُ فِى ظُلَلٍ مِّنَ ٱلْغَمَامِ

hal yanẓurūna illā an yaʾtiyahumu'llāhu fī ẓulalin mina 'l-ghamām

do they await aught save that God come to them in the shadows of the clouds.

Jaʿfar said: *Do they await aught save* God's drawing near to them through the purity[30] (of their being divinely preserved from sin and error) and through God-given success (in goodness)—and so the veils of forgetfulness[31] are drawn back from them and thus they witness His beneficence and kindness; nay, rather, they witness the Beneficent, the Kind [Himself].

وَقُضِىَ ٱلْأَمْرُ

wa quḍiya'l-amr

and the matter is concluded.

Jaʿfar said: *And the matter is concluded*: and the truth of the matter and its hidden (aspects) are unveiled.

---

30 In Shīʿism, the term *ʿiṣmah* (impeccability, infallibility, purity) denotes the imams' purity and infallibility through their being divinely preserved from sin and error.

31 In Sufism, *ghaflah* (forgetfulness or negligence) is the opposite of *dhikr* (the remembrance or recollection of God, especially through the invocation of His name(s) and existentially through harmony with His qualities), as is emphasised throughout this *tafsīr*. This comment provides a concise summary of the spiritual journey, tracing the following steps. 1) The drawing back of the veils of forgetfulness, which corresponds on the ontological level with removing the dirt of opposition (*daran al-mukhālafah*) from the soul, in other words, excising the non-divine qualities. 2) Witnessing the divine quality, which corresponds to the soul being in harmony with the divine qualities. 3) Witnessing the One to whom the qualities belong and from whom they emanate, which corresponds to seeing God.

2:212 زُيِّنَ لِلَّذِينَ كَفَرُوا۟ ٱلْحَيَوٰةُ ٱلدُّنْيَا

zuyyina li'lladhīna kafarū'l-ḥayātu'l-dunyā

to those who deny the truth, the worldly life has been made to appear attractive.

Jaʿfar said: To those who refuse to trust and rely upon their Lord,[32] the adornments of the life of this world are made to appear attractive so much so that they hoard them and take pride in them.

وَيَسْخَرُونَ مِنَ ٱلَّذِينَ ءَامَنُوا۟

wa yaskharūna mina'lladhīna āmanū

and they ridicule those who believe.

That is, (they ridicule) those who have trustingly relied on God in all their affairs, and cast behind them their own management of their affairs, and have turned away from (that)—they are the poor (unto God),[33] the steadfast, the fully-satisfied (with God).

---

32 *Tawakkul* (trusting reliance on God) is a key concept in the teaching of Imām Jaʿfar. In addition to the rest of this comment and the next and their notes, see also the comments on 3:159, where *tawakkul* is an inner state of being 'solely for the Truth'; at 9:40, where *tawakkul* is one of the *junūd* (forces) with which God strengthens His messenger; at 13:27, where objective impersonality, the non-interference of the ego, is related to *tawakkul*; at 18:30 concerning the vast openness of *tawakkul* contrasted to the narrow confines of action that is dependent on oneself; at 25:61, where *tawakkul* is one of the stellar mansions; at 27:61, where *tawakkul* is the mountains mentioned in the verse and at 34:10, where grace is explained as consisting of *tawakkul* together with confidence in God.

33 *Fuqarāʾ*, the poor unto God, is the term by which Sufis refer to themselves. It is based upon Qurʾān 35:15. *Ṣabbār* in addition to 'steadfast', also means 'the very patient, the enduring, those who patiently await the right time for things'; see Qurʾān 14:5, 31:31, 34:19, 42:33. Noticeably, in the Qurʾān, *ṣabbār* always occurs in conjunction with the word *shakūr*, the grateful. *Rāḍūn* (the one fully-satisfied with God), is the plural of *rāḍī*, and again has Qurʾānic references: 5:119, 9:100, 58:22, and 98:8. Such satisfaction is linked in these verse with *al-fawz al-ʿaẓīm* (the tremendous victory); *iḥsān*

2:222 إِنَّ ٱللَّهَ يُحِبُّ ٱلتَّوَّٰبِينَ وَيُحِبُّ ٱلْمُتَطَهِّرِينَ ﴿٢٢٢﴾

inna'llāha yuḥibbu'l-tawwābīna wa yuḥibbu'l-mutaṭahhirīn

verily, God loves those who turn [unto Him] in repentance and He loves those who are purified

Jaʿfar said: He loves those who repent of their own wishful demands. and *those who are purified* of their own desires.[34]

2:284 لِّلَّهِ مَا فِى ٱلسَّمَٰوَٰتِ وَمَا فِى ٱلْأَرْضِ ۗ

Li'llāhi mā fi'l-samāwāti wa mā fi'l-arḍ

To God belongs that which is in the heavens and that which is in the earth

Jaʿfar said: (The heavens and the earth) cut off the one who is preoccupied with them, from God ﷻ; whereas God gives (the heavens and the earth) as possessions to the one who devotes himself to God and relinquishes them.

وَإِن تُبْدُوا۟ مَا فِىٓ أَنفُسِكُمْ

wa in tubdū mā fī anfusikum

and if you declare openly what is within yourselves

Jaʿfar said: [This refers to] surrender unto God (*islām*).

(goodness); *ḥizb Allāh* (the party of God); and *khashyat al-Rabb* (the fear of the Lord).

34 That is, those who are no longer wilful, nor holding to their own wishes against the divine will, unless the two coincide. Such obedience is again a form of *tawakkul* in that the individual will is effaced in the divine will, through trustful reliance on God in the knowledge that what He wills is good, correct and right, the most appropriate, etc.

أَوْ تُخْفُوهُ

2:284

aw tukhfūhu

or you conceal it.

[This refers to] faith (*īmān*).

3

سُورَةُ آلِ عِمْرَانَ

Āl-ʿImrān (The Family of ʿImrān)

3:1 الٓمٓ ①

Alif. Lām. Mīm.

Jaʿfar said: The detached letters in the Qurʾān are allusions to the [divine] onliness, singularity,[35] and permanence, and to the [Self-] existence of the Truth[36] in Himself,[37] having no need of anything other than Himself.

---

35 *Fardānīyah* comprises the concepts of being matchless, unique, and solitary.

36 Al-Ḥaqq (the Truth, the Real) is by far the divine name most frequently mentioned in this commentary, where it is used throughout as a synonym of Allāh—hence in this translation, 'the Truth', with captial T, should be understood as a rendition of the divine name al-Ḥaqq and is to be taken as referring to God the Truth. Its primary importance in Sufism is part of the imam's legacy to this field. See Massignon, *Essai sur les origenes*, p. 203.

37 *Qiyām al-Ḥaqq bi-nafsihi*, 'the existence of the Truth in Himself' (God's Self-existence). This ontological comment reveals an early enunciation on the nature of God, a matter much considered by philosophers and theologians. In later *tafsīr* works such as that of Fakhr al-Dīn al-Rāzī (d. 606/1210), God's unique absolute Self-existence, i.e., that He is the sole self-existent (*qāʾim bi-dhātihi*) and needs nothing outside Himself for His existence, is discussed at some length in the commentary on the divine name al-Qayyūm, as is His being the cause of the existence of everything else. See F. Hamza, S. Rizvi, and F. Mayer (eds.), *An Anthology of Qur'anic Commentaries,* vol. 1: *On the Nature of the Divine* (London: Oxford University Press and the Institute of Ismaili Studies, 2008), pp. 181–7.

3:5 إِنَّ ٱللَّهَ لَا يَخْفَىٰ عَلَيْهِ شَىْءٌ

inna'llāha lā yakhfā ʿalayhi shayʾun

verily, nothing is hidden from God.

Concerning His [above] words, Jaʿfar said: None except God is so thoroughly acquainted with you, such that he sees into your heart; [anyone other than He] would loathe you [if they knew you so well].

3:18 شَهِدَ ٱللَّهُ

shahida'llāhu

God bears witness.

Concerning His [above] words, Jaʿfar said: God bears witness through His onliness, His oneness, and His absolute self-sufficiency; *the angels and those endowed with knowledge* (3:18) bear witness to Him by (believing in and) affirming[38] that which He Himself testified for Himself.

Jaʿfar was asked what the essential reality of this testimony is and he said: It is built upon four pillars, the first of which is observation of (what is) commanded, the second is avoidance of the prohibited, the third is temperance (*qanāʿah*), and the fourth is contentment (*riḍā*).

3:19 إِنَّ ٱلدِّينَ عِندَ ٱللَّهِ ٱلْإِسْلَٰمُ

inna'l-dīna ʿinda'llāhi'l-islām

verily, religion in the sight of God is surrender (unto Him).

Jaʿfar said: (*Islām*) is such that the one who possesses it is preserved from the whisperings of the devil, anxieties, and misgivings of the soul, and (from) the chastisement of the hereafter.

38 *Taṣdīq* comprises the meanings of believing something, giving credence to it, as well as affirming it.

3:28 وَيُحَذِّرُكُمُ ٱللَّهُ نَفْسَهُۥ

wa yuḥadhdhirukumu'llāhu nafsahu

and God warns you Himself.

Jaʿfar said: *God warns you Himself*[39] that you provide evidence for your soul through righteousness,[40] because he who has precedence in merit[41] [shall find that] it is manifest at his end.

3:31 قُلْ إِن كُنتُمْ تُحِبُّونَ ٱللَّهَ فَٱتَّبِعُونِى

qul in kuntum tuḥibbūna'llāha fa'ttabiʿūnī

say, if you love God, then follow me.

Jaʿfar said, concerning His words (above): The inmost selves of the truthful have been bound[42] to following Muḥammad ﷺ, in order that they know that although their states are exalted and their ranks are elevated, they are unable to exceed him or [even] touch him.

---

39 This Qurʾānic phrase may be understood in more than one way. In addition to the rendition above, it could mean 'God warns you of Himself' or 'God warns you of His chastisement' for some commentators take *nafsa* to mean 'chastisement'. See Lane at *nafs* under *n-f-s*.

40 In addition to 'righteousness', *ṣalāḥ* refers to 'goodness, probity, correctness and godliness'. See Wehr at *ṣ-l-ḥ*.

41 The term *sābiqah* is used in early Islamic epistles to signify 'precedence in merit', acquired by the earliest converts to Islam at the time of the Prophet. For the Shīʿah, ʿAlī's *sābiqah* is part of the basis of his entitlement to the succession. (My thanks to Feras Hamza for drawing my attention to this.)

42 *Quyyida*; the use of the past perfect here, combined with the fact that it refers to the *asrār*, indicates that the 'binding' took place *fī'l-azal*.

3:35 إِنِّي نَذَرْتُ لَكَ مَا فِي بَطْنِي مُحَرَّرًا

innī nadhartu laka mā fī baṭnī muḥarraran

verily, I have dedicated to You that which is in my womb, (as) consecrated (to You).

Jaʿfar said [concerning *consecrated (to God)*]:[43] Free from bondage to the world and its inhabitants.

He [also] said [again about] *consecrated*: A pure, exclusive slave of Yours, who is not enslaved by anything among beings.

3:37 فَتَقَبَّلَهَا رَبُّهَا . . . أَنَّىٰ لَكِ هَٰذَا قَالَتْ هُوَ مِنْ عِندِ ٱللَّهِ

fa-taqabbalahā Rabbuhā . . . annā laki hādhā qālat huwa min ʿindi'llāhi

her Lord accepted her . . . whence have you this? She said: It is from God

Jaʿfar said: He accepted her so much that the prophets, despite their exalted ranks, marvel at the magnitude of her rank with God. Do you not see that Zakarīyā said to her: *whence have you this? She said: It is from God*, that is, 'it is from the one who accepted me'.

3:39 وَسَيِّدًا وَحَصُورًا

wa sayyidan wa ḥaṣūran

and a lord, a chaste one.

Jaʿfar said: *A lord* distinct from creation in quality, state, and nature.

43 *Muḥarraran* is from the second verbal form *ḥ-rr-r* which, in addition to meaning 'to consecrate to God' also has the spiritually closely related meaning of 'setting free, emancipating, liberating'.

3:61 فَمَنْ حَآجَّكَ فِيهِ مِنۢ بَعْدِ مَا جَآءَكَ مِنَ ٱلْعِلْمِ

fa-man ḥājjaka fīhi min baʿdi mā jāʾaka mina'l-ʿilm

then who disputes with you concerning it after this knowledge has come to you.

Jaʿfar said: This is an allusion concerning the disclosure of imposters to those who know the deepest realities, so that (the imposters) may be exposed in their pretensions when the effects of the lights of realisation and the falsity of the darknesses of untruthful pretensions are made manifest.

3:68 إِنَّ أَوْلَى ٱلنَّاسِ بِإِبْرَٰهِيمَ لَلَّذِينَ ٱتَّبَعُوهُ وَهَٰذَا ٱلنَّبِيُّ

inna awlā'l-nāsi bi-Ibrāhīma la'lladhīna'ttabaʿūhu wa hādhā'l-nabīyu

verily the people with the best claim to Abraham are those who followed him and this Prophet

Jaʿfar said: *Those who followed him* in their laws and ways of life. *And this Prophet* because of the proximity of Abraham's state to that of the Prophet, may God's blessings be upon the [two of] them, more than to other prophets, and because of the proximity in their laws [which are closer to each other] than to other laws.

وَٱلَّذِينَ ءَامَنُوا۟ۗ

wa'lladhīna āmanū

and those who believe

Because of the proximity of their state to that of Abraham.

وَٱللَّهُ وَلِيُّ ٱلْمُؤْمِنِينَ ﴿٦٨﴾

wa'llāhu walīyu'l-mu'minīn

and God is the Friend of the believers.

(*And God is the Friend of the believers*) in elevating them to reach the station of 'the friend',[44] ﵇ because proximity to Him is a rank of love, (as seen) in His words: *He loves them, and they love Him* (5:54).

3:76 بَلَىٰ مَنْ أَوْفَىٰ بِعَهْدِهِۦ وَٱتَّقَىٰ فَإِنَّ ٱللَّهَ يُحِبُّ ٱلْمُتَّقِينَ ﴿٧٦﴾

balā man awfā bi-ʿahdihi wa'ttaqā fa-inna'llāha yuḥibbu'l-muttaqīn

rather, the one who fulfils his pledge and is God-aware; for verily God loves the God-aware.[45]

Jaʿfar said: [This is a reference to] him who fulfils the pledge that fell to him in the first covenant[46] and who *is God-aware* and purifies that

44 *Al-khalīl*, 'the friend' and *khalīlu'llāh*, 'the friend of God', are epithets of the prophet Abraham ﵇.

45 Throughout this translation, the words *muttaqī, muttaqīn, taqwā*, etc. have been rendered as 'the God-aware (person)', 'the God-aware ones', 'God-awareness' respectively. The line of thought behind these uncommon renditions is as follows: *taqwā* literally means 'to fear God'; to fear God is to be wary of Him in the sense of being aware of Him. It is felt that the terms God-aware/God-awareness convey these implied connotations of the Arabic words.

46 Pledge (*ʿahd*); covenant (*mīthāq*). The 'first covenant' refers to the event described in 7:172: God brings forth the seed of the Children of Adam and asks them '*Am I not your Lord*' to which they reply '*Yea, verily. We testify [to that]*.' The pledge, then, is to acknowledge and affirm God's Lordship (*rubūbīyah*) over mankind and, consequently, mankind's slavehood (*ʿubūdīyah*) vis-à-vis Him. The degrees of this acknowledgement and affirmation distinguish the levels of *ʿubūdīyah*. The Qur'ānic phrase in question makes it clear that fulfilling the pledge means being aware of God, of His absolute lordship over everything. The comment underlines this: the upholder of the pledge is named 'lover'; the lover is the beloved of God; the beloved of God is the God-aware one; the God-aware one is he

pledge and that covenant from its being polluted with falsehood. The fulfilment of the pledge is being with Him by excising that which is other than Him. That is why the Prophet ﷺ said: 'The truest word that an Arab spoke was the saying of Labīd, "Verily, everything except God is false".' He who fulfills the pledge is named 'lover' and *God loves the God-aware.*

3:79 كُونُوا۟ رَبَّـٰنِيِّـۧنَ

kūnū rabbānīyīn

be godly.

Jaʿfar said [glossing *godly*]: Those who listen with the hearing of the heart and who see with eyes of the unseen [i.e., with spiritual vision].[47]

3:92 لَن تَنَالُوا۟ ٱلْبِرَّ حَتَّىٰ تُنفِقُوا۟ مِمَّا تُحِبُّونَ

lan tanālū'l-birra ḥattā tunfiqū mimmā tuḥibbūna

you shall not attain (to true) beneficence until you spend of that which you love.

Jaʿfar said: Through expending his life the slave [of God] arrives at his Beloved's beneficence and his Lord's proximity. Jaʿfar [also] said: They shall not attain unto the Truth until they detach themselves from what is other than Him.

---

who sees that everything other than God 'is naught'; to see that everything other than God 'is naught', is the acknowledgement and affirmation of God's absolute Lordship. See also the immediately preceding note for our rendition of *taqwā* as 'God-awareness'.

47 Elsewhere in the commentary, the heart is explained as 'a hearing, understanding, seeing heart. Thus whenever it hears the oration of God, most high, without any intermediary in that which is between it and the Truth, it understands what He bestowed upon it . . . in pre-eternity.' This 'oration of God most high without any intermediary' is God's direct communication to the heart. To facilitate the English text in this sentence, the Arabic plurals *qulūb* (hearts) and *ghuyūb* (unseen) were rendered in the singular.

3:97 وَمَن دَخَلَهُۥ كَانَ ءَامِنًاۗ

man dakhalahu kāna āminan

and whoever enters it is safe.

Concerning (these) words of God, Jaʿfar said: He into whose heart faith has entered is safe from disbelief.

3:101 وَمَن يَعْتَصِم بِٱللَّهِ فَقَدْ هُدِىَ إِلَىٰ صِرَٰطٍ مُّسْتَقِيمٍ ١٠١

wa man yaʿtaṣim bi'llāhi fa-qad hudiya ilā ṣirāṭin mustaqīm

and whoever holds fast to God has indeed been guided to a harmonious way.[48]

Concerning this verse, Jaʿfar said: Whoever knows Him is, through Him, independent of all mankind.

3:102 يَـٰٓأَيُّهَا ٱلَّذِينَ ءَامَنُوا۟ ٱتَّقُوا۟ ٱللَّهَ حَقَّ تُقَاتِهِۦ

(Yā ayyuhā'lladhīna āmanū) 'ttaqū'llāha ḥaqqa tuqātihi

(O you who believe) be God-aware with the awareness due to Him.

Jaʿfar said: God-awareness is that you see[49] nothing in your heart other than Him.

48 *Mustaqīm*, usually rendered as 'straight', has also the less commonly appreciated meanings of harmonious, honest, proportionate, and sound. Given the emphasis in this *tafsīr* on harmony with God, the word 'harmonious' is the obvious choice as the translation of *mustaqīm*.

49 *Ra'a* (to see) also means 'to discern'; in other words, to discern and understand that there is nothing other than God in one's heart. In the spiritual realm, the 'seeing' is literal but it is subtle, not in the dense physical manner; so one literally sees with spiritual eyes that there is only God in one's spiritual heart. This seeing of God in the heart may be in the form of the letters of the divine name, in other words, the living inscription of the *ḥaqīqah* in the spiritual heart—the *living ḥaqīqah-inscription*; or it

3:110 تَأْمُرُونَ بِٱلْمَعْرُوفِ

taʾmurūna[50] biʾl-maʿrūf

they counsel that which is good.

Jaʿfar said: *They counsel that which is good:* the *good* is in harmony with the Book and the custom (of the Prophet ﷺ).

3:138 هَٰذَا بَيَانٌ لِّلنَّاسِ وَهُدًى وَمَوْعِظَةٌ لِّلْمُتَّقِينَ ﴿١٣٨﴾

hādhā bayānun liʾl-nās wa hudan wa mawʿiẓatun liʾl-muttaqīn

this is a clear declaration for mankind and a guidance and spiritual counsel for the God-aware.

Jaʿfar said: The Declaration[51] has been made manifest to mankind, but only he perceives it clearly who is supported by Him with the light of certainty and purity of inmost self.[52] Do you not see Him say: *and a guidance and spiritual counsel for the God-aware.* Indeed, to be guided by the guidance of the Declaration and to be counselled by it is for those

---

might be the divine lights that are seen—the letters in any case consist of divine light; or it may be the divine face that is seen. . . The infinite God may manifest Himself as He chooses to His creatures.

50 Nwyia's edition has *yaʾmurūna* (*they counsel*) instead of *taʾmurūna* (*you counsel*).

51 *Al-bayān*, here rendered as the 'Declaration' is one of the names by which the Qurʾān is referred to.

52 There are clear resonances here of the Shīʿī doctrine that only the imams understand the Qurʾān correctly because only they are granted the requisite light of certainty and purity of inmost self by God. For their part, the Sufis did not confine the bestowal of such perception, certainty and purity to the imams alone but held that it extends to include others too, from among the Prophet's spiritual progeny. *Sirr*, rendered in this text as 'inmost self' or 'inmost secret', literally means secret, heart, inmost kernal. In the *tafsīr*, it refers to the deepest reality, the *ḥaqīqah,* of the human being, the divine secret placed in the deepest reaches of the spiritual heart. For later Sufi definitions, see ʿAbd al-Razzāq Qāshānī, *Iṣṭilāḥāt al-Ṣūfiyah*, trans. Nabil Safwat as *A Glossary of Sufi Technical Terms* (London: Octagon Press Ltd., 1991), pp. 60–61.

who are God-aware—those who guard (themselves) against everything other than Him.

3:150 بَلِ ٱللَّهُ مَوْلَىٰكُمْ ۖ

bali'llāhu mawlākum

rather God is your protecting patron.

Jaʿfar said: [He is] in charge of all your affairs, from the beginning to the end.

3:159 فَإِذَا عَزَمْتَ فَتَوَكَّلْ عَلَى ٱللَّهِ ۚ

fa-idhā ʿazamta fa-tawakkal ʿalā'llāh

so when you have decided [*upon something*] *then trustfully rely on God.*

Jaʿfar said: He (God) has ordered rectitude of the outward in relation to creation, and the exclusive isolation of one's inner (aspect) for the Truth. Do you not see Him say *so when you have decided . . .*

3:191 ٱلَّذِينَ يَذْكُرُونَ ٱللَّهَ قِيَٰمًا وَقُعُودًا وَعَلَىٰ جُنُوبِهِمْ

(A)'lladhīna yadhkurūna'llāha qiyāman wa quʿūdan wa ʿalā junūbihim

those who remember God standing and sitting and upon their sides.

Jaʿfar said: They *remember God standing* in the witnessings of the Lordship; *and sitting* in the performance of service; *and upon their sides* in the seeing[53] (that comes from) being near (to God).

53 The word *ruʾyah* means to see or perceive, either with the physical eye or in the mind; whereas, the word *ruʾyā* refers more to a vision in the sense of apparition or mental vision. See Lane at *r-ʾ-ā*. For *mushāhadāt* (sing. *mushāhadah*), see following note.

3:200 ٱصۡبِرُواْ وَصَابِرُواْ وَرَابِطُواْ وَٱتَّقُواْ ٱللَّهَ لَعَلَّكُمۡ تُفۡلِحُونَ ﴿٢٠٠﴾

(i)ṣbirū wa ṣābirū wa rābiṭū wa'ttaqū'llāha laʿallakum tufliḥūn

restrain yourselves and persevere stoutly and station yourselves; and be aware of God that you may succeed.

Jaʿfar said: *Restrain yourselves* from disobedience (to God), *persevere* in acts of obedience (to Him), *and station* (your) spirits in the witnessing;[54] *and be aware of God*, that is, avoid being presumptuous[55] with the truth, *that you may succeed*, that you attain the way stations of the people of sincerity, for that is the locus of success.

---

54 *Mushāhadah* (witnessing), is the verbal noun of the third form of the verbal root *sh-h-d* (to see with one's own eyes, to view, watch, observe, witness). It is a term of significance in the *tafsīr*. In this comment, the witnessing is of the divine Lordship by the human slave. Elsewhere, on 25:20, the comment states that the inmost selves of the prophets are in the divine grasp, and do not disengage from the *mushāhadah*. In later mystical usage, *mushāhadah* comes to mean, at the highest level, witnessing God in the mystery of annihilation of all else including the creature-witness themselves: God alone witnesses Himself. Cf. Sells, *Early Islamic Mysticism*, pp. 98, 130–1.

55 The term *inbisāṭ* (presumption) covers the ideas of frivolity, flippancy, arrogance, forwardness. See Lane at *b-s-ṭ*.

❴ 4 ❵

سُورَةُ النِّسَاءِ

al-Nisāʾ (Women)

4:1 يَـٰٓأَيُّهَا ٱلنَّاسُ

Yā ayyuhā'l-nās

O you people.

Concerning His [above] words, Jaʿfar said: That means, be among those people who are (truly) human and do not be forgetful of God. For whoever has recognised that he is from that human being whose nature (God) endowed with that with which He endowed it, his fervour becomes too great [for him] to seek [only] the lower (spiritual) stations, and his rank is raised until the Truth [Himself] is his final ending. *And that to your Lord is the final end* (53:42). The eminence of his fervour comes through the privileges of communication and inspiration with which he has been favoured.[56]

4:9 فَلْيَتَّقُوا۟ ٱللَّهَ وَلْيَقُولُوا۟ قَوْلًا سَدِيدًا ﴿٩﴾

fal-yattaqū'llāha wal-yaqūlū qawlan sadīdan

then let them be aware of God and let them speak correctly.

Jaʿfar said: Truthfulness and God-awareness increase sustenance and expand livelihood.

---

56 Note that the eminent fervour mentioned is a consequence of the heavenly disclosures, among which is the recognition of the true human status, as expounded throughout this *tafsīr*. On the ontological level, to forget God is to obscure the radiance of His qualities in one's soul and not to be a message of God is to be less than a true human.

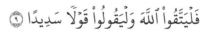

4:59 أَطِيعُواْ ٱللَّهَ وَأَطِيعُواْ ٱلرَّسُولَ وَأُوْلِي ٱلۡأَمۡرِ مِنكُمۡۖ

aṭīʿū'llāha wa aṭīʿū'l-rasūla wa ūlī'l-amri minkum

obey God and obey the Messenger and those of you with authority.

Jaʿfar al-Ṣādiq said: Three norms are unavoidable for the believing slave of God: the norm of God, the norm of the prophets and the norm of the friends (of God). The norm of God is to conceal the secret; God has said: *He is the knower of the unseen and He does not reveal His [knowledge of the] unseen to anyone* (72:26). The norm [or convention] of the Messenger ﷺ is gentle courtesy (towards) creation. And the norm [or convention] of the friends is the fulfilment the pledge and (to have) patience in times of suffering and distress.

4:64 وَلَوۡ أَنَّهُمۡ إِذ ظَّلَمُوٓاْ أَنفُسَهُمۡ جَآءُوكَ

wa law annahum idh ẓalamū anfusahum jāʾūka

would that they, when they wronged their souls, came to you (O Muḥammad).

Jaʿfar said: Whoever aims not for Us according to your way and customs and guidance (O Muḥammad), has gone astray and is misguided.

4:80 مَّن يُطِعِ ٱلرَّسُولَ فَقَدۡ أَطَاعَ ٱللَّهَۖ

man yuṭiʿi'l-rasūla fa-qad aṭāʿa'llāha

whoever obeys the Messenger, verily he has obeyed God.

Jaʿfar b. Muḥammad said [in paraphrase]: 'Whoever acknowledges you in (your) messengership and prophethood, has acknowledged Me in (My) Lordship and Divinity.'

4:125 وَٱتَّخَذَ ٱللَّهُ إِبْرَٰهِيمَ خَلِيلًا ﴿١٢٥﴾

(wa)'ttakhadha'llāhu Ibrāhīma khalīlan

and God took Abraham as a friend.

Concerning His [above] words, [it is related] from Jaʿfar b. Muḥammad, [that] he said: (God) proclaimed the title of friendship for Abraham, for the friend is obvious in meaning. But He kept hidden the title of love for Muḥammad ﷺ because of the perfection of his state. For the lover does not like to disclose the status of His beloved. Rather, He likes to conceal and veil it lest anyone other than He becomes acquainted with it or intrudes upon that which is between the two of them. He said to His Prophet and pure, bosom friend, Muḥammad ﷺ when He manifested to him the state of love: *Say, if you love God, then follow me* (3:31). That is to say, there is no way to the love of God except in following His beloved; nor is access to the Beloved[57] sought with anything better than pledging allegiance to (His) beloved[58] and seeking his contentment.

57 *Ḥabīb* is used predominantly to refer to the beloved; however, it may also be used for 'lover', in which case the rendition at this point could be 'Lover'. My interpretation of the different referents of *ḥabīb* is indicated by the case of the initial letter.

58 Reading *ḥabībihi* for *ḥabībah*.

5

سُورَةُ المَائِدَةِ

al-Mā'idah (The Table-Spread)

5:1 يَـٰٓأَيُّهَا ٱلَّذِينَ ءَامَنُوٓاْ

Yā ayyuhā'lladhīna āmanū

O you who believe.

Concerning His [above] words, Jaʿfar b. Muḥammad said: Therein are four characteristics: a vocative; a metonymy; an allusion; and an attestation. The [word] *yā* is the vocative, and *ayyu* is the particularisation of the vocative; the *hā* is the metonymy; the [word] *alladhīna* is the allusion; and [the word] *āmanū* is the attestation.

5:1 إِنَّ ٱللَّهَ يَحْكُمُ مَا يُرِيدُ ﴿١﴾

inna'llāha yaḥkumu mā yurīd

verily God ordains what He intends.

Jaʿfar said: (God) ordains what He intends (to ordain) and then brings to pass His intention and His will.[59] Then he who is content with His

59 'Intention' renders *irādah*, while 'will' renders *mashī'ah*. Both Arabic terms are linguistically interchangeable. It is interesting to note that the word *ḥukm* (here translated as 'ordinance') is understood as the divine ruling/decree, and that it is associated, in keeping with the words of this Qur'ānic verse, with the divine intention. In later commentaries, the terms *qaḍā'* and *qadar* are used for divine determination with, respectively, the former for ordinances of a general nature and fate, and the latter for particular divine decrees and individual destiny. Later commentators associate divine ordinances variously with the divine will, knowledge, or power. See Hamza, Rizvi, and Mayer, *On the Nature of the Divine*, ch. 5.

ordinance is at ease and has been guided to the way of his good conduct; while he who resents His ordinance nevertheless must undergo it, but has in it resentment and disgrace.

5:3 ٱلْيَوْمَ أَكْمَلْتُ لَكُمْ دِينَكُمْ

(a)l-yawma akmaltu lakum dīnakum

this day I have perfected for you your faith.

Jaʿfar b. Muḥammad said: *This day* is a reference to the day that Muḥammad the Messenger of God ﷺ was sent, and the day of his prophetic message/mission.

5:18 يَغْفِرُ لِمَن يَشَآءُ وَيُعَذِّبُ مَن يَشَآءُ

yaghfiru liman yashāʾu wa yuʿadhdhibu man yashāʾu

He forgives whom He wills (to forgive) and He chastises whom He wills (to chastise).

Jaʿfar said: *He forgives whom He wills (to forgive)*, as a grace to them; *and He chastises whom He wills (to chastise)*, justly.[60]

5:35 وَٱبْتَغُوٓا۟ إِلَيْهِ ٱلْوَسِيلَةَ

waʾbtaghū ilayhiʾl-wasīlah

and seek unto Him a means of approach.

Jaʿfar said: Seek from Him closeness (to Him).

60 That is, He is within His rights to chastise them. The comment does not preclude that His chastisement is often, if not always, less severe than it should strictly be, thanks to the divine mercy.

6

سُورَةُ الأَنعَامِ

al-Anʿām (Cattle)

6:59 ﴿وَعِندَهُۥ مَفَاتِحُ ٱلْغَيْبِ

wa ʿindahu mafātiḥu'l-ghayb

and with Him are the keys of the unseen.

About [these] words of His, Jaʿfar said: Through hearts He unlocks guidance; through concern, care; through tongues, narratives; and through limbs, conduct and an indication.[61]

6:79 إِنِّي وَجَّهْتُ وَجْهِيَ

innī wajahtu wajhiya

verily I have turned my face

Jaʿfar said: That means: I have surrendered my heart to Him who created it and I have dedicated myself to Him excluding every preoccupation and distraction.

---

61 That is, when God causes faith to enter the heart; also, it is through understanding with the heart, seat of the subtle intellect, that the ultimate guidance for people is unlocked by God. 'Through concern, care' may be understood in two ways: first, that people learn to be careful through being concerned about matters and the consequences of thought, word and deed; second, that it is in the face of their concerns, personal and universal, that people begin to appreciate the divine protective care. 'An indication'—i.e., of the inner state.

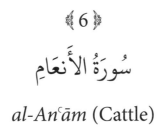

لِلَّذِى فَطَرَ ٱلسَّمَٰوَٰتِ وَٱلْأَرْضَ

li'lladhī faṭara'l-samāwāti wa'l-arḍ

toward Him who has created the heavens and the earth.

Jaʿfar said: [Toward Him] who raised the firmament without any pillars and manifested therein the marvels of His handiwork, [He who] is totally and perfectly able to protect my heart from blameworthy thoughts and harmful whisperings which are not suited to the Truth.

6:122 أَوَ مَن كَانَ مَيْتًا فَأَحْيَيْنَٰهُ

a-wa man kāna maytan fa-aḥyaynāhu

is he who was lifeless and whom We then enlivened

Concerning [these] words of His, Jaʿfar said: *Lifeless* without Us and whom We enlivened through Us and made a leader by whose light those estranged (from God)[62] are rightly-guided and the one astray returns to Him.

كَمَن مَّثَلُهُۥ فِى ٱلظُّلُمَٰتِ

kaman mathaluhu fī ẓulumāt

as one the likeness of whom is in [layers of] darkness.[63]

'Like one who has been abandoned to his passion and desire and is not

---

62 *Ajānib* also means 'strangers'.

63 This Qurʾānic phrase contains a very important, implicit, subtle identification, namely, the reference to the spiritual correspondence of a person. In *man mathaluhu fī ẓulumāti, the likeness of whom is in [layers] of darkness*, the *mathal*/likeness refers to the spiritual body of the person. This likeness is not metaphorical but actual in the spiritual realm; what is inward in the physical realm is outwardly visible in the spiritual realm, the substance of which is subtle, divine light. Consequently, to the extent that a person's soul obscures light with the dirt of its contrary acts, to that extent their spiritual body is dark. The spiritual body of such a person,

(in any way) supported by the fragrances of closeness to God and the intimacy of the [divine] Presence.'

Jaʿfar [also] said, concerning His words *Is he who was lifeless*: '(*Lifeless*) through dependence upon acts of obedience; *and whom We then enlivened*: to whom We then granted the light of humble supplication and remorse.'[64]

6:153 وَأَنَّ هَٰذَا صِرَاطِي مُسْتَقِيمًا

wa anna hādhā ṣirāṭī mustaqīman

and that this is My way, harmonious.

Jaʿfar b. Muḥammad said: (It is) a way from the heart to God through turning away from that which is other than Him.

---

the correspondence of their soul, is in literal darkness in the spiritual realm. The plurality of darknesses referred to in the Qurʾānic phrase refers to the product of different sins (hatred, for example, produces a very deep darkness and doubt is like thick mud which is why the *tafsīr* says when doubt fills a heart it veils the person from perceiving. The soul-body, which is to say the spiritual body (which is visibly manifest in the spiritual realm) is the *simultaneous correspondence* of the state of soul of a person in the physical realm. The two occupy their places in the different realms at one and the same time. In other words, the spiritual realm contains not only posthumous and non-incarnate souls but also the soul-bodies/spiritual bodies that correspond to incarnated souls on earth in the present. The subtle body in the spiritual realm manifests visibly the hidden inner state of soul of a person on earth. The transition described in 6:122, from lifelessness to enlivenment, corresponds to the transition from opacity of soul to transparency.

64 In other words, acts of obedience are sterile unless enlivened with humility (humble supplication) and with neediness (remorse). Neediness, in general, means seeing that everything is totally dependent upon Him always, while remorse includes an awareness that all good belongs to God and that what is not good belongs to us.

7

سُورَةُ الأَعْرَافِ

al-Aʿrāf (The Heights)

7:31 خُذُوا۟ زِينَتَكُمْ عِندَ كُلِّ مَسْجِدٍ

khudhū zīnatakum ʿinda kulli masjidin

don your adornment at every place of worship.

Jaʿfar said: Keep the members of your body away from contact with anything after God has made them an instrument wherewith the religious obligations (that He has ordained) are fulfilled.[65]

7:120 وَأُلْقِىَ ٱلسَّحَرَةُ سَٰجِدِينَ ﴿١٢٠﴾

wa ulqiya'l-saḥaratu sājidīna

and the magicians fell down in prostration.

Jaʿfar said: They found the breath of the winds of pre-existent (divine) care with them and hastened to prostrate themselves [before God] in gratitude. And, *They said, we have believed in the Lord of the worlds* (7:121).

7:142 ۞وَوَٰعَدْنَا مُوسَىٰ ثَلَٰثِينَ لَيْلَةً

wa wāʿadnā Mūsā thalāthīna laylatan

and We appointed for Moses thirty nights.

---

65 From the point of view of the *sharīʿah*, this ritual purity is the adornment mentioned in the Qurʾānic verse. The avoidance recommended in the comment would pertain to what might 'break' the state of ritual purity.

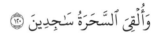

Jaʿfar said: His promise was of thirty nights and he kept[66] the tryst of his Lord. (When) the appointed time for his coming [to meet God] reached [its end], then He drew him forth beyond his term and his norm, and He honoured Moses by speaking to him; and His glory became evident to him [in a manner] beyond human norms, such that he heard what he heard from his Lord, not through himself or his knowledge, and in (a) time other than that which he had given to his people[67]—showing that the 'descents of the Divinity'[68] are beyond (physical) human norms.

7:143 وَلَمَّا جَآءَ مُوسَىٰ لِمِيقَٰتِنَا وَكَلَّمَهُۥ رَبُّهُۥ

wa lammā jāʾa Mūsā li-mīqātinā wa kallamahu Rabbuhu

and when Moses came to Our appointed tryst and his Lord spoke to him.

Jaʿfar said: The *appointed tryst* is seeking to see (God).

Jaʿfar said [also]: He heard a speech extrinsic[69] to his human state.[70] He [God] made the speech rest upon him[71] and spoke to him through

66 In his edition of the Arabic text, Paul Nwyia prefers to use the phrase *fal-yawma* (the day) instead of *fa-iltazama* (he adhered to; he kept). He notes *iltazama* in his apparatus, as the word used in this place in one of the manuscripts which he consulted. As *iltazama* makes more obvious sense in the context, we have chosen it for the English text.

67 That is, in the last ten nights which God added to the appointed thirty, according to this verse of the Qurʾān.

68 *Manāzil al-rubūbīyah* may also be translated more literally as 'the halting places of the Lordship/Divinity'.

69 *Khārijan ʿan* means 'extrinsic to, beyond a thing, outside it, separate from'; while *khārijan min* would mean 'emanating from, coming forth from'. See Lane at *khārij*.

70 *Basharīyatihi*: his humanity. Given what follows, it would seem that *basharīyah* here refers to the physical, corporeal condition of the human state on earth, and to the qualities that pertain to this incarnate state.

71 *Aḍāfa ilā*—for this fourth form of the verbal root *ḍ-y-f*, Lane cites the meaning 'to make incline towards, to rest or lean upon'. This is in keeping with the significance of the preceding sentence—the speech that Moses heard was extrinsic to his physical state; it descended upon his inner self. With the descent of the divine speech, Moses's soul was purged of all that was not in harmony with the divine. God spoke to Moses through the

Moses' inner disposition[72] and his slavehood[73] and Moses disappeared from his soul and was effaced[74] from his qualities; then his Lord spoke to him through the deepest realities of his praiseworthy qualities[75] and Moses heard, from his Lord, the description of Moses. Muḥammad heard, from his Lord, the description of his Lord, for he was the most praised of the praiseworthy, in the sight of his Lord. Hence, the station of Muḥammad ﷺ was the lote tree at the utmost limit while the station of Moses was the mountain.[76] Since God spoke to Moses

---

perfect *ʿubūdīyah* of his inner self—i.e., the self that had nothing of its own, but only that which came from its Lord (*Rabb*).

72 *Nafsīyatihi*, which also implies his inner state of soul.

73 It should be noted that, although on one level the human state is nothing but slavehood because the human creature is *ʿabd Allāh*, the slave of God (it is in this sense that the word 'slave' is used in other parts of the translation to render the word *ʿabd*), here a distinction is made between the 'human state' and the 'inner self and slavehood'. 'Slavehood' (*ʿubūdīyah*), in this sense, is pure receptivity towards God's Lordship, pure emptiness in the face of it; hence its association with Moses's inner self rather than with the outer 'human state'. The multiple function of the word *ʿabd* is to be found in the Qurʾān itself where it is used at times to designate mankind in general and at other times to distinguish God's special slaves, such as the prophets (18:1; 19:1; 54:9), certain categories of excellent right-doing believers (e.g., *ʿibād al-Raḥmān*, 25:63; *ʿibād Allāh*, 76:6) and those who have special status with Him (*ʿabdan min ʿibādinā*; 18:65).

74 Moses's human qualities were effaced. With the non-divine totally extinguished, the divine speaks.

75 Two different words are used here for qualities. First, the Arabic word is *ṣifāt*—which in later theology is used almost exclusively for the qualities or attributes of God; it is the plural of the word *ṣifah* (quality), which occurs near the end of the sentence of our text. Second, the Arabic word for qualities is *maʿānī*, which, in addition to meaning and significance, has the meaning of good qualities. See Lane at *maʿānī*. Through the profoundest *taʾwīl* (returning to the source or root) the good (praised) qualities are shown to stem from the divine qualities themselves.

76 This is one of the comments that displays the microcosmic significances of the prophets. In this comment, Moses represents the *ʿabd*, the soul that is empty for God; while the Prophet Muḥammad represents the *rasūl*, the heart that is replete with the divine qualities. The two stages are in fact simultaneous; Moses became a perfect *ʿabd* when the divine speech came upon his heart and passed through him; and with the coming of the message (*risālah*) he became messenger (*rasūl*). Likewise, in the commentary on 24:35 we are told of the Prophet: 'he stands with God,

on the mountain, He effaced its quality and never shall there appear thereon any vegetation or human settlement.

قَالَ رَبِّ أَرِنِيٓ أَنظُرۡ إِلَيۡكَۚ قَالَ لَن تَرَىٰنِي وَلَٰكِنِ ٱنظُرۡ إِلَى ٱلۡجَبَلِ

qāla Rabbī arinī anẓur ilayka. qāla lan tarānī wa'lākin anẓur ilā'l-jabal

he said: my Lord, show [*Yourself to*] *me that I may gaze upon You. But gaze at the mountain.*

Jaʿfar said: He was unreserved with his Lord concerning the meaning of the sight he saw, for he saw the subtle image of His speech upon his heart, and through that he was emboldened towards his Lord [about seeing Him]. Then (God) said to him: *you shall not see Me*, that is to say: 'you are unable to see Me for you are a transient (creature) and how should the transient have access to the eternally subsistent?'[77] *but gaze at the mountain*; Jaʿfar said: The knowledge of beholding (God) (imminently) alighted upon the mountain and it was reduced to dust and scattered. The mountain ceased to be at the [very] mention of beholding its Lord, and Moses fainted at seeing the flattened mountain. Then how could he have [sustained] seeing his Lord with his eyes, eye to eye?[78] The slave's beholding of God [entails that] the slave is effaced; and the Lord's seeing of the slave [entails] the eternal subsistence of the slave in/through his Lord.[79]

---

through the condition of having perfected slavehood (*ʿubūdīyah*) and love'.

77 How should the corporeal have access to the Subtlest One? And how should the non-divine have access to the divine? How should that which is other than God have access to God? *Fānin* (transient) and *bāqin* (eternally abiding) become key Sufi terms.

78 Things spiritual are perceivable only through spiritual vision and not through physical vision.

79 In other words, the unveiled, direct gaze of God effaces all that is in contrast to Him—so to look at God unveiled, one must be effaced in Him; just as the descent of the divine speech annihilated Moses, except inasmuch as he was naught but pure receptivity to God. At the same time, the gaze of God conveys the divine light—and in/through that divine light, the purified slave subsists as a harmonious continuum.

(Jaʿfar) [also] said: Three [things] are impossible for the slaves unto their Lord: the divine Self-disclosure, means for attachment and gnosis. For no eye sees Him, no heart attains to Him, no intelligence knows Him—because the basis for gnosis lies in being apart; the basis for connection lies in distance; and the basis for witnessing lies in separation.[80]

Concerning His words: *you shall not see Me but gaze at the mountain*, Jaʿfar said: (God) occupied (Moses) with the mountain, then manifested Himself. Were it not for his being occupied with the mountain, Moses would have died, losing consciousness never to recover.

سُبْحَٰنَكَ تُبْتُ إِلَيْكَ وَأَنَا۠ أَوَّلُ ٱلْمُؤْمِنِينَ ﴿١٤٣﴾

subḥānaka tubtu ilayka wa-ānā awwalu al-muʾminīn

glorified are You! I turn to You repentant and I am foremost among the believers.

Concerning His words: *glorified are You! I turn to You repentant*, Jaʿfar said: (Moses) affirmed his Lord's transcendence,[81] and acknowledged his total incapacity to Him, and acquitted himself of his intelligence. *I turn to You repentant* [may be glossed] 'I return to You, [turning away] from my ego, nor am I inclined to my knowledge—for [true] knowledge is that which You have taught me and [true] intelligence is that which You have honoured me with.' *And I am foremost among the believers*: 'Verily You are not to be seen in this world.'[82]

---

80 This comment refers to the total disparity between the creature and the Divinity. No created thing can attain to Him. Even within the incarnate person it is only the divine elements, the divine qualities and graces that accomplish the work. He is to be approached and known only through Himself—His qualities and graces; He is approached and known only by what is His own.

81 Students of theology should note that the verb here is *nazzaha* from which comes the term *tanzīh*, which became coterminus with de-anthropomorphism.

82 In other words, God is not to be seen unveiled in this world, which is

7:157 وَيَضَعُ عَنْهُمْ إِصْرَهُمْ وَٱلْأَغْلَٰلَ

wa yaḍaʿu ʿanhum iṣrahum wa'l-aghlāl

and (he) removes from them their burden and the shackles.

Jaʿfar said [explaining the words *burden* and *shackles*]: The heavy weight of setting up associates with God, the shame of oppositions [to God] and the fetter of heedlessness.

7:160 فَٱنۢبَجَسَتْ مِنْهُ ٱثْنَتَا عَشْرَةَ عَيْنًا ۖ

fa'nbajasat minhu'thnatā ʿashrata ʿaynan

and from it gushed forth twelve springs.

Concerning this verse [it is reported] from Jaʿfar b. Muḥammad [that] he said: From gnosis there gush forth twelve springs. All people drink from one of those springs, in a [given] rank, at a [given] station, according to their scope.

The first of these springs is that of professing God's unity. The second is the spring of slavehood and joy in it. The third is the spring of faithfulness. The fourth is the spring of sincerity. The fifth is the spring of humility. The sixth is the spring of contentment and entrustment [of all things to God]. The seventh is the spring of the Peace (of God's Presence)[83] and dignity. The eighth is the spring of liberality and confidence in God. The ninth is the spring of certainty. The tenth is the spring of the intellect. The eleventh is the spring of love. The twelfth is the spring of intimacy and solitude [with God]; this is the very spring of gnosis itself and from it gush forth these [other] springs. Whoever drinks from one of these springs finds its sweetness and strives hopefully for the spring which is higher than it—from spring to spring until he attains the origin. When he reaches the origin he realises the Truth.

---

the lowest realm (*al-dunyā*), the realm of dense physical matter. The transcendent God is not to be seen by physical eyes.

83 *Sakīnah* is a potent word that primarily means, in Islamic mysticism, the peace of the Presence of God.

7:196 وَهُوَ يَتَوَلَّى ٱلصَّٰلِحِينَ ﴿١٩٦﴾

wa huwa yatawallā'l-ṣāliḥīn

and He is in charge of those who do good.

Jaʿfar was asked about the wisdom in [the above] words of God, given that we know that God is in charge of [and governs all] the worlds. Jaʿfar said: Governance has two aspects. [There is] the governance to do with establishing and origination, and there is the governance to do with care and protection for the establishment of the Truth.[84]

84 The word *iqāmah* (establishing; establishment) used in defining both aspects of *tawliyah* (governance) means 'to set up' in the sense of founding and starting something; it also means 'to put something right'. As in the second usage in the text above, *iqāmah* also means 'to establish firmly', 'to abide, reside, remain'; it also means, much like *tawliyah*, 'to commission someone with the management of something'. In the comment, the first 'establishing' relates to the origination of creation; the second concerns firmly establishing knowledge and awareness of the Truth within creation.

﴾ 8 ﴿

سُورَةُ الأَنفَالِ

al-Anfāl (Spoils of War)

8:17 وَلِيُبْلِيَ ٱلْمُؤْمِنِينَ مِنْهُ بَلَآءً حَسَنًا

wa li-yubliya'l-muʾminīna minhu balāʾan ḥasanan

and that He prove the believers to be sound, through Him.[85]

Jaʿfar said: That He might efface them from their souls; then when He has effaced them from their souls, He Himself is the replacement of their souls for them.[86]

8:24 ٱسْتَجِيبُوا۟ لِلَّهِ وَلِلرَّسُولِ

(i)'stajībū li'llāhi wa li'l-rasūl

respond positively to God and the Messenger.

Jaʿfar said: Respond to Him/him with obedience, that therewith your hearts may be enlivened.

---

85 This rendition of the Qurʾānic phrase, which is in keeping with the tenor of the comment, is not common among English translations, which generally read, 'that He might test the believers by a fair test from Him'. However, it is grammatically sound, since *ablā balāʾan ḥasanan* means 'to prove brave, stand the test'; see Wehr at the fourth form of *b-l-y/w*. Lane in his discussion of the fourth form of *b-l-y/w*, cites the meaning of 'conferring a great blessing' for the phrase.

86 *Nufūsihim* ('their souls'). In other words, when the qualities of the individual ego are erased, the divine qualities deposited in the heart can permeate the soul which is thus sanctified. This comment serves to underscore the concept of the harmonious soul being full of the radiation of the divine lights.

8:24 إِذَا دَعَاكُمْ لِمَا يُحْيِيكُمْ ۖ

idhā daʿākum limā yuḥyīkum

when He invites you to what enlivens you.

Jaʿfar said: Life is life in God, and that is gnosis. As God, most high, has said: *verily We shall enliven him with a good life* (16:97).

8:44 لِيَقْضِيَ ٱللَّهُ أَمْرًا كَانَ مَفْعُولًا ۗ

li-yaqḍiya'llāhu amran kāna mafʿūlan

in order that God conclude a matter that was [to be] done.

Jaʿfar said: That which He has decreed in pre-eternity, He manifests in moment after moment and instant after instant.[87]

8:53 ذَٰلِكَ بِأَنَّ ٱللَّهَ لَمْ يَكُ مُغَيِّرًا نِّعْمَةً . . .

dhālika bi-anna'llāha lam yaku[88] mughayyiran niʿmatan

that is because God would not alter a blessing.

Jaʿfar said: As long as the slave acknowledges God's blessings upon him, God shall not remove a blessing from him—until he does not know [or acknowledge] a blessing and does not thank God for it, at which point, he becomes deserving of having it stripped from him.

---

87 That is to say, God's pre-eternal decree (*qaḍāʾ*) is incepted in time, at every instant. This comment is suggestive of later ideas on causation enshrined in the 'temporal atomism' of Ashʿarī theology (cf. occasionalism) and the Sufi conception of *tajdīdu'l-khalqi bi'l-anfās*, whereby creation is renewed at every instant, literally 'with every breath'.

88 Nwyia's edition has *yakun* instead of *yaku*.

8:67 تُرِيدُونَ عَرَضَ ٱلدُّنْيَا وَٱللَّهُ يُرِيدُ ٱلْءَاخِرَةَ ۗ

turīdūna ʿaraḍa'l-dunyā wa'llāhu yurīdu'l-ākhirah

you wish for the contingencies of the world while God wishes [for you] the hereafter.

Jaʿfar said [glossing the Qurʾānic phrase]: You wish for this world but God wishes for you the hereafter, and what God wishes for you is better than what you wish for yourselves.

8:69 فَكُلُوا۟ مِمَّا غَنِمْتُمْ حَلَـٰلًا طَيِّبًا ۚ

fa-kulū mimmā ghanimtum ḥalālan ṭayyiban

then consume the lawful and good from among the spoils of war you have taken.

Jaʿfar said: The lawful is that in which God is not disobeyed, and the good is that in which God is not forgotten.

9

سُورَةُ التَّوْبَةِ

al-Tawbah (Repentance)

9:25 لَقَدْ نَصَرَكُمُ ٱللَّهُ فِى مَوَاطِنَ كَثِيرَةٍ

la-qad naṣarakumu'llāhu fī mawāṭina kathīratin

God has granted you victory in many fields.

Jaʿfar said: The procurement of victory lies in one thing: submissiveness and neediness (to God) and [recognition of our] helplessness (before God), according to His words, *God has granted you victory in many fields.* You did not base yourselves, in them (i.e., in those fields), on yourselves, you did not witness your own strength nor your plentiful numbers, and you knew that victory is not found in strength but that God, He is the Bestower of victory and the Helper. When the slave acknowledges the reality of his weakness, God helps him; whereas abandonment by God comes about through one thing: self-conceit.[89] God says: *and on the day of Ḥunayn, when the large quantity of your numbers delighted you, yet they did not benefit you at all* (9:25).[90] When they regarded their strength as proceeding from themselves rather than from God, He cast defeat upon them and the earth was straitened for them. God says: *then you turned away and fled,* [when] left to your (own) might and your (own) strength and your (own) plentiful numbers.

---

89 *ʿUjb*, meaning self-admiration; pride.

90 Historically, this verse refers to the battle of Ḥunayn, where, despite their plentiful numbers, the Muslim army suffered a severe setback initially, but ultimately triumphed.

9:37 زُيِّنَ لَهُمْ سُوٓءُ أَعْمَٰلِهِمْ

zuyyina lahum sūʾu aʿmālihim

the evil of their deeds is made to appear fair to them.

Jaʿfar al-Ṣādiq was asked about His (above) words, and he said: It [refers to] hypocrisy.

9:40 وَأَيَّدَهُۥ بِجُنُودٍ لَّمْ تَرَوْهَا

wa ayyadahu bi-junūdin lam tarawhā

and He strengthened him with armies that you saw not.

Jaʿfar said concerning His [above] words: Those are the armies of certainty, confidence in God and trusting reliance upon God.

۞وَلَوْ أَرَادُوا۟ ٱلْخُرُوجَ لَأَعَدُّوا۟ لَهُۥ عُدَّةً

9:46

wa law arādū'l-khurūja la-aʿaddū lahu ʿuddatan

and had they intended to go forth they would surely have made some preparations for it.[91]

Jaʿfar said: If they knew God, they would surely be ashamed before Him and they would surely part, for Him, from their souls, their spirits and their wealth, in place of[92] one of His commands.

---

91 Nwyia reversed the order of this verse.

92 *Kharaja ʿan* has among its several meanings both 'to part from' and 'to disagree with'.

9:46 وَلَٰكِن كَرِهَ ٱللَّهُ ٱنۢبِعَاثَهُمۡ

walākin kariha'llāhu'nbiʿāthahum

but God was averse to their being sent forth.

Jaʿfar said: He demands of His slaves the Truth; but He did not make them worthy of that; then He did not excuse them but rebuked them for that. Do you not see Him say: *and they say: Do not go forth in the heat* (9:81).

9:91 مَا عَلَى ٱلۡمُحۡسِنِينَ مِن سَبِيلٖۚ

mā ʿalā'l-muḥsinīna min sabīlin

there is no path against those who do good.

Jaʿfar said: He who does good is the one who perfects the etiquette of serving his Lord.[93]

9:100 رَّضِيَ ٱللَّهُ عَنۡهُمۡ وَرَضُواْ عَنۡهُ

raḍiya'llāhu ʿanhum wa raḍū ʿanhu

God is pleased with them and they are pleased with Him.

Jaʿfar said: *God was pleased with them*, in the care and success that was preveniently bestowed on them from God; *and they were pleased with Him* in what He bestowed upon them in their following His Messenger ﷺ and (in) the acceptance of what he brought, and (in)

93 *Sayyidihi*, may also be translated as 'his master'. '*Sayyid*' is one of the titles of the descendants of the Prophet. The Shīʿī implication is that the *muḥsin* is the one who perfects his attitude to the imams. The word *ādāb*, rendered as 'etiquette', refers to behaviour both inward and outward. As noted elsewhere, good manners, be they external or internal, are rooted in virtue, which is divine.

their spending of (their) possessions and expending (their) best efforts [to be pleasing to God].[94]

9:111 ۞إِنَّ ٱللَّهَ ٱشْتَرَىٰ مِنَ ٱلْمُؤْمِنِينَ أَنفُسَهُمْ وَأَمْوَٰلَهُم

inna'llāha'shtarā mina'l-muʾminīna anfusahum wa amwālahum

verily God has purchased from the believers their souls and their possessions.

Jaʿfar said about His [above] words: (God) honours them in [both] the language of reality and in the language of commerce: He has purchased from them their bodies as loci for the coming down of love through their hearts; thus He enlivens them with the means for attachment (to Him).[95]

9:116 إِنَّ ٱللَّهَ لَهُۥ مُلْكُ ٱلسَّمَٰوَٰتِ وَٱلْأَرْضِ

inna'llāha lahu mulku'l-samāwāti wa'l-arḍ

verily God, to Him belongs the sovereignty of the heavens and the earth.

Jaʿfar said: All beings belong to Him—so let not that which belongs to Him distract you from Him.

94 In the context of the Qurʾānic verse, the phrase refers to the early Muslims who emigrated from Mecca to Yathrib (known as the *muhājirūn*, 'emigrants') and to the first Muslims among the native residents of Yathrib (known as the *anṣār*, 'helpers'). Here again, all goodness is seen to proceed from God. Thus human goodness is a blessing received by those who do good.

95 The physical body contains the soul which bears the spiritual heart which is the receptacle of divine love. Divine love is the means for attachment to God.

9:128 لَقَدْ جَآءَكُمْ رَسُولٌ

la-qad jāʾakum rasūlun

there has come to you a messenger.

Jaʿfar al-Ṣādiq said: God knows the weakness of His creatures in obeying Him and He informs them of that so that they know that they cannot attain purity through [their] service to Him. So He has established between Himself and them a creature of their own kind in form. Thus He says:

لَقَدْ جَآءَكُمْ رَسُولٌ مِّنْ أَنفُسِكُمْ عَزِيزٌ عَلَيْهِ مَا عَنِتُّمْ
9:128

la-qad jāʾakum rasūlun min anfusikum, ʿazīzun ʿalayhi mā ʿanittum[96]

there has come to you a messenger from among yourselves for whom what they have (of distress) is hard to bear.

Thus [said Jaʿfar] He clothed him from His quality of pity and mercy and sent him forth to creation as a faithful ambassador. And He made obedience to him obedience to Him and conformity to him conformity to Him for he says: *Whoever obeys the Messenger, verily he has obeyed God* (4:80).

96 In Nwyia's Arabic text, the Qurʾān quotation reads *mā ʿindahum*, instead of *mā ʿanittum, what (distress) afflicts you*, even though the commentary cites the correct form.

10

سُورَةُ يُونُس

Yūnus (Jonah)

10:13 لَمَّا ظَلَمُواْ

lammā ẓalamū

when they did wrong.

Jaʿfar said: When they received Our blessings with ingratitude.

10:25 وَٱللَّهُ يَدۡعُوٓاْ إِلَىٰ دَارِ ٱلسَّلَٰمِ

wa'llāhu yadʿū ilā dāri'l-salām

and God calls to the Abode of Peace.

Jaʿfar said: The invitation is general but the guidance is particular.

He also said: Paradise is good only through the Peace (therein). He has chosen you through these privileges solely so that you shall not choose anyone over Him.

He also said: The invitation acts upon the secret reaches of souls,[97] so that they are liquefied by it and incline to it peacefully.

---

97 *Sarāyir* (*sic.*, for *sarāʾir*), here rendered 'secret reaches of souls', is the plural of *sarīrah* (secret, secret thought, heart, mind, soul). *Rakana ilā* means 'to incline to something such as to become calm of mind'. See Lane at *r-k-n*.

10:57 وَشِفَآءٌ لِّمَا فِى ٱلصُّدُورِ

wa shifāʾun limā fīʾl-ṣudūr

and a healing for what is in the breasts.

Jaʿfar said: *A healing for what is in the breasts,* that is, repose for what is in the secret reaches of souls.

And Jaʿfar said: For some of them there is the healing of gnosis and serenity; and for some is the healing of acceptance and contentment; while for others is the healing of repentance and faithful fulfilment; and for some is the healing of witnessing and the meeting [with God].

10:58 قُلْ بِفَضْلِ ٱللَّهِ وَبِرَحْمَتِهِۦ فَبِذَٰلِكَ فَلْيَفْرَحُوا۟

qul: bi-faḍliʾllāhi wa bi-raḥmatihi fabi-dhālika fal-yafraḥū

say: in God's grace and in His mercy, in those let them delight.

Concerning this verse Jaʿfar said: This is vigilance against forgetfulness or the disruption of submissiveness; (and it is) to move away from the calls of the carnal appetites.

And Jaʿfar said: The grace of God is knowledge of Him, and His mercy is the success He gives.

10:107 وَإِن يَمْسَسْكَ ٱللَّهُ بِضُرٍّ فَلَا كَاشِفَ لَهُۥٓ إِلَّا هُوَ ۖ وَإِن يُرِدْكَ بِخَيْرٍ

wa in yamsaskaʾllāhu bi-ḍurrin falā kāshifa lahu illā huwa
wa in yuridka bi-khayrin

and if God touches you with some hurt or loss, then there is none who can remove it save Him; and if He intends for you some good

Jaʿfar said: God has made the hurt or loss dependent upon your quality but the intention for good for you dependent upon His quality—in order that your hope be greater than your fear.

11

سُورَةُ هُودٍ

Hūd

11:96 وَلَقَدْ أَرْسَلْنَا مُوسَىٰ بِآيَاتِنَا وَسُلْطَانٍ مُّبِينٍ ﴿٩٦﴾

wa la-qad arsalnā Mūsā bi-ayātinā wa sulṭānin mubīnin

and We sent Moses with Our signs and evident authority.

Jaʿfar said: The *signs* are humility towards the friends of God and great *authority* against the enemies of God.[98]

11:112 فَٱسْتَقِمْ كَمَآ أُمِرْتَ

faʾstaqim kamā umirta

then be upright even as you have been commanded.

Jaʿfar al-Ṣādiq said: Be poor unto God with firm resolution.

98 In this comment, *al-āyāt* is taken as a reference to Moses's humility towards the friends of God, such as the wisdom figure whom Moses encounters in *Sūrat al-Kahf* (18), while *al-sulṭān* refers to power against the enemies of God, such as Pharaoh.

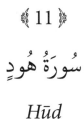

❀ 12 ❀

سُورَةُ يُوسُفَ

Yūsuf (Joseph)

12:19 قَالَ يَٰبُشْرَىٰ هَٰذَا غُلَٰمٌ ۚ وَأَسَرُّوهُ بِضَٰعَةً ۚ

qālā yā bushrā hādhā ghulāmun wa asarrūhu biḍāʿatan

he said: O good news! Here is a slave-boy. And they concealed him for merchandise.

Jaʿfar said: God, most high, had a secret in Joseph. He hid the situation[99] of His secret from them, for had He disclosed to them the reality of what He had deposited in (Joseph), they would have died. Do you not see how they said 'Here is a slave-boy'? Had they known the traces of the [divine] power in him they would have said 'Here is a prophet and a truthful one'. Indeed, when part of the matter was disclosed to the women they said: *this is no human; this is naught but a noble angel* (12:31).[100]

12:20 وَشَرَوْهُ بِثَمَنٍ بَخْسٍ

wa sharawhu bi-thamanin bakhsin

and they sold him for a paltry price.

Jaʿfar said: They sold him for a paltry price because of their ignorance of the subtleties of knowledge and marvellous signs which God had

99 *Mawḍiʿa*, meaning 'rank', 'position', 'location', translated here as 'situation.'

100 Later in the *sūrah* we are told that the wife of the ʿAzīz invited the women of the town, who were gossiping about her love for Joseph, to see for themselves the beauty of Joseph. When she sent him into the room where the women were seated, they exclaimed what is quoted above.

deposited within him.

Jaʿfar [also] said: You are amazed at how Joseph's brothers sold him so very cheaply, yet what you do is more astonishing than that; for you sell your portion of the hereafter for a passionate glance or thought of the world. It may be that a man sells his realisatory knowledge for a paltry sum, and it may be that his good fortune from his Lord escapes him by the very smallest [margin].

Jaʿfar [also] said: God had in Joseph a secret concealed from them. It was already deposited in him at the time they brought him forth out of the pit and he was sold for a paltry sum. Had they witnessed in him the secrets of the Truth that were deposited in him they would all have died in looking at him[101] and their tongues would never have obeyed them in their statement 'here is a slave-boy'. But in their view he was a slave-boy, while in the view of the Truth he was one of the luminaries.

12:30 قَدْ شَغَفَهَا حُبًّا ۖ

qad shaghafahā ḥubban

he has smitten her [heart] with love.

The pericardium is like the clouds: veiling (her) heart from thoughts about anyone other than him and from preoccupation with anything other than him.[102]

---

101 In seeing the secrets of the Truth in Joseph they would have seen the divine secrets in him, and that would have entailed annihilation.

102 The *shaghāf* or pericardium is defined in Lane as 'the fat which clothes the heart'. The meaning is that the love of Joseph acted upon the heart of Zulaykha as clouds act upon the sky, covering and darkening it, thus her heart was closed off from thoughts of anyone or anything other than her beloved. The Arabic text reads 'his heart' after 'veiling', in which case the second half of the comment, rather surprisingly, refers to Joseph instead of to Zulaykha, with the meaning that Joseph's heart was closed off from thoughts about or preoccupation with anything other than God. Or the comment may simply be a general one: 'The pericardium is like the clouds veiling the heart of (a person) from thoughts about anyone/anything other than (his beloved) and from preoccupation with anything other than (the beloved)'. However, in the apparatus, one manuscript is cited as having *qalbuhā* ('her heart'). As this fits in with the overall context, I have opted

12:30 إِنَّا لَنَرَىٰهَا فِي ضَلَٰلٍ مُّبِينٍ ٣٠

innā la-narāhā fī ḍalālin mubīnin

indeed, we consider her to be in evident error.

Jaʿfar b. Muḥammad was asked about passionate love, and he said: (It is) error. Then he recited: *indeed, we consider her to be in evident error*. He said: The meaning of this is: 'in passionate love for something outward'.[103]

12:31 فَلَمَّا رَأَيْنَهُۥٓ أَكْبَرْنَهُۥ

fa-lammā raʾaynahu wa akbarnahu[104]

then when they saw him and they extolled him.

Said Jaʿfar: The awe of prophethood [that fell] upon them overlaid the

---

to use the variant for the English translation at this point.

103 *Fī ʿishqi ẓāhirin* could be read *fī ʿishqin ẓāhirin* ('an outward, passionate love'). This comment displays the early status of *ʿishq* among the Sufis, when it was considered negatively. Later, however, *ʿishq* came to be used for the fervent love of God. In this text, the love of the divine in Joseph's story is manifested in the women of the city (rather than in Zulaykha), who perceiving the inner divine beauty extoll Joseph, proclaiming him 'a noble angel'. So here, Zulaykha, who loved his outer beauty, represents the corporeal person's longing for physical things, while the women who perceived his inner beauty, and through this perception transcended carnal desire, represent the higher lover.

104 The Arabic text has an extra full-sized *waw* here so that the Qurʾān citation seems to read: '*fa-lammā raʾaynahu* *wa* *akbarnahu*'. It may be that it is the original letter which is indicated by the small sized letter to be found at this place in Ḥafṣ. Such small letters 'indicate the fact that there ought to be big ones which are left out in the copies of the Qurʾān compiled and authorized by the Khalifa ʿUthmān and the pronunciation of which is obligatory'. See Abdullah Yusuf Ali, *The Meaning of the Glorious Qur'an* (London: Nadim and Co., 1983), p. xxxi, section ix. However, the small sized *waw* of the Ḥafṣ *muṣḥaf* is attached to the end of *raʾaynahu* and would indicate a long enunciation of the *hu* rather than meaning 'and'.

situation[105] of their desire for him, then they extolled him.

12:67 لَا تَدۡخُلُواْ مِنۢ بَابٖ وَٰحِدٖ

lā tadkhulū min bābin wāḥidin

do not enter through one gate.

Jaʿfar said: In his words, *do not enter through one gate*, Jacob forgot to rely on (divine) protection[106] and [the divine] strength, and (he forgot) that the divine decree overwhelms [all human] planning. Then, helped by God-given success (in goodness, *tawfiq*), he soon corrected (himself) and said: *I cannot avail you aught against God in anything* (12:67).

12:70 أَيَّتُهَا ٱلۡعِيرُ إِنَّكُمۡ لَسَٰرِقُونَ ٧٠

ayyatuhā'l-ʿīru innakum la-sāriqūn

O you caravan, surely you are thieves!

Jaʿfar said: In his order to his crier (to accuse) them of theft, Joseph made a veiled reference to what they did in Joseph's story, with regard to their father [as though saying] 'the deed which you committed (against) your father resembles the deed of a thief.'

12:76 كَذَٰلِكَ كِدۡنَا لِيُوسُفَۖ

ka-dhālika kidnā li-Yūsufa

thus We contrived for Joseph.

Jaʿfar said [glossing]: (Thus) We manifested in Joseph the collective blessings of his sincere/truthful forefathers inasmuch as We protected

---

105 The plural *mawāḍiʿ*, in the comment, is rendered by the English 'situation', as 'situations' would have read inelegantly.

106 *ʿIṣmah* means chastity, innocence, infallibility and also safeguarding, protection, preservation.

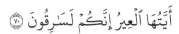

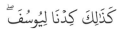

him through (the divine contrivance) in the time of affliction.[107]

12:81 إِنَّ ٱبْنَكَ سَرَقَ

inna'bnaka saraqa

lo, your son has stolen.

Jaʿfar said: The meaning of this [phrase] is 'lo, your son has not stolen'—for how should it be possible that this phrase be used about a prophet [who is the] son of a prophet? This phrase is one of the difficult ones of the Qurʾān; it is like His words in the story of David, *two litigants one of whom has been unjust towards the other* (38:22), while they were not litigants and had not been unjust.

12:92 لَا تَثْرِيبَ عَلَيْكُمُ

lā tathrība ʿalaykum

(there is) no reproof against you.

Jaʿfar said: There is no shame upon you concerning what you did for you were compelled to it as that was predestined for you.

12:93 ٱذْهَبُوا۟ بِقَمِيصِى هَٰذَا

idhhabū bi-qamīṣī hadhā

go with this shirt of mine.

[It is related] from Jaʿfar [that] he said: The intention in [sending] the

107 A comment with strong Shīʿī overtones: The use of the verb *ʿa-ṣ-m* in *ʿaṣimnāhu,* which is rendered 'We protected him', implies the protection of his innocence and chastity, his *ʿiṣmah,* which, on the spiritual register, signifies pure receptivity towards God. Moreover, the imams are held to inherit from their forefathers all the knowledge of the Prophet. See Douglas Crow, *The Teaching of Jaʿfar al-Ṣādiq* (Thesis, McGill University, Montreal 1980).

shirt was that, [since] distress had come to Jacob with the shirt, as stated in His words: *And they came with false blood on his shirt* (12:18), [Joseph] wished that joy should come to him (Jacob) through that wherewith sorrow had come to him.

12:94 قَالَ أَبُوهُمْ إِنِّي لَأَجِدُ رِيحَ يُوسُفَ

qāla abūhum innī la-ajidu rīḥa Yūsuf

their father said: truly I sense the fragrance of Joseph.

Jaʿfar al-Ṣādiq said: It is said that the east wind asked God most high, and said: 'Assign me, that I give him the good news of his son'; and God gave it permission to do that. Jacob was in prostration then raised his head and said: *truly I sense the fragrance of Joseph.* And his children said to him: *surely you are in your old aberrance* (12:95), that is, in your old love [of Joseph]. The fragrance was blended with divine care and compassion and mercy and notification of the end of the severe trial. Even thus, the confirmed believer finds the fragrance of the fresh breeze of faith in his heart and the breath of gnosis (coming) from the divine care, preveniently given to him from God in his inmost self.

12:100 وَقَدْ أَحْسَنَ بِيٓ إِذْ أَخْرَجَنِي مِنَ ٱلسِّجْنِ

wa qad aḥsana bī idh akhrajanī mina'l-sijn

and He was good to me when He brought me out of prison.

Jaʿfar al-Ṣādiq said: Joseph said, *and He was good to me when He brought me out of prison*, and he did not say 'when He brought me out of the well' even though that was the more distressing, because he did not wish to confront his brothers with [the statement]: 'for you treated me cruelly and flung me in the well' after he had said: *(there is) no reproof against you this day* (12:92).

إِنَّ رَبِّى لَطِيفٌ لِّمَا يَشَآءُ ۚ

12:100

inna Rabbī laṭīfun limā yashāʾu

verily my Lord is kind to whom He wills.

Jaʿfar al-Ṣādiq said: He has made His slaves stand under His will. If He wills He chastises them, and if He wills He effaces [their sins] from them; and if He wills He brings them close [to Himself], and if He wills He distances them [from Himself]—in order that the willing and power be His and no one else's. Then He manifests His loving kindness to His special slaves—through love and gnosis and faith; thus His words: *verily my Lord is kind to whom He wills:* to His slaves to whom care and friendship from Him have already been granted.

12:111

عِبْرَةٌ لِّأُو۟لِى ٱلْأَلْبَٰبِ ۗ

ʿibratun li-ūlīʾl-albāb[108]

and a lesson for those who possess spiritual minds.

Jaʿfar al-Ṣādiq said [in paraphrase]: 'For the possessors of secrets with God.'

108 According to the dictionary, *albāb* ('heart, mind, intellect, reason, understanding') is the plural of *lubb* ('kernal, essence, innermost'). *Albāb* is equated in this comment with the inmost self of a person, their secret (*sirr, asrār*). The spiritual mind is the inmost spiritual consciousness of a person. '*Those who possess spiritual minds*' are those in whom the spiritual mind is functioning rather than lying dormant or smothered under *daran*.

13

سُورَةُ الرَّعْدِ

al-Raʿd (Thunder)

13:9 ٱلْكَبِيرُ ٱلْمُتَعَالِ ﴿٩﴾

al-Kabīri'l-Mutaʿāli

the Great, the Exalted.

Jaʿfar said: The place where He alights[109] is of great significance in the hearts of the sages, while [whatever is] other than Him is insignificant in their view. He is exalted above being drawn near to except through His pure generosity.

13:11 إِنَّ ٱللَّهَ لَا يُغَيِّرُ مَا بِقَوْمٍ حَتَّىٰ يُغَيِّرُواْ مَا بِأَنفُسِهِمْ

inna'llāha lā yughayyiru mā bi-qawmin ḥatā yughayyirū mā bi-anfusihim

verily God does not change that which is with a people until they change that which is in their souls.[110]

Jaʿfar al-Ṣādiq said: He does not deem it suitable for them to change their inmost selves, nor does He alter for them their states; were He

---

109 'The place where He alights' translates *maḥall*, which means 'a place where a person or party alights or descends and stops or sojourns . . . or. . . takes up his abode, abides, lodges or settles.' See Lane at *maḥall* under *ḥ-l-l*.

110 This is usually understood to mean that God does not alter the condition of a people until they alter the condition of their souls. See Asad, *Message of the Qurʾān*, p. 360. This Qurʾānic phrase, taken on its own, is a *naṣṣ* that supports the principle of micro-macro cosmic correspondence by showing how changes in the one affect the other. The dynamic flows both ways.

to make suitable for them the changing of their inmost selves and the witnessing of tribulation and need,[111] they would become humble and needy, and through that they would attain to salvation.

13:14 وَمَا دُعَآءُ ٱلْكَٰفِرِينَ إِلَّا فِى ضَلَٰلٍ ﴿١٤﴾

wa mā duʿāʾ-kāfirīna illā fī ḍalālin

and the call of the disbelievers is only in error.

Jaʿfar said: Whoever calls [people] through his [lower] soul[112] calls to his [lower] soul, and that is unbelief and error. That is the place of betrayal and the falling away from the ranks of the loyal. For there are different types of people who summon: there is a caller who calls through the Truth; there is a caller to the Truth; and there is a caller to the way of the Truth. All of these callers invite creation to these ways [but] not through themselves.[113] Thus, these are the ways of the Truth. For the caller who invites through his lower soul, invites to error no matter what he is calling [people] to.[114]

---

111 *Balwā* comprises both the meanings of trial and need. Instead of applying the *bi-qawmin* to the macrocosmic condition, the *tafsīr* applies it to the innermost levels of the microcosm, and shows that when the divine is active or activated in the heart, then the soul is automatically affected positively. It would seem that the issue here is the state of the inmost self—does it breathe freely and easily or is it oppressed by the darkness of the soul. The emphasis in the Qurʾānic citation is on the need for the person to make good the state of their soul, while the *tafsīr* emphasises the precedence of divine activity in both the inner and outward dimensions.

112 *Bi-nafsihi* ('by/of/in himself'; or 'through/of his lower soul'). This implies an element of egoism in such a caller, an egoism that sullies his invitation at a profound level. It is 'the hidden fold of the ego'. In light of the discussion of qualities, this phrase would mean to summon people through your own 'poor and wretched' soul which would not lead to the Truth. This Qurʾānic verse begins with the phrase: *Lahu daʿwatu'l-Ḥaqq*, which may be rendered: 'To Him is the true summons' or 'His is . . .'. The verb *daʿā* means to call, invite, summon. The word *dāʿī*, here rendered caller, has the specific meaning of 'missionary'. In the Shīʿī hierarchy the rank of the *dāʿī* is the one above the ranks of the common believers.

113 *Lā bi-anfusihim*, i.e., with no interference from their lower soul/ego.

114 The point in this comment seems to be that any intrusion of the individual

13:27 إِنَّ ٱللَّهَ يُضِلُّ مَن يَشَآءُ وَيَهۡدِيٓ إِلَيۡهِ مَنۡ أَنَابَ ﴿٢٧﴾

inna'llāha yuḍillu man yashāʾu wa yahdī ilayhi man anāba

verily God lets go astray whom He will and guides to Himself whomever turns to Him repentant.

Jaʿfar said: He lets the person who seeks Him through his lower soul, stray from perceiving Him and His being. Whereas He guides, that is, He causes to attain His deepest truths, the one who seeks Him through Him.[115]

13:38 لِكُلِّ أَجَلٖ كِتَابٞ ﴿٣٨﴾

li-kulli ajalin kitābun

for every appointed time there is a divine prescript.

Jaʿfar said: There is a time for seeing (God).

13:39 يَمۡحُواْ ٱللَّهُ مَا يَشَآءُ وَيُثۡبِتُۖ

yamḥu'llāhu mā yashāʾu wa yuthbitu

God effaces what He will and establishes.

Concerning [the above] words of God, [it is related] from Jaʿfar b. Muḥammad [that] he said: He effaces unbelief and establishes faith; He

ego fatally flaws the work of the summoner—thus only he who is divinely appointed to be a summoner and who is divinely preserved from sin and error (*maʿṣūm*) and has divine assistance (*tawfīq*) is able to convey the summons correctly. This may be understood as having Shīʿī overtones: that the imams are the true and correct summoners to be followed.

115 This continues the point of the previous comment and touches on the theme of *tawakkul*, which is spoken of in several comments: he who relies on himself rather than on God is in error; the guarantee of success is total and trusting reliance on God, for which there must be no reliance on oneself, no subtle, false claims by the ego, for God is All-Powerful and the creature is utterly needy and helpless.

effaces ignorant denial and establishes gnosis; He effaces forgetfulness and establishes the remembrance (of God); He effaces hatred and establishes love; He effaces weakness and establishes strength; He effaces ignorance and establishes knowledge; He effaces doubt and establishes certainty and He effaces passionate inclinations and establishes the intellect, in this manner. The indication of this is in [His words]: *everyday He is concerned with some matter* (55:29), [that is,] effacing and establishing.

وَعِندَهُۥٓ أُمُّ ٱلْكِتَٰبِ ٣٩

13:39

wa ʿindahu ummu'l-kitāb

and with Him is the archetype of the Book.

Jaʿfar said: The Book in which distress and felicity are ordained. Nothing is added to it nor is anything subtracted from it. *The Word with Me is not altered* (50:29). Deeds are signs. Then he for whom felicity was ordained will have felicity at the end, while he for whom distress was ordained will have distress at the end.

14

سُورَةُ إِبْرَاهِيمَ

Ibrāhīm (Abraham)

14:1 كِتَٰبٌ أَنزَلْنَٰهُ إِلَيْكَ لِتُخْرِجَ ٱلنَّاسَ مِنَ ٱلظُّلُمَٰتِ إِلَى ٱلنُّورِ

kitābun anzalnāhu ilayka li-tukhrija'l-nāsa mina'l-ẓulumāti ilā'l-nūr

a Book which We have sent down to you that you may bring forth mankind from the darknesses into light.

Said Jaʿfar: [It is] a pledge with which you have been distinguished. In it is a clear statement of the perdition of previous communities and of the salvation of your community [O Muḥammad]; *which We have sent down to you that you may bring forth* people, by means of it, from the darknesses of disbelief into the light of faith, and from the darknesses of innovation into the lights of [the prophetic] custom and from the darknesses of the [lower] soul into the lights of the heart.

14:26 وَمَثَلُ كَلِمَةٍ خَبِيثَةٍ كَشَجَرَةٍ خَبِيثَةٍ

wa mathalu kalimatin khabīthatin ka-shajaratin khabīthatin

and the likeness of a harmful word is as a harmful tree.[116]

Jaʿfar said: The harmful tree is the carnal appetites; its soil is the lower soul; its water wishful expectation; its leafage is indolence; its fruits disobedience; and its final end is the fire.

116 *Khabīthah* (bad, wicked, evil, malicious, harmful, vicious).

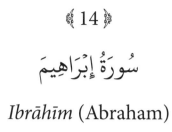

14:32 وَسَخَّرَ لَكُمُ ٱلْفُلْكَ لِتَجْرِيَ فِي ٱلْبَحْرِ بِأَمْرِهِۦ

wa sakhkhara lakumu'l-fulka li-tajriya fi'l-baḥri bi-amrihi

and He has made of service to you ships, that they may wend their way upon the sea by His command.

Jaʿfar said: He has made the heavens of service to you with the rains, and the earth with vegetation, and the two seas as ways for trade. He has made of service to you the sun and the moon which turn around you and cause the benefits of fruits and crops to reach you. He has made the heart of the believer of service to His love and His knowledge. God's share of the slaves is their hearts and nothing else, because the heart is the receptacle of His gaze and the repository of His trust[117] and of the knowledge of His secrets.

14:35 رَبِّ ٱجْعَلْ هَٰذَا ٱلْبَلَدَ ءَامِنًا

(Rabbī) 'jʿal hādhā'l-balada āminan

(my Lord), make this land safe.

Concerning [these] words of His, [it is related] from Jaʿfar b. Muḥammad that he said: (This refers to) the hearts of the sages; 'make them sanctuaries of Your secret and safe from being cut off from You.'

وَٱجْنُبْنِي وَبَنِيَّ أَن نَّعْبُدَ ٱلْأَصْنَامَ ﴿٣٥﴾

wa'jnubnī wa baniyya an naʿbuda'l-aṣnām

and preserve me and my sons from worshipping idols.

Jaʿfar said: Do not take me back to my witnessing the friendship [that I have with You], nor take my offspring back to witnessing the prophethood.[118]

---

117 *Amānah* (a deposit in trust, entrustment, charge, trusteeship). In other words, the spiritual heart contains the theophany, the *ḥaqīqah*.

118 Here the point seems to be that friendship or prophethood are 'idols'

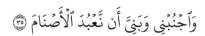

14:37 فَٱجۡعَلۡ أَفۡئِدَةً مِّنَ ٱلنَّاسِ تَهۡوِىٓ إِلَيۡهِمۡ

fa'j'al af'idatan mina'l-nāsi tahwī ilayhim

so incline the hearts of people towards them.

Ja'far said: *so incline the hearts of people towards them* since their hearts are inclined to You.

14:52 هَٰذَا بَلَٰغٌ لِّلنَّاسِ

hādhā balāghun li'l-nāsi

this is a clear message to people.

Ja'far said: (It is) spiritual counsel for creation and a warning for them to avoid evil associates and the gatherings of those who contend [against God]. For when hearts become habituated to sitting with the adversaries [of God] they are perverted and degenerate.

to the extent that they distract from God, and that the awareness even of the elevated status of sanctity or prophethood is an intrusion of ego-consciousness.

15

سُورَةُ الحِجْرِ

al-Ḥijr (The Rocky Tract)

15:9 إِنَّا نَحْنُ نَزَّلْنَا ٱلذِّكْرَ وَإِنَّا لَهُۥ لَحَـٰفِظُونَ ٩

innā naḥnu nazzalnā'l-dhikra wa innā lahu la-ḥāfiẓūn

verily We, but We, sent down the Remembrance and verily We are its guardian.

Jaʿfar said: *and verily We are its guardian*—'[Protecting it] in him for whom We intend good and taking it away from him for whom We intend adversity.'

15:28 إِنِّى خَـٰلِقٌۢ بَشَرًا مِّن صَلْصَـٰلٍ

innī khāliqun basharan min ṣalṣālin

verily, I am creating a human from clay.

Jaʿfar said: He tested them, the angels,[119] in order to prompt them to

119 The angels too keep growing in knowledge of and awe at the wonders of His power, wisdom, and mercy. Concerning the prostration of the angels to Adam, Muslims too often think that this means all angels should bow to all people. So it is worth pointing out that it is to Adam, the first man, that the angels bowed. Moreover, according to some scholars and contrary to popular belief, the angels do have free will (that is why Iblis could chose to refuse to prostrate to Adam). The 'superiority' of the ordinary incarnate human over the angels (to generalise and not to go into the many categories and levels of angelic beings), lies in the fact that the incarnate human contains within his person all levels of being, including the lowest level of dense physical matter—as God on the metacosmic scale contains the whole of being including the hells, in Himself. And

seek understanding so that they should increase in knowledge of the wonders of His power, and their own souls should be nothing in their sight.

15:42 إِنَّ عِبَادِى لَيْسَ لَكَ عَلَيْهِمْ سُلْطَٰنٌ

inna ʿibādī laysa laka ʿalayhim sulṭānun

verily, over My slaves you have no power.

[It is related] from Jaʿfar al-Ṣādiq, concerning God's words: *the slaves of the Gracious* (25:63), that he said: [This phrase is applicable to] creation in its entirety with regard to [its] createdness but not with regard to gnosis. Whereas [God's words] *My slaves*, is a designation of slavehood and gnosis.[120]

15:72 لَعَمْرُكَ إِنَّهُمْ لَفِى سَكْرَتِهِمْ يَعْمَهُونَ ﴿٧٢﴾

la-ʿamruka innahum lafī sakratihim yaʿmahūn

by your life, verily, they rove and stray in their drunkenness.

Concerning [the above] words of God, Jaʿfar said: By your life O Muḥammad, truly they all are in the drunkenness of heedlessness and [under] the veil of remoteness (from Us), except those for whom you are the means and the guide to Us.

---

in the fact that in order to be in harmony with the divine, the incarnate human has to overcome the myriad pulls of density—which the angels do not have to do. It is not difficult for a subtle being of light to choose to obey God, the way it is for a dense creature. But, as God wills, angels have their own lessons to learn, in order to increase them in knowledge and understanding, in wisdom and humility.

120 This seems to pick up on the idea of indiscriminate mercy and discriminating mercy; *ʿubūdīyah* entails and is the consequence of gnosis (*maʿrifah*): to know God is to be no obstacle to Him; it is to be effaced in Him; to be in harmony with the divine.

15:87 وَلَقَدْ ءَاتَيْنَـٰكَ سَبْعًا مِّنَ ٱلْمَثَانِى

wa la-qad ātaynāka sabʿan mina'l-mathānī[121]

and We have given you seven of the oft-repeated.

[It is related] from Jaʿfar, concerning this verse, [that] he said, [in explanatory paraphrase]: 'We have honoured you and revealed to you and sent you [as Our messenger] and inspired you and guided you and established you in authority and power. Then We honoured you with seven miracles,[122] the first of which is right guidance; the second is prophethood; the third is mercy; the fourth is compassion; the fifth is devoted love (*mawaddah*) and intimate love (*ulfah*); the sixth is bliss; and the seventh is the Peace (of the divine Presence) and the exalted Qurʾān in which is the most exalted name of Allāh.'

121 *Al-mathānī* are traditionally taken as referring to the seven verses of the *Fātiḥah*, the opening *sūrah* of the Qurʾān, which is recited in every cycle (*rakʿah*) of every canonical prayer.

122 *Karāmāt*, which could also be rendered 'marks of honour', came to be specifically associated with the miracles performed through saints, the word *muʿjizah* being reserved for the miracles vouchsafed to the prophets.

﴾ 16 ﴿

سُورَةُ النَّحْلِ

al-Naḥl (The Bee)

16:12

وَسَخَّرَ لَكُمُ ٱلَّيْلَ وَٱلنَّهَارَ وَٱلشَّمْسَ وَٱلْقَمَرَ

wa sakhkhara lakumu'l-layla wa'l-nahāra wa'l-shamsa
wa'l-qamar

*and He has placed the night and the day and the sun and the
moon at your service.*

Jaʿfar al-Ṣādiq 🕮 said: He has placed at your service the rains in the
heavens, and the plants and vegetation on earth, and the various
animals, in the day and at night. He has placed at your service the
angels who praise (God) on your behalf; and on earth, the grazing
livestock, domestic animals, the ships, and the [other] creatures.[123] He
has placed everything at your service in order that nothing should busy
you and distract you from Him and so that you can be at the service
of Him who has placed all these things at your service. For indeed, He
has placed all things at your service and has placed your heart at the
service of His love and knowledge of Him—that is the portion allotted
to the slave from his Lord.

---

123 *Khalq* may mean specifically 'mankind'.

16:96 مَا عِندَكُمْ يَنفَدُ وَمَا عِندَ ٱللَّهِ بَاقٍ ۗ

mā ʿindakum yanfadu wa mā ʿindaʾllāhi bāqin

what is with you comes to an end but what is with God is unending.

Jaʿfar said: *What is with you comes to an end* that is, acts such as [the performance of] the religious obligations and supererogatory prayers; but *what is with God is unending*, His qualities and attributes. For what is new is transient but the Pre-existent One is everlasting.[124]

16:97 فَلَنُحْيِيَنَّهُۥ حَيَوٰةً طَيِّبَةً ۖ

fala-nuḥyiyannahu ḥayātan ṭayyibatan

We shall indeed enliven him with a good life.

Jaʿfar said: The 'good life' is knowledge of God, sincerity of station with God and sincerity of standing with God.[125]

Jaʿfar [also] said: The 'good life' is that it be made good for His sake—in that it is all from God and returns to Him.

---

124 *Al-Qadīm*, 'the Pre-existent One', is one of the divine names. *Al-ḥadath* ('the new') implies the occurrence or advent of something which did not previously exist. (Later, philosophers would use the term *ḥādith* for that which is temporally incepted.) Thus everything which at some point did not previously exist is *ḥadath* and is doomed to pass away—only the Uncreated, which always was, shall always be.

125 *Maqām*, 'station', in later Sufism came to mean specifically a permanent realisation of a spiritual station, as opposed to a temporary state (*ḥāl*). *Wuqūf* ('standing'), also means halting, stopping, staying, standing still; it also means cognisance, knowledge, understanding. For the later development of the mystical concept of this 'standing' or 'halting', see A. J. Arberry, ed. and trans., *The Mawāqif and Mukhātabāt of Muḥammad b. ʿAbdi'l-Jabbār al-Niffarī* (Cambridge: Gibb Memorial Trust, 1978), especially the sections on *waqfah* and *wāqif* in Arberry's Introduction.

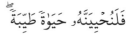

16:125 ٱدۡعُ إِلَىٰ سَبِيلِ رَبِّكَ بِٱلۡحِكۡمَةِ وَٱلۡمَوۡعِظَةِ ٱلۡحَسَنَةِۖ

(u)dʿu ilā sabīli Rabbika bi'l-ḥikmati wa'l-mawʿiẓati ('l-ḥasanah)

call to the way of your Lord with wisdom and good counsel.

Jaʿfar said: Calling with wisdom is that (a person) summons (another) [with a summons] from God to God through God; and good counsel is that creation be seen to be bound by the reins of the divine power—so (the one) who gets it right [should be] thanked and (the one) who rejects [it should be] excused.[126]

16:127 وَٱصۡبِرۡ وَمَا صَبۡرُكَ إِلَّا بِٱللَّهِۚ

wa'ṣbir wa mā ṣabruka illā bi'llāh

and be patient—and your patience can only be through God.

Jaʿfar said: God enjoined patience upon His prophets; and He appointed the highest portion (of patience) for the Prophet ﷺ, inasmuch as He commanded him to be patient through God, not through himself.

126 That is, those who reject the right way and, perhaps more specifically, those who reject the imams. This comment, suggestive as it is of a Jabri-latitudinarian attitude which excuses 'sinners' for what they cannot avoid, is in keeping with the rigorous predestinarian doctrine manifest in this commentary.

﴾ 17 ﴿

سُورَةُ الإِسْرَاءِ

al-Isrāʾ (The Night Journey)

Banī Isrāʾīl (The Children of Israel)

It is said that a man came to Jaʿfar b. Muḥammad and said: Describe for me the ascent (*miʿrāj*).[127] He replied: How should I describe for you a station which even Gabriel, with all the magnitude of his rank, was not able [nor permitted][128] to enter.

---

127 The *isrāʾ* is the famous night journey of the Prophet during which, accompanied by the archangel Gabriel and riding on the heavenly steed named Burāq, he was taken in spirit from Mecca to Jerusalem and thence on the ascent (*miʿrāj*) through the seven heavens ascending to the utmost limit. For the traditional account of this journey, see Martin Lings, *Muhammad* (Rochester, VT: Inner Traditions, 1983), pp. 101–104; and Asad, *Message of the Qurʾān*, Appendix IV. The Qurʾānic verses 53:13–18 are traditionally understood to refer to the *miʿrāj*.

128 *Lam yasiʿ* comprises both the meanings given above of 'not being able' and 'not being allowed'. Tradition tells us that the archangel accompanied the Prophet on his spiritual journey all the way to the furthest boundary beyond which it was not for Gabriel to go. This comment is rather intriguing given that the alchemical theurgy does pertain to a soul's spiritual journey or ascent. Looking closely at the wording some things are clear: 1) The Imam declines to describe a particular station (*maqām*), (rather than the whole journey), which pertains to the Prophet. 2) He refused to give a description of this to the man asking the question, saying 'How should I describe for *you* . . .' 3) Moreover, the unusual way this comment begins, 'It is said that a man came to Jaʿfar', indicates that the questioner was not someone Jaʿfar's circle of students were familiar with. So perhaps it is not at all surprising that the teacher of alchemists refused to provide an extempore description of the whole alchemical journey to an unknown person.

17:65 وَكَفَىٰ بِرَبِّكَ وَكِيلًا ﴿٦٥﴾

wa kafā bi-Rabbika wakīlan

and sufficient is your Lord as trustee.

Jaʿfar said: Sufficient is your Lord as trustee for him who trustfully relies on Him and entrusts his affair to Him.[129]

17:70 ۞وَلَقَدْ كَرَّمْنَا بَنِيٓ ءَادَمَ

wa la-qad karramnā banī Ādam

verily We have honoured the children of Adam.

Jaʿfar said: We have honoured the children of Adam with spiritual knowledge.[130]

17:80 أَدْخِلْنِي مُدْخَلَ صِدْقٍ

adkhilnī mudkhala ṣidqin

make me enter through the portal of sincerity.[131]

Concerning His [above] words, [it is related] from Jaʿfar b. Muḥammad that he said: *Make me enter* therein in the condition of contentment [with You]; *and bring me forth* from it with You content with me (17:80).

He also said: *Bring me forth* from the grave to the standing before You on the path of sincerity with the sincere ones.

And he said: To seek entrustment[132] is that He be the one entrusted

---

129 This is reflected in the *duʿah*, current to this day: *ʿalāʾllāhi tawakkaltu wa ilayhi fawwaḍtu amrī* (upon God I trustfully rely, and to Him I entrust my affair).

130 *Maʿrifah,* 'spiritual knowledge' or 'gnosis', denotes realisatory understanding of spiritual truths.

131 In addition to sincerity, *ṣidq* means faithfulness and truthfulness.

132 *Tawlīyah* is the verbal noun from the second form of the verbal root *w-l-y*, which means 'to seek to appoint someone as governor, ruler, manager; to make someone the head of something, to entrust someone

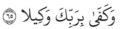

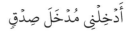

to, that is to say: 'Make me enter the arena of Your gnosis and bring me forth from the witnessing in gnosis to the witnessing in the Essence.'[133]

17:80 وَٱجۡعَل لِّي مِن لَّدُنكَ سُلۡطَٰنٗا

wa'j'al lī min ladunka sulṭānan

and grant me authority directly from Yourself.

Jaʿfar said [interpreting this direct authority]: A strength in religion for me, through which love is awarded to me.[134]

17:101 وَلَقَدۡ ءَاتَيۡنَا مُوسَىٰ تِسۡعَ ءَايَٰتِۭ

wa la-qad ātaynā Mūsā tisʿa āyātin

and indeed We gave Moses nine signs.

Jaʿfar said: Among the signs with which God distinguished him are the making [of Moses for God's own purpose]; the casting of love upon him;[135] speaking (to him); steadfastness in the locus of the (direct, divine) oration; protection on the Nile; the white hand;[136] and the giving

with something, to commission someone' etc. 'Entrustment'—as *tawlīyah* is rendered in the text—is to be understood in the sense of seeking 'to appoint someone as ruler (*wālī*). . .'

133 The phrases 'the witnessing in gnosis' and 'the witnessing in the essence' render '*mushāhadat al-maʿrifah*' and '*mushāhadat al-dhāt*' which might also be translated 'the witnessing of gnosis' and 'the witnessing of the essence'. The translation opted for in the text conveys better the concepts of witnessing God through knowledge of Him and witnessing Him in and through the essence—which is what the Arabic indicates.

134 *Awjaba lī bihā al-maḥabbah* could also be rendered 'through which love is made incumbant for me'.

135 This and the casting of love upon Moses, are a reference to 20:39, 41 where God says to Moses: *I cast love from Me upon you*, and *and I made—or 'took'—you for Myself*. (My thanks again to Feras Hamza for drawing my attention to these references.)

136 One of the possible interpretations of the white hand of Moses is that through it God revealed the hand of Moses's spiritual body—which was

of the tablets [of the Commandments].

17:105 وَبِٱلْحَقِّ أَنزَلْنَٰهُ وَبِٱلْحَقِّ نَزَلَ

wa bi'l-ḥaqqi anzalnāhu wa bi'l-ḥaqqi[137] nazala

and in truth We have sent it down, and with truth has it descended.

Jaʿfar said: The Truth has been sent down upon the hearts of His distinguished ones—from His concealed benefits,[138] the wonders of His beneficence and the subtleties of His handiwork—that wherewith their inmost selves are illumined and their hearts purified and their exteriors adorned; and with the Truth has He sent down these subtleties upon them.[139]

---

fully angelic and made of the white light of God. Cf. the discussion at 28:29, on how Moses became an angelic being when he approached the burning bush and the lights of holiness permeated him and the robes of intimacy enveloped him and the divine speech passed through him.

137 These Qurʾānic words are usually taken to be a reference to the Qurʾān itself. See the translations by Muhammad Pickthall, *The Glorious Koran* (London: George Allen and Unwin, 1980), and Asad, *Message of the Qurʾān*, for example. The phrase *bi'l-ḥaqqi* means both 'with truth' and 'in truth'. The specific use of the divine name *al-Ḥaqq*, as the reference to God in the commentary, should also be kept in mind.

138 *Fawāyid* (*sic.*), plural of *fāʾidah* incorporates the meanings of benefit, profit, or advantage; good; knowledge—which God bestows upon a man such that he consequently seeks it and acquires it. See Lane under *f-y-d*. In this connotation of the *fawāʾid* being benefits that God gives a person to seek and acquire, we meet again that double blessing: the initial, prevenient blessing of seeking the good and the second, subsequent blessing of acquiring that good.

139 That is, the subtleties and benefits bestowed pertain to the Truth; they are illuminating, purifying, adorning truths from God, the Truth.

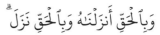

18

سُورَةُ الكَهْفِ

al-Kahf (The Cave)

18:14 وَرَبَطْنَا عَلَىٰ قُلُوبِهِمْ إِذْ قَامُوا۟ فَقَالُوا۟ رَبُّنَا رَبُّ ٱلسَّمَٰوَٰتِ وَٱلْأَرْضِ

wa rabaṭnā ʿalā qulūbihim idh qāmū fa-qālū rabanā rabbu'l-samawāti wa'l-arḍ

and We fortified their hearts when they stood forth and they say our Lord is the Lord of the heavens and the earth

Jaʿfar said: *when they stood forth*, that is to say, (when) they stood [in prayer][140] and were dedicated in supplicating Us.

He said: They stand forth for the Truth, through the Truth, with a seemly standing, and call on Him with sincerity, showing Him correct poverty, and have the best recourse to Him; and they say: *our Lord is the Lord of the heavens and the earth*—proud of Him and magnifying Him. Then the Truth repays them for their standing (thus) by responding to their call with the best response and the most subtle oration,[141] and He manifests in them signs at which [even] the messengers marvel [as] when He said: *had you beheld them you would surely have turned away from them, fleeing* (18:18).[142]

140 The verb *qāma* comprises several meanings including 'to stand forth, rise up' and 'to stand to perform the canonical prayer'. In addition to dedicated, *akhlaṣū* means 'they were devoted, faithful, sincere'.

141 *Khiṭāb:* the direct divine oration in the heart.

142 The end of this verse is *and you would have been filled with utter terror because of them.*

18:17 ذَاتَ ٱلْيَمِينِ . . . ذَاتَ ٱلشِّمَالِ

dhāta'l-yamīni . . . dhāta'l-shimāl

on the right . . . on the left.

Jaʿfar said: A person's 'right' is his heart and his 'left' is his soul. Divine care encircles them; were it not for that (the person) would perish.

18:18 لَوِ ٱطَّلَعْتَ عَلَيْهِمْ لَوَلَّيْتَ مِنْهُمْ فِرَارًا

law iṭṭalaʿta ʿalayhim la-wallayta minhum firāran

had you beheld them you would surely have turned away from them, fleeing.

Jaʿfar said: If you beheld them from your standpoint, you would surely turn from them in flight; but if you beheld them from the standpoint of the Truth you would surely witness in them the meanings[143] of (God's) onliness and things divine.

Jaʿfar said (too): *If you beheld* the traces of Our power and care that were in them and the governance of (Our) custody over them, *you would surely turn from them, fleeing*, that is, you would have been unable to stand steadfast to witness what was in them through awe of Us. Thus the reality of the flight [is that you would be fleeing] from Us not from them, because what showed through them was from Us.[144]

Jaʿfar also said: *If you beheld them from your standpoint* you would have fled; but if you beheld them from My position you would have stayed. That is because the friend of God has states with God [such that] he who looks at (the saint) through his [lower] soul is unable to behold him due to human weakness; (the saint) escapes his seeing (him). Thus did the Prophet ﷺ escape the disbelievers.[145]

---

143 *Maʿānī*, plural of *maʿnan* (meaning, significance, explanation; but also 'good qualities').

144 This is another testification to the sanctified soul. The sleepers of the cave are taken as saints; their sleep is symbolic of the effacement of their souls in the face of the divine, which is why what is in them is overpowering.

145 This elliptical reference to the Prophet is to be understood on the

18:24 وَٱذْكُر رَّبَّكَ إِذَا نَسِيتَ

wa'dhkur Rabbaka idhā nasīta

and remember your Lord when you have forgotten.

Jaʿfar said: *When you have forgotten* others, then draw close to Me with remembrance.[146]

18:30 إِنَّا لَا نُضِيعُ أَجْرَ مَنْ أَحْسَنَ عَمَلًا ﴿٣٠﴾

innā lā nuḍīʿu ajra man aḥsana ʿamalan

verily We do not neglect the recompense of one who does good.

Jaʿfar said: Those who trust God with their provisions and the meeting of their requirements, and who seek [such] provision from His countenance, the seeking of which God has permitted,[147] God truly shall not let their effort in seeking His gratification go to waste. He facilitates for them the way of trusting reliance (upon Him) that they may, thereby, be free of the need for searching and action.[148] Thus He brings them forth from the narrow confines of seeking into the vast openness of trusting reliance (upon Him).

---

spiritual register: the essential reality (*ḥaqīqah*) of the Prophet escaped the disbelievers because they looked at him through their own qualities, with their human limitations. Had they looked at him through the divine qualities, they would have perceived his true status.

146 *Adhkār* (lit. 'remembrances') includes meditative prayers, repetitions of holy formulae and Qurʾānic phrases, and monologic prayer, involving the invocation of the divine name(s). In this comment, the two aspects of the *shahādah*, the negation and the affirmation, are taken up and elaborated: *nasiyu'l-aghyār* (the forgetting of others is the negation, *nafiy*: '*lā ilāha*; no god'); and *dhikru Rabbika* (the remembrance of your Lord is the affirmation, *ithbāt*: '*illā'llāh,* except God').

147 In other words, they seek the *ḥalāl* in a manner that is *ḥalāl.*

148 The word translated as 'action' is *ḥaraka*, which has 'movement' as a primary meaning. It also means 'undertaking' and 'enterprise', which may be more pertinent in the context of the comment.

18:46 وَٱلْبَٰقِيَٰتُ ٱلصَّٰلِحَٰتُ

al-bāqiyātu'l-ṣāliḥāt

enduring good deeds.

[Concerning this phrase] Jaʿfar al-Ṣādiq said: It is to render unadulterated the affirmation of God's unity, for that subsists in the subsistence of the one who professes God's unity in the subsistence of the unified One (*muwaḥḥad*).

18:67 قَالَ إِنَّكَ لَن تَسْتَطِيعَ مَعِىَ صَبْرًا ﴿٦٧﴾

qāla innaka lan tastaṭīʿa maʿiya ṣabran

He said: verily you shall never be able to bear patiently with me.

Jaʿfar said: You are not patient with one who is beneath you [in rank] so how can you be patient with one who is above you?[149]

18:84 وَءَاتَيْنَٰهُ مِن كُلِّ شَىْءٍ سَبَبًا ﴿٨٤﴾

wa ātaynāhu min kulli shayʾin sababan

and We gave him a means to everything.

Jaʿfar said: Verily, God, most high, has made a cause[150] for everything,

149 The Qurʾānic reference is to the mysterious figure of al-Khiḍr who is, on the basis of 18:65, associated with *al-ʿilm al-ladunī* (direct God-given knowledge). In the context of his meeting with al-Khiḍr, Moses represents the exoteric, the outward, the *ẓāhir*, while al-Khidr represents the esoteric, the inward, the *bāṭin*.

150 *Sabab*, plural *asbāb,* can be variously rendered as means, cause, a rope that extends vertically. For the translation we have made use of both 'means' and 'cause(s)' as renditions suited to the context. In the teaching of Imām Jaʿfar, *sabab/asbāb* has an important place as the concept of the means or ropes by which the imam is linked to the divine realm. The *asbāb* have a dual function: first, they convey the spiritual support which the imam receives in his inmost self, for instance, his *ʿilm*, knowledge, which

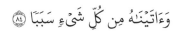

and He has made the causes the qualities of being. Whoever witnesses[151] the cause is detached from the thing caused; while the heart of him who witnesses the making of the thing caused is filled with doubts about the causes. Now when a person's heart is filled with doubt, it comes between him and perception and it veils him from witnessing.

18:101 وَكَانُواْ لَا يَسۡتَطِيعُونَ سَمۡعًا ١٠١

wa kānū lā yastaṭīʿūna samʿan

and they are incapable of listening.

Jaʿfar al-Ṣādiq said: They are incapable of listening to the Word of the Truth, or to the traditions of *al-muṣṭafā* (the Prophet) ﷺ, or to the stories of the lives of the righteous guides among the prophets and the truthful ones, because they have not been placed among those who accept the Truth; and so they are prevented from listening to the oration of the Truth.

18:110 وَلَا يُشۡرِكۡ بِعِبَادَةِ رَبِّهِۦٓ أَحَدَۢا ١١٠

wa-lā yushrik bi-ʿibādati Rabbihi aḥadan

and let him not give a share to anything else in the worship of his Lord.

Jaʿfar said: When he stands before his Lord he does not see anything other than Him, nor is there anything other than Him in his concern or endeavour.

---

includes the correct and complete understanding of the Qurʾān; second, it is the sole means by which God's continual guidance is conveyed to man, through the vehicle of the imam. See further, Crow, *Teaching of Jaʿfar al-Ṣādiq*, pp. 37–38.

151 *Shahida* (to witness, see, experience personally; to attest, confirm, testify; acknowledge). The implication of all these meanings of the verb needs to be borne in mind.

﴾19﴿

سُورَةُ مَرْيَم

Maryam (Mary)

19:6 وَٱجْعَلْهُ رَبِّ رَضِيًّا ﴿٦﴾

wa'j'alhu Rabbi raḍīyan

and make him, my Lord, content.

Jaʿfar said: *Content*, that is, content with what occurs [both] for him and against him.[152]

19:8 قَالَ رَبِّ أَنَّىٰ يَكُونُ لِي غُلَٰمٌ

qāla Rabbi annā yakūnu lī ghulāmun

He said, my Lord, how shall I have a son.

Jaʿfar said: He received the blessing with thanks before it had actually come to pass. *How shall I have a son*—'through what kindness or deed or obedience could I deserve to draw forth from Yourself this answer [to my prayer], this bounty and generosity save through Your prevenient bounty and blessings upon Your slaves in all circumstances; for if I have despaired of my acts, I have not despaired of Your grace.'

152 In keeping with the tone of the *tafsīr*, this contentment may be understood—be it on the level of external life in the world or on the inner level—to be with whatever occurs to the advantage of the higher self and whatever occurs against the lower soul or ego.

19:23 يَٰلَيْتَنِى مِتُّ قَبْلَ هَٰذَا

yā laytanī mittu qabla hādhā

O would that I had died before this.

Jaʿfar said: When she saw no one suitable, no guide, no person of discernment among her folk who might exonerate her against their statements, she (Mary, the Blessed Virgin) said: *O would that I had died before* I saw in my people what I see.

And Jaʿfar said: *O would that I had died before* I saw for my heart any attachment other than God.[153]

19:52 وَقَرَّبْنَٰهُ نَجِيًّا ﴿٥٢﴾

wa qarrabnāhu najīyan

and We drew him near in secret converse.

Jaʿfar said: He who has been brought close to God, most high, has three distinguishing characteristics: When God gives him knowledge, He provides him [the means to] act upon that knowledge; and when He has raised him to act upon that knowledge, He gives him faithfulness in his action. And when He appoints him to the company of those who have submitted to God, He bestows in his heart respect for them and he knows that respect for those who believe is a part of respect for God most high.[154]

---

153 The verb *taʿallaqa* has the meanings of attachment in the sense of both 'suspension from' and 'fondness for'. The words of the blessed Virgin are taken and here used to express the sentiment: What is the point of corporeal life if the heart be dead, for to the extent that al-Ḥayy, the Living One's presence (His spirit /life and light /qualities), does not permeate the heart to that extent the heart is dead. Earthly life is all about striving to let the spiritual heart live in the earth of corporeality. Thus this comment picks up again on that major theme of this commentary: striving to become godly by letting God's life and light extend through the heart and soul.

154 Note the progressive purifications: knowledge granted; action that expresses this knowledge; sincerity in those actions; humble respectfulness

19:85 يَوْمَ نَحْشُرُ ٱلْمُتَّقِينَ

yawma naḥshuru'l-muttaqīn

the day We gather the God-aware.

Jaʿfar said: The God-aware [person] is he who is wary of everything other than God; and the God-aware is he who is wary of following his desires.[155] Whoever is characterised thus is carried by God, flanked by light, to the Presence of witnessing, so that the people at the assembly[156] might know his place among them.

19:93 إِن كُلُّ مَن فِي ٱلسَّمَٰوَٰتِ وَٱلْأَرْضِ إِلَّآ ءَاتِي ٱلرَّحْمَٰنِ عَبْدًا ﴿٩٣﴾

(in kullu man fi'l-samawāti wa'l-arḍi) illā ātī'l-Raḥmāni ʿabdan;

(there is none in the heavens nor the earth) but comes to the Gracious as a slave.

Concerning His (above) words, [it is related] from Jaʿfar b. Muḥammad that he said: (. . .) *but comes to the Gracious as a slave*, either poor and wretched through his own qualities or noble through (and) corroborating the qualities of the Truth.

---

in the knowledge of qualitative oneness.

155 It is difficult to convey in a single English word all that is implied by *hawan* (pl. *ahwāʾ*), rendered here as 'desires'. One should bear in its other meanings: passions, whims, longings, pleasures, inclinations.

156 The Arabic phrase *ahl al-mashhad* ('the people at the assembly') captures, in a way that English does not, the connotation of an assembly of 'witnessers,' or those blessed with '*mushāhadah*', witnessing. Both *mashhad* and *mushāhadah* derive from the verbal root *sh-h-d* (to see with one's own eyes, to witness, to experience personally, to attend, to be present).

﴿ 20 ﴾

سُورَةُ طه

Ṭā' Hā'

20:3 إِلَّا تَذْكِرَةً لِّمَن يَخْشَىٰ ۝٣

illā tadhkiratan liman yakhshā

but only as a reminder for him who fears.

Jaʿfar said: God sent down the Qurʾān as a spiritual counsel for those who fear, as a mercy for the believers and as an intimacy for the lovers. Thus He said: *We did not send down the Qurʾān to you that you should be troubled. But only as a reminder for him who fears* (20:2–3).

20:11–12 فَلَمَّآ أَتَىٰهَا نُودِيَ يَٰمُوسَىٰٓ ۝١١ إِنِّيٓ أَنَا۠ رَبُّكَ

fa-lammā atāhā nūdiya yā Mūsā. Innī anā Rabbuka

then when he came to it, he was summoned: O Moses. Verily I am I, your Lord.[157]

Jaʿfar said: It was said to Moses ﷺ 'How did you know that the call was the call of the Truth?' He said: 'Because it effaced me and pervaded me; it was as though every hair of mine was addressed by a call from all directions and it was as though they, of themselves, expressed a response. Then, when the lights of awe had pervaded me and the lights of glory and omnipotence had surrounded me, I knew that I was being addressed from the precinct of the Truth. Since the beginning of the

157 *Innī Anā Rabbuka*, is often rendered with the likes of 'Verily I, I am your Lord.' Carl Ernst translates it: 'I am I, your Lord' which we feel conveys more accurately the tremendous nature of this phrase. See Ernst, *Words of Ecstasy in Sufism*, p. 10.

oration was [the phrase] *Innī; verily I*, followed immediately by [the word] *Anā; I*—I knew that no one has the right to refer to himself with these two phrases together, consecutively, except for the Truth. I marvelled; and that was the locus of effacement. I said: "You are You, who never ceased and never ceases; Moses has no standing with You nor has he the courage to speak unless You allow him to subsist through Your eternal subsistence and (unless) You qualify him with Your character so that You are wholly the orator and the one addressed." Then He said: "None bears My oration other than Me, nor answers Me except Me—I am the speaker and the one spoken to, while you are in the middle, a corporeal form[158] in whom lies the locus of the oration"."

20:12 فَٱخْلَعْ نَعْلَيْكَ

fa'khla' na'layka

so put off your two sandals.

Jaʿfar said [glossing this phrase]: So excise attachments from yourself, for you are under Our eye.[159]

158 *Shabḥun* means a bodily, corporeal form (see Lane); it also means apparition, indistinct shape, ghost, phantom, spirit, figure, person (see Wehr).

159 *Bi-aʿyuninā* (lit., 'in Our eyes'); this Qurʾānic phrase, which also occurs at 11:37, is rendered by some as 'in Our view' (see Lane under *ʿayn*). In effect, the phrase denotes being under God's gaze, but since I use this latter to render *naẓar*, I have opted to reflect the difference of Arabic terms. To engage in *taʾwīl*, the use of the word *ʿalāʾiq* (attachments) brings to mind another pertinent word from the same verbal root: *ʿulayqah*, as in the phrase *ʿulayqat Mūsā* (see Wehr at *ʿ-l-q*), a reference to the burning bush. When Moses is at the *ʿulayqah*, where he is fully cognisant of being under God's gaze, where he is fully aware of God's eternal Presence, there is no possibility of any attachment (*ʿalāʾiq*) to other than God, just as there simply cannot be any water in flaming fire.

20:18 وَلِىَ فِيهَا مَـَٔارِبُ أُخْرَىٰ ﴿١٨﴾

wa liya fīhā maʾāribu ukhrā

and I have other uses for it.

Jaʿfar said [glossing *other uses*]: Various benefits, the greatest benefit for me in it being Your addressing me with the words: *And what is that in your right hand O Moses?* (20:17).

20:27 وَٱحْلُلْ عُقْدَةً مِّن لِّسَانِى ﴿٢٧﴾

wa'ḥlul ʿuqdatan min lisānī

and undo the knot from my tongue.

Jaʿfar said: When God spoke to Moses, He tied back his tongue from talk with other than Him. Then, when He commanded him to go to Pharaoh, he whispered to Him with his inmost self and said: *And undo the knot from my tongue* that I may fulfil (Your) command in the most perfect tone.[160]

---

160 The word *maqām* is the name for musical modes and can mean, literally, 'tonality,' implying both the sound quality of the voice and the style of discourse. The spiritual significance of 'the most perfect tone' (*atamm maqām*) is that the tone is purely divine with no interference from the individual mouthpiece. In other words, when God spoke to him, the attribute of speech iṇ Moses was divine; and Moses's request was that after the loosening of the knot from his tongue, which here means after indiviudal, human speech was restored to him, the attribute of individual, human speech in Moses would not interfere in his delivery of the divine message. For more on the spiritual significance of sound see J. Godwin, *Harmonies of Heaven and Earth* (London: Thames and Hudson, 1987), and S. Pearce, *Alchemy of Voice* (London: Hodder Mobius, 2005). In addition, *maqām* means 'standing, position, rank', with the following possible rendition of the Arabic phrase *atamm maqām*: 'that I may fulfil (Your) command from the most/more perfect standing'. The same interpretation holds—for the most perfect standing is the one in which the divine qualities flow through Moses unimpeded by his individual human attributes.

20:33 كَيْ نُسَبِّحَكَ كَثِيرًا ﴿٣٣﴾

kay nusabbiḥaka kathīran

so that we praise You much.

Said Jaʿfar: It was said to Moses: 'You consider your praise of Me much and that you utter *lā ilāha illā'llāh* and *Allāhu Akbar* much and you have forgotten Our initial graces upon you in protecting you on the river and restoring you to your mother and nurturing you in the chambers of your enemy. And much more than all this, Our oration with you and Our speaking to you; and more than that, Our notification that We have made you for Us.'[161]

20:82 وَإِنِّي لَغَفَّارٌ لِّمَن تَابَ

wa innī la-ghaffārun liman tāba

and verily I am indeed forgiving to he who repents.

Jaʿfar said: *And verily I am* [*indeed*] *forgiving to he who repents*, 'to him who has recourse to Me in his affairs and does not turn to anyone other than Me'; *and believes*, 'and who witnesses Me and does not witness alongside with Me anyone other than Me'; *and who does good*, 'who dedicates his heart faithfully and sincerely to Me'; *and thereafter follows right guidance*, 'and thereafter never opposes the Sunnah of the Prophet ﷺ.'[162]

161 The comment emphasises that man's thanks and praise, even that of the prophets, can never equal God's graciousness, nor is there ever parity between the graces bestowed and the praise offered.

162 On the spiritual register, the Sunnah of the *nabī* is perfect receptivity to God (*ʿubūdīyah*) and the manifestation of the divine qualities in the cosmos. It is to be in harmony with the inner *nabī* or the 'imam of your being' (*imām wujūdika*). For the Shīʿah this harmony with the microcosmic imam coincides with being in harmony with the macrocosmic imam.

20:115 وَلَقَدْ عَهِدْنَآ إِلَىٰٓ ءَادَمَ مِن قَبْلُ فَنَسِىَ

wa la-qad ʿahidnā ilā Ādama min qablu fa-nasiya

and We had indeed entrusted a pledge to Adam before, but then he forgot.

Jaʿfar said: We entrusted a pledge to Adam that he not forget Us in (any) state, but he forgot Us and was preoccupied with the garden. Then he was tried with transgressing the prohibition. That [transgression occurred] because the bliss distracted him from the Benefactor. Thus he fell from the blessing through the trial and was expelled from the bliss and the garden so that he would know that the bliss lies in being close to the Benefactor, not in the enjoyment of eating and drinking.

20:121 وَعَصَىٰٓ ءَادَمُ رَبَّهُۥ فَغَوَىٰ

wa ʿaṣā Ādamu Rabbahu fa-ghawā

and Adam disobeyed his Lord and thus went astray.

Jaʿfar said: He viewed paradise and its bliss with his eye and so it was proclaimed against him, until the day of judgement: *and Adam disobeyed his Lord.* Had he looked at it with his heart, a complete abandonment would have been proclaimed against him for all eternity. But then God had compassion on him and was merciful to him, (as seen) in His words: *then his Lord chose him and relented towards him and guided (him)* (20:122).

20:124 وَمَنْ أَعْرَضَ عَن ذِكْرِى

wa man aʿraḍa ʿan dhikrī

but whoever turns away from My remembrance.

Concerning this verse, Jaʿfar said: If they knew Me they would not turn away from Me. Whoever turns away from Me, him I return to [a state of] preoccupation with the species and beings appropriate to him.

21

سُورَةُ الأَنبيَاءِ

al-Anbiyāʾ (The Prophets)

۞وَأَيُّوبَ إِذْ نَادَىٰ رَبَّهُۥٓ أَنِّي مَسَّنِيَ ٱلضُّرُّ وَأَنتَ أَرْحَمُ ٱلرَّٰحِمِينَ ٨٣ 21:83

wa Ayyūba idh nādā Rabbahu annī massaniya'l-ḍurru wa anta arḥamu'l-rāḥimīn

and Job, when he cried out to his Lord that 'Verily adversity has befallen me and You are the Most Merciful of the merciful'.

Jaʿfar said: These words emerged from him, not as a complaint, but as part of his secret converse [with God] seeking a response from the Truth that would reassure him.

Jaʿfar [also] said: When God subjected Job to the trial and lengthened its duration, Satan came to Job and said: 'If you wish to be free from this trial then bow down to me once.' Upon hearing this Job said: *Satan has touched me with disease* (38:41). And (he said): '*Adversity has befallen me* in that Satan hopes for me to bow down to him.'

Jaʿfar also said: When Job had attained a high degree in the trial and he found it sweet, the trial became [as it were] a home for him. Then when his soul was at ease in (the trial) and he dwelt calmly with it, people extolled him for his patience and praised him. But he said: *adversity has befallen me*, for the loss of patience.

[It is further related] from Jaʿfar concerning His words: *adversity has befallen me,* that he said: Revelation was withheld from Job for forty days, [which made him] fear being abandoned by his Lord and being cut off [from Him]; thus he said: *adversity has befallen me.*

21:89 وَزَكَرِيَّآ إِذْ نَادَىٰ رَبَّهُۥ رَبِّ لَا تَذَرْنِى فَرْدًا

wa Zakarīyā idh nādā Rabbahu, Rabbi lā tadharnī fardan

and Zakarīyā, when he called to his Lord, my Lord do not leave me alone.[163]

Jaʿfar said [in paraphrase]: Do not make me one of those who has no way to secret converse with You or to adorn [myself] with the ornaments of service to You.

He [also] said [concerning] *alone*: [That is, separated] from You, there being for me no access to You.

163 *Fardan* ('solitary, alone'). English translations of the Qurʾān often render this term as 'childless,' given the Qurʾānic context. I prefer the more general rendition, especially as the comments imply that Zakarīyā is saying, 'Do not leave me alone, separated in Being without any means of direct access to You.'

22

سُورَةُ الحَجِّ

al-Ḥajj (The Pilgrimage)

22:2 وَتَرَى ٱلنَّاسَ سُكَـٰرَىٰ

wa tarā'l-nāsa sukārā

and you see mankind [behaving] as [though they are] intoxicated.

Jaʿfar said: They are intoxicated by what they see of the unfolding of [His] glory, the sovereignty of [His] omnipotence and the pavillions of [His] grandeur; until the prophets resort to saying 'my soul, my soul!'

22:26 وَطَهِّرْ بَيْتِيَ لِلطَّآئِفِينَ وَٱلْقَآئِمِينَ وَٱلرُّكَّعِ ٱلسُّجُودِ ﴿٢٦﴾

wa ṭahhir baytiya li'l-ṭā'ifīn wa'l-qā'imīna wa'l-rukkaʿi al-sujūd

and purify My house for those who circumambulate and those who stand and those who bow and prostrate [to God]

Concerning His [above] words, [it is related] from Jaʿfar b. Muḥammad [that] he said: Purify yourself/your soul from keeping company with those who are opposed[164] [to the Truth] and from associating with other than the Truth. *And those who stand* with [a] mind [like that] of the sages standing with Him upon the carpets of intimacy and service. *and those who bow and prostrate* [*to God*], [that is,] the foremost imams, who return to the beginning from the utmost end.

---

164 *Mukhālifīn* includes the meaning of 'those who are inconsistent and/or incompatible (with the Truth)'. It is from *kh-l-f*, the same verbal root as *mukhālafah*.

22:28 لِّيَشْهَدُوا۟ مَنَـٰفِعَ لَهُمْ

li-yashhadū manāfiʿa lahum

that they may witness [things that are] of benefit to them.

Jaʿfar said: (This is a reference to) what they witness, in that place, of the beneficence of the Truth, in that He grants them the success of witnessing that tremendous assembly. Furthermore, their benefits (are) the increase, blessings, and responses (to prayers) that are promised to them for it [i.e., promised to them as their due upon their performance of the pilgrimage].[165]

22:34 وَبَشِّرِ ٱلْمُخْبِتِينَ ﴿٣٤﴾

wa bashshiri'l-mukhbitīn

and give glad tidings to the humble.

Concerning the (above) words of God, [it is related] from Jaʿfar b. Muḥammad [that] he said [defining *the humble*]: Whoever obeys Me and moreover fears Me in his obedience and is humble for My sake. *And give glad tidings* to him whose heart trembles with an ardent longing to meet Me; *and give glad tidings* to him who remembers Me when alighting in My neighbourhood;[166] *and give glad tidings* to him whose eyes shed tears in fear of being left separated from Me. Give them (all) the *glad tidings* that My mercy surpasses My anger.[167]

---

165 *Ḥajj*: the pilgrimage to the Holy Kaʿbah in Mecca, which every Muslim is required to perform at least once in his/her life, if possible. The physical pilgrimage is an ectype of the spiritual journey of the soul. However, the whole of an incarnate person's life is the ongoing manifestation on earth of that soul's journey in the spiritual realm—although the correspondences are not always easily recognised or understood correctly.

166 That is, at the holy house; but also more generally, when alighting in the vicinity or environs of God's direct Presence, for instance, at the times of the canonical rites.

167 *Sabaqat raḥmatī ghaḍabī*, a *ḥadīth qudsī* (a sacred saying). The *aḥadīth qudsīyah* are a distinct category of the traditions from the Prophet. Although uttered on the tongue of the Prophet they are of purely divine origin; God

(Jaʿfar) also said (explaining the nature of the *glad tidings*): Authority in intercession.[168]

(Jaʿfar) also said: *Give glad tidings* to those who long to gaze at My face.

(Jaʿfar) also said: The humble person, in his humility, is like the earth that bears all dirt and conceals every impurity and all dross.[169]

22:78 فَنِعْمَ ٱلْمَوْلَىٰ وَنِعْمَ ٱلنَّصِيرُ ﴿٧٨﴾

fa-niʿma'l-mawlā wa niʿma'l-naṣīr

a perfect Patron and a perfect Granter of victory.

Jaʿfar said: [God is] the perfect helper (*muʿīn*) for those who turn to Him for help; and *the perfect Granter of victory* to those who seek His assistance.

---

is the Speaker—but they are not part of the Qurʾān. Concerning *sabaqat*, rendered above as 'surpasses', the meanings of 'precedence', 'forestalling,' and 'outstripping' are essential to the verb, and are, clearly, all meant to be understood in this phrase. God's mercy comes *before* His anger as it is an essential aspect of God's nature in a way that anger is not; His mercy *forestalls* or restrains His legitimate anger; His mercy *overrides* His anger.

168 The humble are to be given glad tidings of receiving the power/ authority (*mulk*) of intercession for others.

169 This comment is susceptible of more than one interpretation. 1) That the humble do not react except peaceably when they encounter the *daran* of others' misdeeds and mistakes, and that when they witness the impurities and shortcomings of others, they do not reveal them; with regard to their own impurities and shortcomings—they do not flaunt them, correctly being ashamed of them. 2) That the humble person is the one who has been brought to the state of 'universal man' and that, as a microcosmic being, they bear the spiritual pollution of all on earth in that they seek to cleanse the whole earth, i.e., to wash away the sins of the world by offering to God their prayers and righteous acts on behalf of the whole collectivity of souls on earth. This links back to the glad tidings of the authority to intercede for others.

24

سُورَةُ النُّورِ

al-Nūr (The Light)

24:30 قُل لِّلْمُؤْمِنِينَ يَغُضُّواْ مِنْ أَبْصَٰرِهِمْ

qul li'l-mu'minīna yaghuḍḍū min abṣārihim

tell the believers that they [should] lower their gaze.

Concerning this verse, Jaʿfar al-Ṣādiq said: Lowering the gaze from that which is forbidden and from that which is not related to the Truth is an obligation upon the slaves [of God]. The injunction of the obligation is to avert one's thought(s) from all that which the slave regards as legitimate, and its meaning is the protection of the heart and its thoughts from gazing at Being, lest through that it (the heart) be banished [from God's Presence], (or be) forgetful [of God], (or) veiled [from God]—even though (such thoughts) be permissible in the manifest [realm].

24:35 ۞ٱللَّهُ نُورُ ٱلسَّمَٰوَٰتِ وَٱلْأَرْضِ

Allāhu nūru'l-samāwāti wa'l-arḍ

God is the light of the heavens and the earth.

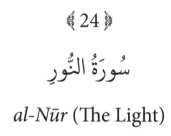

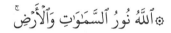

Jaʿfar b. Muḥammad said: The lights are varied: the first of them is the light of the protection of the heart; then there is the light of fear; then the light of hope; then the light of recollection; then there is perception through the light of knowledge; then the light of shame; then there is the light of the sweetness of faith; then the light of surrender; then the light of goodness; then there is the light of blessing; then the light of grace; then the light of favours; then the light of generosity; then the light of compassion; then the light of the heart; then there is the light of encompassment; then the light of awe; then the light of bewilderment; then the light of life; then the light of intimacy; then the light of integrity; then there is the light of quiescence; then there is the light of tranquillity.[170] Then there is the light of sublimity; then the light of majesty; then the light of power; then the light of strength;[171] then there is the light of Godhood; then the light of the (divine) onliness; then there is the light of the (divine) singularity; then is the light of (God's) eternal future; then the light of beginningless and endless eternity; then there is the light of permanence; then the light of (God's) eternal past; then the light of eternal subsistence; then there is the light of totality; then there is the light of the Ipseity.[172]

Each one of these lights has its people; it has its state and its locus. All (the lights) are from the lights of the Truth, which God, most high, has mentioned in His words: *God is the light of the heavens and the earth*. Each one of His slaves has a drinking place at one of these lights; and it might be that (a slave) has an apportioned lot from two lights or three. These lights are never perfected[173] except for *al-muṣṭafā*,

---

170 The lights so far pertain either to God in His relationship with the soul (protection, generosity, compassion, grace, etc.) or to states of soul that open the soul to the divine influx (fear, hope, shame, surrender). Now come the purely divine lights—the qualities pertaining to God in Himself—of which the other lights are extensions.

171 Paul Nwyia notes in his apparatus that one of the manuscripts has a variant reading of *qūwah* (strength), instead of the repetition of *jalāl*, majesty.

172 Since the full list is introduced by the phrase *awwaluhā* ('the first of which'), followed by . . . *thumma* . . . *thumma* . . . ('then . . .then . . .'), it might seem that there is a strict order of ascendence. However, the list may be taken as offering a schema of categories some of which are on the same level while others are self-evidently higher—especially if the relevant Arabic word is read as *thamma* which means 'there', and, in this context, 'there is'. In our English text, we read *thumma* as 'then', while the words 'there is' are due to the nominative case of the phrases.

173 The Arabic verb *tamma* means 'to complete, perfect, to finish, to accomplish'. Thus the phrase *lan tatimm li* could have been translated as: 'These lights are never accomplished (or attained) except by the Chosen One'. The rendition given in the body text has the benefit of conveying the receptive nature of the perfection, which the comment itself goes on to point out. Thus the lights are perfected for the perfect ʿ*abd*, the perfectly receptive one, by God the Light Himself. The Prophet here, as the perfect

the Chosen One 🌸—for he stands with God most high through the condition of having perfected slavehood and love. For He is light, and he from his Lord is in possession of light.[174]

[It is also related] from Jaʿfar b. Muḥammad al-Ṣādiq, concerning this verse, [that] he said: [God] has illumined the heavens with the light of the stars and the sun and the moon; and He has illumined the earths with the light of the plants: the red ones, the white, the yellow, and others; and He has illumined the heart of the believer with the light of faith and surrender. He has illumined the paths[175] to God with the light of Abū Bakr, ʿUmar, ʿUthmān, and ʿAlī 🌸—it is for this reason that the Prophet 🌸 said: My companions are like the stars—whomever of them you choose to follow, you shall be rightly-guided.

[Jaʿfar] also said, concerning this verse: (God) illumined the heavens through four: Jibrāʾīl (Gabriel), Mīkāʾīl (Michael), Isrāfīl (Seraphiel), and ʿIzrāʾīl (Azrael) 🌸 and He illumined the earth through Abū Bakr, ʿUmar, ʿUthmān, and ʿAlī 🌸.

24:35

لَّا شَرْقِيَّةٍ وَلَا غَرْبِيَّةٍ

lā sharqīyatin wa-lā gharbīyatin

neither eastern nor western.

Concerning this verse, Jaʿfar said: Neither fear which imposes despair, nor hope which brings about an extensive delight. Thus he stands [balanced] between fear and hope.

---

muṣṭafā, is the *insān kāmil*, the perfect/complete human.

174 The choice of words here recalls the Qurʾānic phrase: *fa-huwa ʿalā nūrin min Rabbihi; and so he is in possession of light from/through his Lord* (39:22). *ʿAlā nūrin* has been rendered here as 'in possession of light' since *ʿalā* has 'in possession of' as one of its usages. See Wehr at *ʿa-l-y*.

175 The word *ṭuruq* immediately evokes the later Sufi orders, all of which trace their lineages back to one of the aforementioned companions of the Prophet 🌸.

24:37 رِجَالٌ لَّا تُلْهِيهِمْ تِجَـٰرَةٌ وَلَا بَيْعٌ عَن ذِكْرِ ٱللَّهِ

rijālun lā tulhīhim tijāratun wa-lā bayʿun ʿan dhikri'llāh

men whom neither trade nor commerce distract from the remembrance of God.

Said Jaʿfar: In reality, these are the (true) men from among men, for God, most high, has preserved their inmost selves from returning to that which is other than Him and from noticing other than Him. Thus (neither) the trade of this lower world, its blessings and attraction, nor the hereafter and its rewards divert them from God, most high—for they are in the gardens of intimacy and the meadows of remembrance.

24:39 وَٱلَّذِينَ كَفَرُوٓاْ أَعْمَـٰلُهُمْ كَسَرَابٍۭ

wa'lladhīna kafarū aʿmāluhum ka-sarābin

as for those who disbelieve, their deeds are as a mirage.

Jaʿfar said: The tyranny of the company of other than God has overshadowed them and so there is something like a mirage over their hearts;[176] it does not benefit them and it does not lead them to the Truth. Were they to find the way to God, the secret reaches of their souls would be illumined and thus would be as God, most high, has said: *light upon light* (24:35).

176 Tyranny (*ẓulm*); overshadowed (*aẓallat*); both the Arabic terms have the attendant connotation of darkness—a wordplay that English cannot quite reproduce. *Ẓalama* in particular means both 'to sin or transgress' and 'to darken or oppress'. The deeds of those who deny God by veiling the lights of His qualities through their *kufr* cast the dark shadow of their own contradictory qualities over their hearts.

24:63 لَّا تَجْعَلُوا۟ دُعَآءَ ٱلرَّسُولِ بَيْنَكُمْ كَدُعَآءِ بَعْضِكُم بَعْضًا

lā tajʿalū duʿāʾaʾl-rasūli baynakum ka-duʿāʾi baʿḍikum baʿḍan

do not take the summons of the Messenger among you as (though it were only like) the summons of one of you to another.

Jaʿfar said: The sacred things[177] follow one upon the other. He who breaches the sanctity of creatures has breached the sanctity of the believers. He who breaches the sanctity of the believers has breached the sanctity of the saints. He who breaches the sanctity of the saints has breached the sanctity of the prophet; and he who has breached the sanctity of the prophet has breached the sanctity of God.[178] He who does not respect the sanctity of God, most high, has entered the divan of the wretched damned. The best of good morals is to safeguard respect for the sacred.[179] He from whose heart respect for the sacred has fallen, becomes careless about the religious obligations and the customs (of the prophets).[180]

---

177 *Ḥurumāt* (sing. *ḥurmah*) has been renderd as 'sacred things' and 'respect for the sacred', as the word encompasses both the meanings of sanctity, holiness, sacredness and respect, reverence, veneration. *Ḥurmah* is rendered as sanctity. See Wehr at *ḥurmah* under *ḥ-r-m*.

178 This comment demarcates graphically the ontological empathy and continuity of God with His creatures—since the sanctity of God in Himself, Beyond Being, is absolutely inviolable.

179 See Qurʾān 4:139; 10:65; 35:10, where it is stated *inna'l-ʿizzata li'llāhi jamīʿan; verily, all dignity/honour belongs to God*. For *ʿizzah* see Asad, *Message of the Qurʾān*, 4:139; 10:65 and note 86.

180 *Ḥurumāt* is also applied specifically to the divinely ordained prohibitions and the inviolable ordinances of God. In this sentence, the imam connects respect for the sacred with upholding God's ordinances. The concept of 'respect for the sacred' being the best of morals and manners is of great importance in later Sufism. *Ādāb al-sulūk*, 'Etiquette of the Spiritual Journey' is a whole discipline within Sufism. Ibn ʿArabī discusses the subject in depth in his treatment of *Adab* which has been called 'one of the foundations of his hermeneutics'. See Denis Grill, 'Adab and Revelation,' pp. 228–263 in *Muhyiddin b. ʿArabi, A Commemorative Volume*, ed. Hirtenstein & Tiernan (Rockport, MA: Element Books, 1993).

25

سُورَةُ الفُرْقَانِ

al-Furqān (The Criterion)

25:7 مَالِ هَٰذَا ٱلرَّسُولِ يَأْكُلُ ٱلطَّعَامَ وَيَمْشِي فِي ٱلْأَسْوَاقِ

mā li-hādhā'l-rasūli yaʾkulu'l-ṭaʿāma wa yamshī fī'l-aswāq

what is this Messenger that he eats food and walks in the markets.

Jaʿfar said: They blamed the messengers for (their) humility and happiness and they did not realise that (the humility and happiness) was most perfect due to their awe (of God) and (was) a most strong manifestation of the reverence due to them. That [ignorant attitude] was because (those who blamed) had witnessed in (the messengers) only the external aspect of (their) nature. Had they witnessed in them the special characteristics of their privileges, it would have kept them back from their words *what is this Messenger . . .*

25:20 وَمَآ أَرْسَلْنَا قَبْلَكَ مِنَ ٱلْمُرْسَلِينَ إِلَّآ إِنَّهُمْ لَيَأْكُلُونَ ٱلطَّعَامَ

wa mā arsalnā qablaka mina'l-mursalīna illā innahum la-yaʾkulūna'l-ṭaʿām

and We have not sent before you messengers except that they ate food.

Jaʿfar said: That is: God, most high, never sent a messenger without revealing his external aspect to mankind through the messenger's being with them in the human condition; but He kept (the messenger's) inmost self from noticing them and from being preoccupied with them—for the inmost selves of the prophets are in the (divine) grasp and do not in any state disengage from the witnessing.

25:61 تَبَارَكَ ٱلَّذِى جَعَلَ فِى ٱلسَّمَآءِ بُرُوجًا

tabāraka'lladhī ja'ala fi'l-samā'i burūjan

blessed is He who placed in the sky stellar mansions.

[It is related] from Jaʿfar b. Muḥammad, concerning [the above] words [of God] ﷻ (that) he said: The sky (*samā'*) has been so named because of its height. Now the heart is a sky because through faith and gnosis it rises[181] without limit or end. Just as the one known has no limit to Him, even so, knowledge of Him has no limit.

The mansions of the sky are the orbits of the sun and moon. They are Aries, Taurus, Gemini, Cancer, Leo, Virgo, Libra, Scorpio, Sagittarius, Capricorn, Aquarius, and Pisces. There are mansions in the heart too and they are the mansion of faith, the mansion of gnosis, the mansion of the intellect, the mansion of certainty, the mansion of submission, the mansion of goodness, the mansion of trusting reliance upon God, the mansion of fear, the mansion of hope, the mansion of love, the mansion of yearning, and the mansion of rapture. The continued well-being of the heart is through these twelve mansions just as through the twelve [zodiacal] mansions, Aries, Taurus, etc., is the well-being of the transient realm and its folk.

25:63 ٱلَّذِينَ يَمْشُونَ عَلَى ٱلْأَرْضِ هَوْنًا

alladhīna yamshūna 'alā'l-arḍī hawnan

those who walk upon the earth gently.

Jaʿfar said: [*Those who walk*] without pride or conceit, without swaggering pompously but with humility and the Peace (of the Presence of God) and dignity and serenity; of good moral character;[182] and of

181 The verbal root *s-m-w* from which the words *samā'* (sky) and *yasmū* (rises) are derived, means 'to be high'.

182 *Ḥusn al-khulq* also comprises the meanings of 'well-mannered' and 'good-natured'. Good manners are, after all, rooted in virtue.

joyful countenance—even as the Prophet ﷺ described the believers when he said: 'Gentle and mild, like a compliant camel;[183] if it is led, it goes along, and if it is made to kneel upon a rock, it kneels down.' That is due to what they have observed of the exaltedness of the Truth and His awesomeness, and what they have witnessed of His magnificence and majesty; because of this their spirits are humble and their souls have surrendered, for it imposes humility and submissiveness upon them.

25:71 يَتُوبُ إِلَى ٱللَّهِ مَتَابًا ﴿٧١﴾

yatūbu ilā'llāhi matāban

he repents to God with true repentance.

Jaʿfar said: He does not resort to the Truth who has recourse to other than Him. (Only when) he resorts to God and none other than Him, (both) externally and inwardly, only then is he repentant to Him.

25:72 وَٱلَّذِينَ لَا يَشْهَدُونَ ٱلزُّورَ

wa'lladhīna lā yashhadūna'l-zūr[184]

and those who do not testify to falsehood.

Jaʿfar said: *falsehood* is [a reference to] the desirous demands[185] of the

183 *Anf* means 'pride', but here it denotes self-respect. *Jamal anf* describes a camel that does not require being shouted at or hit to do what its master requires of it; like a camel led by the nose. (Thanks to Feras Hamza for pointing this out.)

184 The word *zūr* means 'falsehood' not only in a general sense but also in the very specific sense of something false that is taken as lord or worshipped in place of God. Thus the phrase *lā yashhadūna'l-zūr; who do not testify to falsehood* means: 'not bearing false witness', but also 'not testifying to false gods'. This sense is also evoked by the word *yashhadūna* itself, which comes from the same verbal root as the word *shahādah* (the Islamic testimonial of faith: there is no god but God). The lower soul (*nafs*), then, is a false god.

185 *Amānī* (desires, demands, claims, longings) is the plural of *umnīyah* from the root verb *manā*.

lower soul and the following of its caprices.

25:74 هَبْ لَنَا مِنْ أَزْوَٰجِنَا وَذُرِّيَّٰتِنَا قُرَّةَ أَعْيُنٍ

hab lanā min azwājinā wa dhurrīyātinā qurrata aʿyunin

grant us joy through our spouses and our offspring.

Jaʿfar said: Grant us in our spouses help in obeying You and in our children a balm that we may be delighted by them.[186]

186 A possible alternative translation, taking the *min* as redundant, and reading *barrahum* instead of *barhamun*, is as follows: 'God grant us spouses that help in obeying You and the most dutiful of children, that we may be delighted by them.'

﴾ 26 ﴿

سُورَةُ الشُّعَرَاءِ

al-Shuʿarāʾ (The Poets)

26:50 قَالُوا۟ لَا ضَيْرَ ۖ إِنَّآ إِلَىٰ رَبِّنَا مُنقَلِبُونَ ﴿٥٠﴾

qālū lā ḍayra; innā ilā Rabbinā munqalibūn

they said: No harm; verily to our Lord we return.

Jaʿfar said: Whoever feels a trial in love, is no lover; indeed, whoever observes a trial in love is no lover. Indeed, whoever does not delight in a trial in love, is no lover. Do you not see how, when the first stages of love came to the magicians, their [extrinsic] fortunes abandoned them yet it was easy for them to sacrifice their lives in the witnessing of their Beloved; and so they said: *no harm.*

26:62 قَالَ كَلَّآ ۖ إِنَّ مَعِىَ رَبِّى سَيَهْدِينِ ﴿٦٢﴾

qāla kallā; inna maʿiya Rabbī sa-yahdīni[187]

He said: Never; for verily my Lord is with me, He will guide me.

Jaʿfar said: Whoever is in the care of the Truth and under His protection is not affected by anything among [secondary] causes nor is he alarmed by the dangers of the way[188] for he is under the protecting shelter of the Truth and in His grasp. As for him who is [engaged] in witnessing (God) and is in [the divine] Presence, how should he be affected by that which proceeds from him or redounds to him? Do you not see how

187 Nwyia has *yahdīnī*, with the final long i.

188 *Mawārid* is the plural of both *mawrid* and *mawridah* (watering place; a road or way to water). See Lane under *w-r-d.*

God has related of him to whom He spoke, in His words: *for verily my Lord is with me, He will guide me.*

26:80 وَإِذَا مَرِضْتُ فَهُوَ يَشْفِينِ ﴿٨٠﴾

wa idhā mariḍtu fa-huwa yashfīni

and when I am ill He heals me.

Jaʿfar said: And when I am sickened by the sight of my deeds and my states, He heals me with the reminder of (His) grace and generosity.

26:114 وَمَآ أَنَا۠ بِطَارِدِ ٱلْمُؤْمِنِينَ ﴿١١٤﴾

wa mā anā bi-ṭāridi'l-muʾminīn

and I am not [*one*] *to reject the believers.*

Jaʿfar said: I do not give the lie to the truthful.

26:127 وَمَآ أَسْـَٔلُكُمْ عَلَيْهِ مِنْ أَجْرٍ ۖ

wa mā asʾalukum ʿalayhi min ajrin

and I do not ask of you any recompense for it.

Jaʿfar said: Ambition is removed from all the messengers, because of its baseness. Thus every messenger gives notification of himself with His words:

26:212 إِنَّهُمْ عَنِ ٱلسَّمْعِ لَمَعْزُولُونَ ﴿٢١٢﴾

innahum ʿani'l-samʿi la-maʿzūlūn

verily they are cut off from hearing.

Jaʿfar said: This is to hear spiritual counsel but pay no heed to it.

26:220 إِنَّهُۥ هُوَ ٱلسَّمِيعُ ٱلْعَلِيمُ ﴿٢٢٠﴾

innahu huwa'l-Samīʿu'l-ʿAlīm

verily He, even He is the Hearer, the Knower.

Said Jaʿfar: *The Hearer* is He who hears the secret converse of the inmost self and *the Knower* is He who knows the volitions[189] of the conscience.

189 In addition to 'volitions,' *irādāt* means 'intentions, decrees, desires, wishes'. In this comment, *al-asrār* and *al-ḍamāyir* (for *al-ḍamāʾir*) have been rendered in the singular as 'the inmost self' and 'the conscience'. Alternatively, the definite article could have been dropped: 'inmost selves' and 'consciences'.

27

سُورَةُ النَّمْلِ

al-Naml (The Ants)

27:21 لَأُعَذِّبَنَّهُۥ عَذَابًا شَدِيدًا

la-uʿadhdhibannahu ʿadhāban shadīdan

I shall indeed chastise him with a severe chastisement.

Jaʿfar said [glossing]: Indeed I shall try him with a dispersed inmost self.[190]

27:34 إِنَّ ٱلْمُلُوكَ إِذَا دَخَلُواْ قَرْيَةً أَفْسَدُوهَا

inna'l-mulūka idhā dakhalū qaryatan afsadūhā

verily, kings, when they enter a town, destroy it.

Jaʿfar said: (In this) He alluded to the hearts of the believers. For when gnosis enters hearts, it removes from them all demands and all desires—so that there is no place in the heart for anything other than God most high.

---

190 These Qurʾānic words are those spoken by Solomon, concerning the hoopoe who was not present at Solomon's great gathering. The comment treats the hoopoe as a symbol of man. On this basis, an equation is being made between a dispersed inmost self and the chastisement for not being present at the King's gathering; dispersion being the opposite of recollection. In recollection one is gathered together in the presence of the King; in dispersion one is separated from Him and scattered far and wide. There is a connection with 29:21, where the chastisement is a dispersal or division of concern, while here it is far more severe: the dispersal or division of the inmost self.

27:36 بَلۡ أَنتُم بِهَدِيَّتِكُمۡ تَفۡرَحُونَ ٣٦

bal antum bi-hadīyatikum tafraḥūn

rather it is you who exult and delight in your gift.

Jaʿfar said: In the sight of God and His prophets and His friends, the world is too small for them to delight in it or sorrow over it.[191]

27:50 وَمَكَرُواْ مَكۡرٗا وَمَكَرۡنَا مَكۡرٗا

wa makarū makran wa makarnā makran

so they plotted a plot and We plotted a plot.

Jaʿfar said: God's plot is more hidden than the crawling of an ant upon a black rock on a pitch-black night.

27:61 أَمَّن جَعَلَ ٱلۡأَرۡضَ قَرَارٗا

am-man jaʿala'l-arḍa qarāran

or He who made the earth stable

Concerning these words of His, Jaʿfar said: That is to say, He who made the hearts of His friends the dwelling place of His spiritual knowledge and placed therein rivers of increase from His beneficence in every breath, and consolidated them with the mountains of trusting reliance upon God, and beautified them with the lights of faithfulness, certainty, and love.

191 This should not be misunderstood as a lack of concern for the well-being of creation. Rather, it is a lack of worldliness; an inner detachment through transcendence.

27:61 وَجَعَلَ بَيْنَ ٱلْبَحْرَيْنِ حَاجِزًا ۗ

wa jaʿala bayna'l-baḥrayn ḥājizan

and placed between the two seas a barrier.

That is to say: between the heart and the lower soul, lest the lower soul should overwhelm the heart with its darknesses and thus oppress it. So He placed God-given success and the intellect (*ʿaql*) as the barrier between the two.

27:88 وَتَرَى ٱلْجِبَالَ تَحْسَبُهَا جَامِدَةً وَهِىَ تَمُرُّ مَرَّ ٱلسَّحَابِ ۚ

wa tarā'l-jibāla taḥsabuhā jāmidatan wa hia tammurru marra al-saḥābi

and you see the mountains which you deem rigid (and motionless) and they pass along as do the clouds.

Jaʿfar said: You see the soul *rigid (and motionless)* when the spirit goes forth;[192] while the spirit enters deep into *Firdaws*,[193] betaking itself to its place under the divine throne.

Jaʿfar [also] said: The light of the hearts of those who profess God's unity and the restlessness of the plaintive moans of those who yearn *pass along as do the clouds* until they see the Truth—then they rest at peace.

---

192 The soul is a corpse when the individuated and differentiated spirit within it sheds it; just as the body is a corpse without the soul. This comment emphasises that the enlivenment of the soul lies in the presence of the divine Spirit within it. To the extent that the divine permeates the soul, to that extent is the soul alive.

193 Speaking of a spirit that has a place under the divine throne means that *Firdaws* is the realm of the undifferentiated but individuated spirits that are the archetypes, the realities (*ḥaqāʾiq*), of all beings. See also Abū Bakr Sirāj ad-Dīn, *The Book of Certainty* (Cambridge: Islamic Texts Society, 1992), pp. 6–7.

28

سُورَةُ القَصَصِ

al-Qaṣaṣ (The Story)

وَأَصْبَحَ فُؤَادُ أُمِّ مُوسَىٰ فَـٰرِغًا إِن كَادَتْ لَتُبْدِى بِهِۦ لَوْلَآ
أَن رَّبَطْنَا عَلَىٰ قَلْبِهَا 28:10

wa aṣbaḥa fuʾādu ummi Mūsā fārighan; in kādat la-tubdī bihi lawlā an rabaṭnā ʿalā qalbihā

and the mind of Moses' mother became desolate; she almost disclosed him, had We not strengthened her heart.

Jaʿfar said: The breast is the fount of consent; the heart is the fount of certainty; the mind[194] is the fount of perception; the conscience is the fount of the inmost self and the soul is the sheltering place of every good deed and every misdeed.

وَلَمَّا تَوَجَّهَ تِلْقَآءَ مَدْيَنَ 28:22

wa lammā tawajjaha tilqāʾa Madyan

and when he turned his face towards Midian.

Jaʿfar said: He turned his face in the direction of Midian, and he turned his heart towards his Lord, seeking from Him the way of guidance.[195]

---

194 *Fuʾād*, here rendered 'mind' (as in Lane's *Lexicon* and in keeping with the context), is often translated as 'heart'. But it tends to signify only the physical heart, whereas *qalb* signifies the essential, spiritual heart. See Lane at *fuʾād* under *f-ʾ-d* and *qalb* under *q-l-b*.

195 This is a reference to the rest of this Qurʾānic verse: *he said: it might be*

So God, most high, honoured him by speaking [to him]. Whoever dedicates himself entirely to God, most high—God, most high, makes that which he hopes for reach him.

28:24 إِنِّي لِمَآ أَنزَلْتَ إِلَيَّ مِنْ خَيْرٍ فَقِيرٌ ٢٤

innī limā anzalta ilayya min khayrin faqīrun

truly I am in need of whatever good You send down upon me.

Jaʿfar said: In need of You, seeking from You an increase in neediness to You; for only You suffice me against need of You.

He also said: Needy at all times (every instant), not resorting to miracles and divine signs without neediness to You and drawing near to You.

28:29 ءَانَسَ مِن جَانِبِ ٱلطُّورِ نَارًاۖ

ānasa min jānibi'l-ṭūri nāran

he perceived, on the side of the mountain, a fire.

Jaʿfar said: [Moses] saw a fire—an indication of the [divine] lights, for he saw light in the form of the fire. When he drew near to it, the lights of holiness pervaded him and the robes of intimacy encompassed him. Then he was addressed with the subtlest oration and the most beautiful response was called for from him. Through that he became a noble angel brought close [to God]. He was given what he requested and was made safe from that which he feared. Thus His words: *he perceived, on the side of the mountain, a fire.*

---

that my Lord will [thus] guide me along the right way.

28:35 وَنَجْعَلُ لَكُمَا سُلْطَٰنًا

wa najʿalu lakumā sulṭānan

and We will grant you both authority.

Said Jaʿfar: Dread in the hearts of the enemies and love in the hearts of the friends (of God).

❁ 29 ❁

سُورَةُ العَنكَبُوتِ

al-ʿAnkabūt (The Spider)

29:21 يُعَذِّبُ مَن يَشَآءُ وَيَرْحَمُ مَن يَشَآءُ

yuʿadhdhibu man yashāʾu wa yarḥamu man yashāʾu

He chastises whom He intends (to) and He is merciful to whom He intends.

Jaʿfar said: *He chastises whom He intends* with the dispersal[196] of [their] concern; *and He is merciful to whom He intends* by bringing together [their] concern for Him [alone].

29:45 إِنَّ ٱلصَّلَوٰةَ تَنْهَىٰ عَنِ ٱلْفَحْشَآءِ وَٱلْمُنكَرِ

inna'l-ṣalāta tanhā ʿani'l-faḥshāʾi wa'l-munkar

verily prayer restrains from vile deeds and (from) that which is repugnant.

Jaʿfar said: When prayer is acceptable, it restrains one from proclaiming deeds and from seeking recompense.

196 *Shatāt*, here rendered 'dispersal,' means 'dispersed, separated, scattered, broken'. 'Bringing together their concern for Him alone' is not as limiting as it might sound, but the opposite, since He is infinite and contains everything. However, 'their concern' in all things at all levels will be God and His qualities: peace, mercy, justice, love, compassion. The extension of the divine qualities pertains to both microcosm and macrocosm.

29:69 وَٱلَّذِينَ جَٰهَدُوا۟ فِينَا

wa'lladhīna jāhadū fīnā

but those who strive for Us.

Jaʿfar said: The spiritual struggle is sincere neediness (to God) and that is the detachment of the slave from his soul, and his attachment to his Lord.[197] The spiritual struggle frees the slave from all that he is attached to. The spiritual struggle is the generous expending of one's spirit[198] for the satisfaction of (God) the Truth.

He also said: Whoever strives with his soul for his soul[199] attains the munificence of his Lord; while he who strives with his soul for his Lord attains to his Lord.

197 Detachment (*infiṣāl*) and attachment (*ittiṣāl*). Thus the *nafī* and the *ithbāt,* respectively, of the *shahādah* constitute *mujāhadah.*

198 *Badhl al-rūḥ*. Since spirit (*rūḥ*) is the divine breath of life breathed into man at his creation, *badhl al-rūḥ* means to expend the whole of life, appropriately, at all levels, in satisfying the One who breathes through and in all creatures. Ṣafā too has its service to God, its *khidmah.*

199 Fearing hell or hoping for paradise; to such a person, God's generosity shall grant avoidance of hell or entry into paradise. The striving of the soul for God is the *khidmah* or *murūwah* of Marwah.

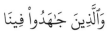

30

سُورَةُ الرُّومِ

al-Rūm (The Byzantines)

30:17 فَسُبْحَـٰنَ ٱللَّهِ حِينَ تُمْسُونَ وَحِينَ تُصْبِحُونَ ﴿١٧﴾

fa-subḥāna'llāhi ḥīna tumsūna wa ḥīna tuṣbiḥūn

then glorify God when you enter the evening and when you enter the morning.

Jaʿfar said: So begin your morning with God and with Him draw your evening to a close. For whoever has his beginning with God and his end with Him will not be troubled in what lies between the two.

30:40 ٱللَّهُ ٱلَّذِى خَلَقَكُمْ ثُمَّ رَزَقَكُمْ

Allāhu'lladhī khalaqakum thumma razaqakum

God is the one who created you, then provided for you.

Jaʿfar said: *Created you, then provided for you*—moved you to the manifestation of the effects of the Lordship in you; *then He deadens you, then He enlivens you,* through [His] Self-veiling and Self-disclosure.

30:53 وَمَآ أَنتَ بِهَـٰدِ ٱلْعُمْىِ

wa mā anta bi-hādi'l-ʿumyi

and you cannot guide the blind.

Jaʿfar said: The manifestation of the signs of your messages are for those to whom the Truth, in pre-eternity, manifested the signs of felicity and whom He adorned with the ornament of distinction—because your summons to such a one is a reminder and spiritual counsel but [it is] not an initial summons. For it is not possible for you to bring someone to the place of felicity if felicity has not already been bestowed upon them in pre-eternity. You are the summoner and the warner; God is the guide. Do you not see Him say: *And you cannot guide the blind.*

﴾ 32 ﴿

سُورَةُ السَّجْدَةِ

al-Sajdah (Prostration)

32:16 يَدْعُونَ رَبَّهُمْ خَوْفًا وَطَمَعًا

yadʿūna Rabbahum khawfan wa ṭamaʿan

who call to their Lord in fear and in hope.

Said Jaʿfar: Fearing Him and hopeful in Him.

33

سُورَةُ الأَحْزَابِ

al-Aḥzāb (The Confederates)

33:35 وَٱلصَّٰدِقِينَ وَٱلصَّٰدِقَٰتِ

wa'l-ṣādiqīna wa'l-ṣādiqāt

and the truthful men and the truthful women.

Jaʿfar said: The truthful person is one who describes for you the good of the hereafter, not the good of the world, and who shows you the best moral qualities, not the worst; and who gives you his heart, not his limbs.[200]

33:46 وَدَاعِيًا إِلَى ٱللَّهِ بِإِذْنِهِۦ وَسِرَاجًا مُّنِيرًا ﴿٤٦﴾

wa dāʿiyan ilā'llāhi bi-idhnihi wa sirājan munīran

and as a summoner to God, with His permission, and as an illuminating lamp.

Jaʿfar said: A summoner to God, not to himself, he glories in his slavehood, not in his prophethood, that thereby his call to his [Lord-] Master may be sound. Then the summons becomes, for the one who responds to it, an illuminating lamp which leads him upon the way of right guidance, and enables him to see the faults and offences of the soul.

200 A comment that is in keeping with the text's emphasis on qualities—for good manners are rooted in virtue and virtue is the presence of the divine qualities. 'Who gives you his heart . . .' i.e., who is sincerely with you, and not just in outward appearance.

34

سُورَةُ سَبَإٍ

Sabāʾ (Sheba)

34:10 ۞ وَلَقَدْ ءَاتَيْنَا دَاوُۥدَ مِنَّا فَضْلًا ۖ

wa la-qad ātaynā Dāwūda minnā faḍlan

and indeed We gave David grace from Us.

Jaʿfar said: *Grace*—confidence in God and trusting reliance upon Him.

❁ 35 ❁

سُورَةُ فَاطِرٍ

al-Fāṭir (The Originator)

al-Malāʾikah (The Angels)

35:1 يَزِيدُ فِي ٱلْخَلْقِ مَا يَشَآءُ ۚ

yazīdu fi'l-khalqi mā yashāʾu

He augments in creation what He wills.

Jaʿfar said: [Augments with] soundness of natural disposition and the power of spiritual sight.

35:28 إِنَّمَا يَخْشَى ٱللَّهَ مِنْ عِبَادِهِ ٱلْعُلَمَـٰٓؤُا۟ ۗ

innamā[201] yakhshā'llāha min ʿibādihi'l-ʿulamāʾu

only the knowledgeable among His slaves [*truly*] *fear God.*

Jaʿfar said: The knowledgeable fear the abandonment of reverence[202] in (the rites of) worship; and the abandonment of reverence when informing about the Truth; and the abandonment of reverence when following the Messenger ﷺ; and the abandonment of reverence when serving the friends (of God) and the sincere, truthful ones.

---

201 The particle *innamā* could be taken as governing the phrase *yakhshā'llāha* (as Pickthall has done), in which case the rendition would be: 'the knowledgeable among His slaves fear God alone'.

202 *Ḥurmah* also means holiness, sacredness, sanctity, respect, veneration, inviolability, and hence dignity.

ثُمَّ أَوۡرَثۡنَا ٱلۡكِتَٰبَ ٱلَّذِينَ ٱصۡطَفَيۡنَا مِنۡ عِبَادِنَاۖ

35:32 فَمِنۡهُمۡ ظَالِمٞ لِّنَفۡسِهِۦ وَمِنۡهُم مُّقۡتَصِدٞ وَمِنۡهُمۡ سَابِقُۢ بِٱلۡخَيۡرَٰتِ

(thumma awrathnā'l-kitāba'lladhīna'ṣṭafaynā min 'ibādinā) fa-minhum ẓālimun li-nafsihi wa minhum muqtaṣidun wa minhum sābiqun bi'l-khayrāt

(then We made those of Our slaves whom We chose to inherit the Book;) among them is he who wrongs his own soul; and among them is he who is moderate; and among them is he who is foremost through good deeds.[203]

Concerning these words of God, most high, Jaʿfar said: God, most high, distinguished [in the Book] three categories of believers. First of all He called them *muʾminīn; believers*; then He called them *ʿibādinā; Our slaves*, thus attaching them to Himself as a grace and generosity from Himself; then He said *(alladhīna) iṣṭafaynā; (whom) We chose*—He made them all [specially chosen] bosom friends knowing their different stations. Then, at the end of the verse, He put them all together, at the entry into paradise, for He said: *gardens of Eden which they enter* (35:33). Moreover, He commenced with those who wrong their souls, by way of informing [us] that He shall not be drawn close to except purely by His generosity. For wrongfulness has no effect on [divine] pre-election. Then He (mentions) next the moderate, for they are between fear and hope. Then He sets the seal with the foremost lest anyone feel safe from His plot. All of them are in paradise because of the sanctity of one word, that is, the word 'faithfulness'.

Jaʿfar [also] said: The lower soul is wrongful; the heart is moderate; and the spirit is foremost.

He also said: Who looks with his soul to the world is wrongful; who looks with his heart to the hereafter is moderate; who looks with his spirit to the Truth is foremost.

---

203 *Khayrāt* rendered as 'good deeds' also means 'blessings'. The full Qurʾānic verse has been given because the commentary refers to it, even though part of the verse is not explicitly cited in the Arabic edition.

36

سُورَةُ يسٓ

Yā Sīn

36:1 يسٓ ①

Yā Sīn.

Jaʿfar al-Ṣādiq said about His words *Yā Sīn*: They mean, *Yā Sayyid*; O lord (and are) addressed to His Prophet. That is why the Prophet said: '*Anā sayyidukum*; I am your lord'. In that he was not praising himself, rather he was relating the meaning of the Truth's addressing him with His words *Yā Sīn*.

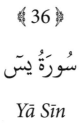

﴾ 37 ﴿

سُورَةُ الصَّافَّاتِ

al-Ṣāffāt (Those Ranged in Ranks)

37:103 فَلَمَّآ أَسۡلَمَا

fa-lammā aslamā

then, when the two of them had surrendered.

Said Jaʿfar: Abraham expelled from his heart the love of his son; and Ishmael expelled from his heart the love of life.[204]

37:164 وَمَا مِنَّآ إِلَّا لَهُۥ مَقَامٞ مَّعۡلُومٞ ١٦٤

wa mā minnā illā lahu maqāmun maʿlūmun;

there is none of us but has his known station.

Jaʿfar said: Creatures have different stations with God. Whoever oversteps his bounds perishes.[205] The prophets have the station of witnessing; the messenger(s) have the station of eye witnessing; the angels have the station of awe; the believers have the station of proximity and service; the disobedient have the station of repentance; and the unbelievers have the station of banishment and the lack of God-awareness. This is the meaning of the words of (God) most high: *There is none of us but has his known station.*

---

204 The context is the trial of Abraham and Ishmael, when Abraham saw in a dream vision that he was to sacrifice his son. See the verses that immediately precede this one in the Qurʾān for their story.

205 This hierarchy is to be applied on both the microcosmic and macrocosmic levels.

38

سُورَةُ صٓ

Ṣād

38:20 وَءَاتَيْنَٰهُ ٱلْحِكْمَةَ وَفَصْلَ ٱلْخِطَابِ ۝٢٠

wa ātaynāhu'l-ḥikmatah wa faṣla'l-khiṭāb

and We gave him wisdom and decisive oration.

Jaʿfar said: Sincerity of word, integrity in vows, and constancy in matters.

38:24[206] وَظَنَّ دَاوُۥدُ أَنَّمَا فَتَنَّٰهُ فَٱسْتَغْفَرَ رَبَّهُۥ

wa ẓanna Dāwūda annamā fatannāhu fa'staghfara Rabbahu;

and David guessed that We had tried him; so he begged forgiveness of his Lord.

Jaʿfar said: Part of that is what God, most high, mentions about His trying David and his trial and test, and what was brought forth for him in the way of immense renunciation, remorse, continual weeping, sorrow, and immense fear, such that he clung close to his Lord.[207] Thus although the occasioning sin therein was extensive, its final outcome

206 Nwyia has this as 38:25.

207 Given that *laḥiqa bi* ('to cling close to'), also means 'to reach, join, catch up with', another equally possible rendition of the last phrase would be: 'until he reached his Lord'. Indeed, in clinging close to his Lord, he reaches his Lord. Although *laḥiqa bi-Rabbihi* is commonly used to mean simply 'he died', this does not fit in with the implication of the comment, nor with the tenor of the commentary.

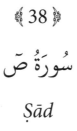

was immense, glorious and exalted—because through it, God gave (David) intimate closeness and the favoured state of being beloved.[208]

38:35 وَهَبْ لِي مُلْكًا

wa-hab lī mulkan

bestow upon me a kingdom.

Jaʿfar said: *Bestow upon me a kingdom*, that is, contentment with Your apportionment such that I have no choice alongside Your choice.

38:78 وَإِنَّ عَلَيْكَ لَعْنَتِيٓ إِلَىٰ يَوْمِ ٱلدِّينِ ﴿٧٨﴾

wa inna ʿalayka laʿnatī ilā yawmiʾl-dīni

and verily, My curse is upon you until the day of judgement.[209]

Jaʿfar said: My displeasure, which ceases not flowing from Me upon you, reaching you at your ordained times, in your bygone days.[210]

---

208 *Ḥuẓwah*: 'a state of fortunateness or happiness; nearness to the heart; a state of favour, of being beloved, of being in high estimation; high rank or standing'.

209 God's words addressed to Satan.

210 At first glance this is an unusual instance of severity in the commentary. The 'unceasing' nature of the divine displeasure is to be understood in terms of the Qurʾānic context, where it is Satan's pride and disobedience to God that evokes it. However, the comment explains that effects of this divine displeasure touch the recipients only at specific, ordained moments in 'bygone days' i.e., in time before the Day of Judgment, which was the Qurʾānic cut off point—thereby emphasising that God's displeasure is not unceasing or eternal.

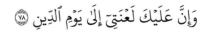

39

سُورَةُ الزُّمَرِ

al-Zumar (The Groups)

39:29 ٱلْحَمْدُ لِلَّهِ ۚ بَلْ أَكْثَرُهُمْ لَا يَعْلَمُونَ ﴿٢٩﴾

al-ḥamdu li'llāhi, bal aktharuhum lā yaʿlamūn

praise belongs to God, but most of them do not know.

Jaʿfar said: They do not know that no one among the slaves of God attains the requisite in His praise, nor [do they attain to] that praise which is rightfully due from the slaves of God, for His blessings; [nor do they know] that no one praises Him as is His due—save [He in] His praise of Himself.

39:30 إِنَّكَ مَيِّتٌ وَإِنَّهُم مَّيِّتُونَ ﴿٣٠﴾

innaka mayyitun wa innahum mayyitūn

verily you are dead and verily they are dead.[211]

Jaʿfar said: *Verily you are dead* to the preoccupation they are in—with themselves, their children and their world; *and verily they are dead*, that is, far-removed from the different kinds of miracles by which you

211 Concerning the words *mayyit* and *mayyitūn*, some scholars assert that these words pertain to that which is dying but as yet has life in it; other scholars hold that they pertain to what is already dead. See Lane at *mayyit* under *m-y-t*. Translators of the Qurʾān usually take these words in this phrase in the sense of 'are bound to die', 'will one day die'. See Asad, *Message of the Qurʾān* and ʿAli, *Meaning of the Glorious Qur'an*. We have translated the words as 'dead' since this is how they seem to be taken in the comment.

are distinguished.

39:65 لَئِنْ أَشْرَكْتَ لَيَحْبَطَنَّ عَمَلُكَ

la-in ashrakta la-yaḥbaṭanna ʿamaluka

if you associate aught with God (as His equal or partner), your works shall be to no avail.

Jaʿfar said: If you look at[212] other than Him, you will, in the hereafter, be debarred from meeting Him.

212 The verb used is *naẓara ilā*, which means 'to look at with the eyes, to pay attention to, to contemplate or consider'. *Naẓar* is the word used for God's gaze which is received by the subtle heart. In the light of the earlier interpretation of God's gaze—as that which transmits His qualities—the comment here implies that if you look at other than Him, with the gaze of your inner being, you will close your subtle receptivity towards Him, you will obscure your *ḥaqīqah*; and if you do that, you will remain with your own wretched qualities, which will be a barrier between you and God, for you will not be *qualified* to meet God. To 'meet' God in the profoundest sense, you have to be godly. Looking at God means being effaced in Him as expounded at 7:143, 83:24. The effacement in God is the ultimately beatific meeting with God, a matter of the very dearest importance. The principle enunciated in the comment stands—it is part of the spiritual economy. However, mercy has the last word: if, despite all your failings and shortcomings, you actually love what God is (which is to say that you love God) and you *want* to meet God, then from His tremendous grace and infinite mercy, He will accept the very minimum effort from you towards that, and render it victorious, by Himself picking you up and carrying you to Him. He will ensure that you look at Him properly. God's grace and mercy are potent—the creature has but to receive them. The Qurʾānic phrase itself implies that if you attribute any of God's qualities to other than God, then you commit *shirk*. Goodness, beauty, mercy, and so forth all belong to God no matter where they manifest. So while it can be said 'so and so is wise or beautiful', it should be known in the heart whose wisdom and beauty is manifest in the locus of that creature.

39:74 ٱلْحَمْدُ لِلَّهِ ٱلَّذِى صَدَقَنَا وَعْدَهُۥ

al-ḥamdu li'llāhi'lladhī ṣadaqanā waʿdahu

praise belongs to God who has fulfilled for us His promise.

Jaʿfar said: *Praise belongs to God who has fulfilled for us His promise,* is the praise of the sages who dwell in the abode of stability with God most high. While His words: *praise belongs to God who has put sorrow away from us* (35:34), is the praise of those who have attained [to God].

40

سُورَةُ غَافِرٍ

Ghāfir (Forgiving)

al-Muʾmin (The Believer)

40:16 لِّمَنِ ٱلْمُلْكُ ٱلْيَوْمَ لِلَّهِ ٱلْوَٰحِدِ ٱلْقَهَّارِ ﴿١٦﴾

limani'l-mulku'l-yawm lillāh al-Waḥid al-Qahār

to whom belongs sovereignty this day to God, the Only, the Irresistible.

Jaʿfar said: He reduced the beings endowed with spirits to silence, (and kept them) from answering His question in His words: *to whom belongs sovereignty*. No one at all could dare to answer, nor was anyone other than Him qualified to answer His question. Then when mankind was silenced from answering, He answered Himself with the requisite response; thus He said: *to God, the Only, the Irresistible.*

40:51 إِنَّا لَنَنصُرُ رُسُلَنَا وَٱلَّذِينَ ءَامَنُوا۟

innā[213] la-nanṣuru rusulanā wa'lladhīna āmanū

truly We do indeed help Our messengers and those who believe.

Jaʿfar said [in interpretive paraphrase]: Through the believers We help Our messengers in outward (matters); and through the messengers We help the believers in inner (matters).[214]

---

213 In Nwyia's edition, this is written as *innanā*. The meaning is exactly the same in both cases; it is simply a difference of orthography.

214 In outward (matters) this is *ẓāhiran*; in inner (matters), it is *bāṭinan*; i.e., in external, worldly matters and inner, spiritual matters respectively.

40:66 وَأُمِرْتُ أَنْ أُسْلِمَ لِرَبِّ ٱلْعَٰلَمِينَ ﴿٦٦﴾

wa umirtu an uslima li-Rabbi'l-ʿālamīn

and I am commanded to submit to the Lord of the worlds.

Jaʿfar said: I [take refuge in and] resort to none but Him; nor do I humble myself save before Him—for resorting to Him is the locus of joy; and humility before Him is the fount of honour.

41

سُورَةُ فُصِّلَتْ

Fuṣṣilat (Detailed Signs)

41:12 وَزَيَّنَّا ٱلسَّمَآءَ ٱلدُّنْيَا بِمَصَٰبِيحَ

wa zayyannā'l-samā'a'l-dunyā bi-maṣābīḥ

and We adorned the lower heaven with lights.

Jaʿfar said: We have adorned the limbs of the believers through service.

41:31 نَحْنُ أَوْلِيَآؤُكُمْ فِى ٱلْحَيَوٰةِ ٱلدُّنْيَا

Naḥnu awliyā'ukum fi'l-ḥayāti'l-dunyā

We are your friends in the lower life.

Jaʿfar said: The angels are the protecting friends[215] of the person who perceives merit and recompense in his works. And God is the protecting friend of the person who is proved true[216] in his deeds and performs them witnessing the [divine] command (in them)—for God, most high, says: *God is the protecting friend of those who believe* (2:257).

215 *Awliyā'*, singular *walī* (friend, close helper, supporter, patron, protector). See also the comment and relevant note on 4:59.

216 *Tuḥuqqiqa*, he whose deeds affirm and extend his *ḥaqīqah*, and who perceives the divine activity in them.

41:44 قُلْ هُوَ لِلَّذِينَ ءَامَنُوا۟ هُدًى وَشِفَآءٌ ۖ

qul huwa li-lladhīna āmanū hudan wa shifāʾun

say: It is guidance and healing for those who believe.

Jaʿfar said: The Qurʾān is a healing for him who is in the shade of impeccability,[217] while it is inscrutable[218] for him who is in the darkness of being abandoned.

217 In Shīʿism, the term ʿ*iṣmah* (impeccability, infallibility, innocence, purity) is applied to the prophets and the imams—hence the title 'the infallible imam'. The implication in this comment, therefore, could be that the Qurʾān is a healing for those who follow the infallible imam. This is underlined by the Shīʿī doctrine that the imam is the '*Qurʾān nāṭiq*, the speaking Qurʾān', and so the one who knows the true meaning of the Book.

218 For a full discussion of the term ʿ*aman* see Lane at ʿ*amāʾun* under ʿ*-m-y*, where it is stated that ʿ*aman* refers to 'anything that the intellectual faculties cannot perceive, and to the definition of which the describer cannot attain'.

﴿ 42 ﴾

سُورَةُ الشُّورَىٰ

al-Shūrā (Counsel)

42:9 وَهُوَ يُحْيِ ٱلْمَوْتَىٰ

wa huwa yuḥyi'l-mawtā

and He enlivens the dead.

Jaʿfar said: He enlivens the souls of the believers through service to Him; and He deadens the souls of the hypocrites through opposition to Him.[219]

42:23 قُل لَّآ أَسْـَٔلُكُمْ عَلَيْهِ أَجْرًا إِلَّا ٱلْمَوَدَّةَ

qul lā asʾalukum ʿalayhi ajran illā'l-mawaddah

say: I do not seek of you recompense for it, only devoted love.

Jaʿfar said: Only that you show devoted love towards me by means of deeds that draw you closer to your Lord.

219 We have here again the concepts of enlivenment and deadening, where enlivenment is equated with *muwāfaqah* (harmony with God) and the deadening of souls is equated with opposition to God (*mukhālafah*). In the comment here, we are told that the enlivenment of the soul consists in its service (*khidmah*) to God. So we have an equation between *muwāfaqah* and *khidmah*. The matter of service to God is related directly to the heroic soul in the commentary on Marwah. Thus the service of the soul lies in its efforts to harmonise itself with God; in other words, in its efforts to be godly. And we are back to the equation: The soul's service of the Lord (*khidmat al-Rabb*), consists in harmony with God (*muwāfaqah bi'llāh*).

43

سُورَةُ الزُّخْرُفِ

al-Zukhruf (Ornaments of Gold)

43:68 لَا خَوْفٌ عَلَيْكُمُ ٱلْيَوْمَ وَلَآ أَنتُمْ تَحْزَنُونَ ﴿٦٨﴾

lā khawfun ʿalaykumu'l-yawma wa-lā antum taḥzanūn

no fear is on you this day nor do you grieve.

Said Jaʿfar ﷺ [in paraphrase]: No fear is upon those who obeyed Me in (My) commands and religious obligations and who followed the customs established by the Messenger.[220]

He also said: In the hereafter, no fear is upon the one who feared Me in the world. No fear is upon the one who loved Me and eliminated the love of others from his heart. No fear is upon the one who safeguarded what I placed with him, namely faith and spiritual knowledge. No fear is upon the one who thought good of Me—I shall give him that which he hoped for.

Fear (befalls) the limbs while grief (befalls) the heart for fear of being cut off (from God).

43:71 وَفِيهَا مَا تَشْتَهِيهِ ٱلْأَنفُسُ وَتَلَذُّ ٱلْأَعْيُنُ

wa fīhā mā tashtahī'l-anfusu wa taladhdhu'l-aʿyun[221]

and therein is that which the souls desire and enraptures the eye.

Jaʿfar said: What a difference between what the souls desire and that

220 The *sunnat al-nabī* is important to both Sunnīs and Shīʿīs. For the latter, of course, it is conveyed foremost by the imams.

221 The text of the *tafsīr* has *tashtahī* without the final pronominal suffix *hi*—which may simply be a scribal error. The meaning is not altered. *Aʿyun* is

which enraptures the eye. For all the blessings, desirable things and delights of paradise are, in comparison with the rapture of the eye, as a finger dipped in the ocean—because the desirable things of paradise have a limit and an end, for they are created. But in the ever-abiding abode the eye is enraptured only in gazing upon the Ever-abiding [Himself] ﷻ! And that has no limit, nor description, nor end.

the plural of ʿ*ayn*, which means not only 'eye' but also 'essence or source' and 'spring or fountain'.

46

سُورَةُ الأَحْقَافِ

al-Aḥqāf (The Winding Sand-Tracts)

46:9 مَا كُنتُ بِدْعًا مِّنَ ٱلرُّسُلِ

mā kuntu bidʿan[222] mina'l-rusul

I am not a new thing among the messengers.

Concerning this verse, Jaʿfar said [in explanatory paraphrase]: There is nothing to do with me in my prophethood. It is purely something which I was given, not because of me but rather by grace from God when He made me suitable for His message and described me in the earlier books of the prophets ﷺ.

46:13 إِنَّ ٱلَّذِينَ قَالُواْ رَبُّنَا ٱللَّهُ ثُمَّ ٱسْتَقَـٰمُواْ

inna'lladhīna qālū Rabbuna'llāhu thumma'staqāmū

verily, those who say our Lord is God and then stand soundly.

Said Jaʿfar: They stand soundly with God, most high, in the movements

---

222 *Bidʿan* may be understood in either of two ways: 1) Something that is a novelty or new thing or a 'first', in which case the meaning of the Qurʾānic verse is 'I am not the first of the messengers'; 2) Someone that is an innovator, with the meaning 'I am not an innovator among the messengers,' i.e., my message is not an innovation. See Lane at *bidʿun* under *b-d-ʿ*. In its Qurʾānic context, this verse and the ones immediately before and after it, contain a protestation for the authenticity of the revelation given to the Prophet. There is also a reference (46:10) to what is interpreted as a Biblical anticipation of the Arab Prophet, which the *tafsīr* picks up on: '. . . and described me in the earlier Books of the prophets . . .' See Asad, *Message of the Qurʾān*, 46:10, note 12, p. 771.

of the heart with the witnessings of the oneness of God.[223]

46:30 يَهْدِىٓ إِلَى ٱلْحَقِّ وَإِلَىٰ طَرِيقٍ مُّسْتَقِيمٍ ٣٠

yahdī ilā'l-Ḥaqqi wa ilā ṭarīqin mustaqīmin

guiding to the Truth and to a harmonious path.

Jaʿfar said: He/it leads to the way of the Truth, by bringing (people) forth from known things and rituals,[224] and (to) the realisation of the Truth[225]—that is the harmonious way.

223 *Tawḥīd* (monotheism) denotes both the *belief* in the oneness of God, and also, by extension, the oneness of God itself, as rendered in the text.

224 'Rituals' translates *marsūmāt* which, in the singular, refers to that which is recorded in writing and sealed, hence prescripts, edicts, regulations, ceremonies, etiquette, and rituals. This comment might easily be taken as antinomian, however, his point may be that the purpose of all rites and rituals is the realisation of the Truth. So the bringing forth from 'known things and rituals' is the attainment of this realisation. It does not necessarily mean the abandonment of rites and rituals, but rather following them through to their profoundest end—this seems to be confirmed by the following comment. Nevertheless, it presents the following perspective: religion and knowledge are for the purpose of God-realisation; they, in themselves, are not the goal but only a means to the end.

225 *Al-taḥqīq bi'l-Ḥaqq* is to be read in apposition to *ṭarīqi'l-Ḥaqq*, both phrases being governed by the *ʿalā* that immediately precedes *ṭarīq*. The comment reflects the dual guidance of the Qurʾānic phrase.

﴾ 47 ﴿

سُورَةُ مُحَمَّدٍ

Muḥammad

47:3 ٱلَّذِينَ كَفَرُوا۟ ٱتَّبَعُوا۟ ٱلْبَٰطِلَ

(a)lladhīna kafarū'ttaba'ū'l-bāṭila

those who disbelieve follow falsehood.

Jaʿfar said: He who does not order the foundational principles of his states in accordance with the Truth is not successful in following the path of the Truth. He who neglects the foundational principles of his states—what hope is there of him reaching the end of (the path)?

47:19 أَنَّهُۥ لَآ إِلَٰهَ إِلَّا ٱللَّهُ

annahu lā ilāha illā'llāh

that there is no god except God.

Concerning (these) words of His, Jaʿfar said: He eliminates causes[226] from the Lordship and declares the Truth to be beyond perception.

226 In other words, He eliminates the possibility of there being a cause beyond God; God being the Uncaused Cause. *ʿIlal,* as the plural of *ʿillah*, also means 'weaknesses, deficiencies'.

﴾ 48 ﴿

سُورَةُ الفَتْحِ

al-Fatḥ (Victory)

48:2 وَيُتِمَّ نِعْمَتَهُۥ عَلَيْكَ

wa yutimma niʿmatahu ʿalayka

and to complete His blessing upon you.

Jaʿfar said: Part of the perfection of the blessing upon His Prophet ﷺ is that He made him His beloved; and [that] He swore by his life;[227] and that through him, He superseded all the revealed laws of the [earlier] messengers; and [that] He made him ascend to the place of closest proximity and protected him in the ascent, such that *(his gaze) did not waver; nor did it/he overstep the bounds* (53:17); and [that] He sent him to black people and white; and that He made spoils of war lawful for him and his community; and [that] He made him an intercessor [with God] whose intercession is accepted; and He made him the lord of the progeny of Adam; and [that] He has joined his remembrance with His remembrance, and his satisfaction with His satisfaction;[228] and [that] He has made him one of the two pillars of monotheism.[229] This and the like thereof are among the perfection of the blessing upon (the Prophet) and, through him and his rank, upon his community.

227 For instance, *La-ʿamruka; By your life* (15:72).

228 As exemplified in numerous Qurʾānic verses such as: *Obey God and obey His Messenger* (64:12); *Whoever obeys the Messenger, verily he has obeyed God.* (4:80); see also Qurʾān 48:17, 33:71, 4:13, 3:32, etc.

229 This is a reference to the two testimonials of the Islamic faith: that there is no god except God and that Muḥammad is His Messenger.

48:26 حَمِيَّةَ ٱلْجَٰهِلِيَّةِ

ḥamīyata'l-jāhilīyah

the raging fury[230] *of the state of ignorance.*

Jaʿfar said: Reprehensible raging fury which oversteps the limits into vengefulness.

230 *Ḥāmīyah* also means fanaticism, zeal, violence. *Jāhilīyah* is often used for the pre-Islamic period in Arabia. Given the spiritual register of this *tafsīr*, I have rendered it more generally.

﴾ 49 ﴿

سُورَةُ الحُجُرَاتِ

al-Ḥujurāt (The Private Rooms)

49:13 إِنَّ أَكْرَمَكُمْ عِندَ ٱللَّهِ أَتْقَىٰكُمْ ۚ

inna akramakum ʿinda'llāhi atqākum

verily, the noblest of you in the sight of God is the one who is most God-aware.

Jaʿfar said: The noble one is the God-aware one in reality; and the God-aware one is cut off from beings, (attached only) to God.[231]

231 The noble person, imbued with good qualities and characteristics, is God-aware existentially as well as with the mind.

50

سُورَةُ قٓ

Qāf

50:37 لِمَن كَانَ لَهُۥ قَلْبٌ

liman kāna lahu qalbun

for whoever has a heart.

Concerning His [above] words, Jaʿfar said: That means, a hearing, understanding, seeing heart. Thus whenever it hears the oration[232] of God, most high, without any intermediary in that which is between it and the Truth, it understands what He bestowed upon it through [granting it] faith and surrender—without any request [being made by it], or (any) intercessor or means that it might have had with God, in pre-eternity.[233] And he sees the power of the All-Powerful, the Creator, in himself, His kingdom, His earth, and His heaven. Through this he is guided to God's onliness, His power, and His will.

232 *Khiṭāb,* rather than *kalām* which is the term usually used to refer to God's revealed Word, the Qurʾān. This brings to mind Muḥammad b. ʿAbd al-Jabbār al-Niffarī (d. 354 AH) and his use of the word *mukhaṭabāt* to describe God's direct speech addressed to his heart. See Arberry, (ed. and trans.), *Mawāqif and Mukhātabāt.*

233 That is to say, the heart is addressed directly and privately by God. And when it hears such an address the heart understands God's gratuitous gift of faith and surrender which He bestowed upon it in pre-eternity, before the heart had made any request for these things, without the heart having any intercessor to intercede for it or means by which to approach God. Pre-eternity pertains to beyond being.

﴾ 51 ﴿

سُورَةُ الذَّارِيَاتِ

al-Dhāriyāt (The Scattering Winds)

51:24 ضَيْفِ إِبْرَٰهِيمَ ٱلْمُكْرَمِينَ ﴿٢٤﴾

ḍayfi Ibrāhīma'l-mukramīn

the honoured guests of Abraham.

Concerning these words of (God) most high, Jaʿfar said: *honoured*, inasmuch as they were given hospitality by the noblest of creatures, the most manifest of them in chivalry,[234] the most distinguished of them in soul, the most exalted of them in fervour, [namely] the Friend, God's blessings and peace upon him.[235]

---

234 *Futūwah*, in addition to chivalry, means honourableness, bountifulness, generosity, liberality, nobility, the sum of the noble qualities of manliness. Later, it became famously connected with the chivalric Sufi orders of Islam. The *Tāj al-ʿArūs* of Murtaḍā al-Zabīdī notes that the first one who mentioned this term is Jaʿfar al-Ṣādiq (see Lane at *futūwah* under *f-t-w*). Here then may be another aspect of the imam's legacy to Sufism and to Islam in general.

235 Clearly the implication is that the angelic visitors of Abraham were 'his honoured guests' not only because they are most honourable in themselves or because he showed them much respect and honour, but also because *he* was the one receiving them. The application of such honorifics to a prophet other than the Prophet Muḥammad is an example of the universalism of Islam in keeping with Q. 2:285: *we make no difference between any of His messengers.*

51:49 وَمِن كُلِّ شَىْءٍ خَلَقْنَا زَوْجَيْنِ لَعَلَّكُمْ تَذَكَّرُونَ ﴿٤٩﴾

wa min kulli shayʾin khalaqnā zawjayni laʿallakum tadhakkarūn

and of everything We created pairs that you might reflect.

Jaʿfar said: In order that the one who professes God's unity might look at (those) other [than God] and see them as pairs, doubles and fours, and [seeing this] flee from them, and return to the Only, the One so that thereby the profession of God's unity is a verified fact for him.

51:55 وَذَكِّرْ فَإِنَّ ٱلذِّكْرَىٰ تَنفَعُ ٱلْمُؤْمِنِينَ ﴿٥٥﴾

wa dhakkir fa-innaʾl-dhikrā tanfaʿuʾl-muʾminīn

and remind; for verily, remembrance benefits the believers.

Jaʿfar al-Ṣādiq said: This means: O Muḥammad, remind My slaves of My open-handed bestowing and generosity, My favours and blessings and My prevenient mercy to your community specifically. The remembrance,[236] which benefits the believers is the slave's remembrance[237] of God, most high, and (of) the pre-existent (divine)

236 *Dhikrā* denotes remembering after being reminded. See Lane at *dhikrā* under *dh-k-r*. In the course of the discussion of this comment in the next few notes, the reader should keep in mind the ontological nature of *dhikr* that this commentary highlights.

237 The translation in the body text takes the particle *li* as indicating possession (*kitābun li* is 'a book by' or 'a book belonging to'), thereby taking the slave as the grammatical subject and God as the object. This rendition implies that the beneficial reminder to the believers is a person's own remembrance of God and of His graces; a de facto reminder by example: be as you would have others be. However, if God is taken as the subject and the slave as the object, then the phrase would mean: 'The remembrance . . . believers, is God most high's remembrance of the slave and [the expression of this remembrance in] the ancient, prevenient divine care . . .' Alternatively, since *dhakara li* means 'to tell', 'to relate to', this phrase could be understood to mean 'the remembrance due to being reminded, *al-dhikrā*, which benefits the believers is [that when] God most high reminds the slave and [in the recollection of] the ancient . . .' In this rendition, God's reminder is through His gaze in the heart, which the

care [manifest] in faith, gnosis, the God-given success to obey (God) and the preservation from sins.

Jaʿfar said: Whoever remembers God, most high, but then forgets His remembrance, was untouched[238] by His remembrance. The remembrance of God, most high, is His oneness, His prior eternity, His will, His power, and His knowledge—never does any forgetfulness or unawareness befall Him for they are among human qualities. Whoever, then, remembers God, most high, remembers Him through His remembrance of him.[239]

---

soul extends through harmonising with the gaze.

238 *Majhūlan*, literally means 'unknown'. It is tempting to read it simply as a synonym of *jāhil* (ignorant): 'was ignorant/unaware of His remembrance'. However, the implicit connotation of *majhūl* in the phrase *nāqatun majhūlatun* provides a key to the literal text. *Nāqatun majhūlatun* refers to a she-camel that has never been milked, nor yet conceived, or that *has no brand* upon her (see Lane at *majhūl* under *j-h-l*). Thus, rather than rendering the phrase *kānā majhūlan* as 'was unknown', we have preferred 'was untouched', especially since that seems to be the implication of the comment: that those who engage in a transient *dhikr* are untouched by the divine *dhikr* which is the act of God Himself. True *dhikr* is only through absorption into the divine *dhikr*. The theme of how that which is human falls woefully short of the mark is to be found in other comments of the *tafsīr*.

239 An alternative interpretation of the last sentence of the comment could well be: 'Whoever (would) remember God, let him remember Him through His remembrance of Him.' The distinction being drawn here is between a remembrance of God which is transient and lapses into forgetfulness, and which pertains to the human, and the true remembrance of God which is His own eternal, unceasing remembrance and awareness of Himself. Thus, as is explained in the comment, whoever truly remembers God does so through this divine 'Self-remembrance' and never lapses into forgetfulness. The true remembrance of God then, is His own eternal, uninterrupted Self-awareness, and from the human point of view it is an uninterrupted participation in this through the constant receptivity in the heart, of God's gaze which conveys His Presence and qualities, and in the extension of these through the soul. The ceaseless remembrance of God is literally a state of being—that of harmony with the divine qualities.

51:56 وَمَا خَلَقْتُ ٱلْجِنَّ وَٱلْإِنسَ إِلَّا لِيَعْبُدُونِ ﴿٥٦﴾

wa-mā khalaqtu'l-jinna wa'l-insa illā li-yaʿbudūni[240]

and I did not create the jinn and mankind except for them to worship Me.

Concerning His [above] words, Jaʿfar said: Except for them to know Me, then to worship Me on the carpets of spiritual knowledge, so that they absolve themselves of hypocrisy and [the seeking of] a good reputation.

240 Nwyia's edition reads *yaʿbudūnī*, with a long i.

﴾ 52 ﴿

سُورَةُ الطُّورِ

al-Ṭūr (The Mount)

52:1 وَٱلطُّورِ ۝١

wa'l-ṭūr

by the Mount.

Jaʿfar said: [This is an allusion to] the intimacy in My remembrance and the sweet delight in My love that comes suddenly upon the hearts of My beloved lovers.[241]

52:2 وَكِتَٰبٍ مَّسْطُورٍ ۝٢

wa kitābin masṭūrin

and by a Book inscribed in lines.

[This is a reference to] the drawing close and the proximity that the Truth has inscribed upon Himself[242] for them [His beloved lovers].

---

241 Thus, if the *min* is taken as partitive. Alternatively, '[This is an allusion to] what unexpectedly befalls the hearts of My beloved lovers through the intimacy in My remembrance and the sweet delight in My love.'

242 The phrase *kataba ʿalā nafsihi*, which is used in the comment, is itself Qurʾānic, occurring at 6:12 and 6:54 as follows: *kataba ʿalā nafsihi'l-raḥmah; He has inscribed mercy upon His self*. The phrase *katabaʿalā nafsihi* is often rendered as 'He has prescribed for Himself.' However, the very literal rendition is used above in the translation, given its propensity for mystical interpretation.

52:48 وَٱصْبِرْ لِحُكْمِ رَبِّكَ فَإِنَّكَ بِأَعْيُنِنَا ۖ

wa'ṣbir li-ḥukmi Rabbika fa-innaka bi-aʿyuninā[243]

then endure patiently the decree of your Lord, for verily you are under Our eye.

Jaʿfar said: At this oration, the cultivation of patience and the bearing of his burden were made easy for him [the Prophet]. Even so, every state benefits the slave in the locus of witnessing.[244]

243 Nwyia has *fa* instead of the standard *wa* at the beginning of this phrase.

244 Here the *maḥall al-mushāhadah* (the locus of witnessing) seems to be an interpretation specifically of the Qurʾānic phrase *bi-aʿyuninā, 'under Our eye'*. Thus, being under God's eye or gaze is identified as the locus of *mushāhadah*.

﴾ 53 ﴿

سُورَةُ النَّجْمِ

al-Najm (The Unfolding Star)

53:1 وَٱلنَّجْمِ إِذَا هَوَىٰ ①

wa'l-najmi idhā hawā

by the unfolding star when it comes down.[245]

Jaʿfar said: It is the locus of the [divine] Self-disclosure and Self-veiling among the hearts of the people of gnosis.

[It is also related] from Jaʿfar b. Muḥammad, concerning these [above] words of (God) most high, that he said: *The unfolding star* is Muḥammad ﷺ; as he came down, lights radiated from him.

(Jaʿfar also) said: *The unfolding star* is the heart of Muḥammad; *when it comes down* [is an allusion to] when it is cut off from everything other than God.

245 This verse is often rendered literally: 'By the star when it sets'. I have preferred to incorporate Asad's understanding which is based on the interpretation given to the above verse by ʿAbd Allāh b. ʿAbbās, who referred to ʿAlī b. Abī Ṭālib as his master in *tafsīr*, as quoted in Ṭabarī's commentary. Asad's understanding and rendition are appropriate, given both the Qurʾānic context and the comment. See Asad, *Message of the Qurʾān*, note 1 on 53:1. However, reading the phrase on the *tafsīr*'s spiritual register, I retain the word 'star', because, in the subtlest realms beyond being, a star is an archetypal essence. The archetypal essence of a *rasūl-safīr* is a sun-star. (The manifold categories of beings have their archetypes in manifold categories and exceedingly intricate combinations of levels of individuation within undifferentiated Spirit. 'The unfolding star' thus describes the 'descent' of an essence/essential archetype into being and down through the levels of being to the lowest level of dense, physical matter, *al-dunyā*. This 'descent' is an extension rather than a departure from the origin.

53:2 مَا ضَلَّ صَاحِبُكُمْ وَمَا غَوَىٰ ﴿٢﴾

mā ḍalla ṣāḥibukum wa mā ghawā

your companion has not strayed nor is he deluded.

Jaʿfar said: He has not strayed from His nearness for even the twinkling of an eye.

53:3 وَمَا يَنطِقُ عَنِ ٱلْهَوَىٰٓ ﴿٣﴾

wa mā yanṭiqu ʿani'l-hawā

nor does he speak from capricious desire.

Jaʿfar said: How could he speak out of capricious desire, he who pronounced the declaration of monotheism and the completion of the revealed law (*sharīʿah*) and the ethics of commanding and forbidding? Nay, but he spoke only by a [divine] command and was silent only by a [divine] command. (When) he commanded, his command was a closeness to the Truth; (when) he forbade, his forbidding was protective and preventative.

53:8 ثُمَّ دَنَا فَتَدَلَّىٰ ﴿٨﴾

thumma danā fa-tadallā[246]

then He/he drew near, reaching down He/he[247] *drew nearer.*

Jaʿfar said: The question of 'how?' was cut off from [that] nearness. Do

246 In this particular comment, the Prophet is taken as the subject of the verbs *danā* and *tadallā*. Through and indeed in the depths of his spiritual heart, the receptacle of God's gaze, God drew him close to Himself, the Most High. Microcosmic depth = macrocosmic height.

247 Most translators of this Qurʾānic verse take the 'he' to refer to the archangel Gabriel. Clearly the *tafsīr* does not. The drawing near takes place between God and the Prophet. In keeping with the tone of the comments we have presented both possible renditions of the subject of the verbs: He/he. With this in mind, and without wishing to intrude on the 'how' of this

you not see that God, most high, veiled Gabriel from (the Prophet's) nearness [to God] and from his Lord's nearness to him (the Prophet).

He also said: Muḥammad ﷺ drew close[248] to the gnosis and faith which had been placed in his heart. Then, through the peace/tranquillity of his heart he reached down (drawing close) to that which drew him near; and doubt and misgiving vanished from his heart.

53:9 فَكَانَ قَابَ قَوْسَيْنِ أَوْ أَدْنَىٰ ﴿٩﴾

fa-kānā qāba qawsayni aw adnā

so that He was but the distance of two half-bows' length or even nearer.

Jaʿfar said: He drew him near to Him until He was as at [the short distance of] two half-bows' length from him.[249] The drawing near to

nearness, it should be noted that the word *tadallā* is remarkably evocative. *Danā* means to come close, draw near; *tadallā* means to hang down, draw near, descend. Discussing this verse, some traditional commentators understand the verb *tadallā* to denote a coming down without leaving the highest place, hence my translation 'reaching down'—which is applicable to both a non-spatial or spatial context. See Lane at *tadallā*. These verses (53:1–12) then, may be taken as describing a 'divine descent' or extension, while the following verses (13–18) describe the human ascent.

248 *Mā adnāhu*, in keeping with the general tone of this comment and taking into account the following comment, is understood to mean that the Prophet was drawn by God to His Presence, through the tranquillity and peace (which is the qualitative aura of the divine Presence) in his heart. Both words being from the same verbal root, the use of the word *sukūn* for tranquillity/peace, evokes *Sakīnah*—the Peace of the divine Presence. Furthermore, as explained in comments elsewhere, the heart is the conveyor of the means for attachment to God. There the means is the divine love; here it is the divine peace. This comment expresses the mystery of the spiritual journey: the 'movement' seems to be from the human but the pull and conveyance are in fact divine.

249 The word *qāba* refers to the short distance between the middle and the end of a bow. The phrase *qāba qawsayni* is used idiomatically to mean 'very close; imminent'.

God, most high, has no limit; but the drawing near to the slave has limits.[250]

53:10 فَأَوْحَىٰٓ إِلَىٰ عَبْدِهِۦ مَآ أَوْحَىٰ ﴿١٠﴾

fa awḥā ilā ʿabdihi mā awḥā

then He revealed to His slave what He revealed.

Jaʿfar said: [*He revealed*], without any intermediary in what was between Him and him, a secret to his heart which none but he knows;[251] without any intermediary except at the end when He grants him intercession on behalf of his community.[252]

And (Jaʿfar) al-Ṣādiq said, about His words: *He drew near, reaching down He drew nearer*: When the Beloved drew so extremely close to the beloved, extreme awe befell him. So the Truth treated him with extreme kindness—for only extreme kindness can alleviate extreme awe.

And those are His words: *Then He revealed to His slave what He revealed*, that is, what was, was; what came to pass, came to pass; and the Beloved said what the Beloved says to His beloved; and He showed him the kindness (and courtesy) of the Beloved to His beloved, and

250 God is infinite and transcends all limits, and in approaching Him, finitude has to be shed—only the Infinite can reach the Infinite. The slave is created and while the slave remains within the realm of the finite, though he is approaching God and is approached by Him, his full situation is governed by the last restrictions of finitude and, while in the world, the last restrictive differences between the spiritual and physical realms. This comment should be read keeping in mind what is said elsewhere in the commentary, particularly on the vision of God.

251 The comment that this *waḥy* ('revelation') was a secret revealed directly to the Prophet's heart—without any intermediary and not as part of the Qurʾān which is for all and which was brought to the Prophet by the archangel Gabriel—underlines the identification of God as the one who descends and draws close.

252 The connection between the end of this comment and the rest of it seems to be the matter of the intermediary. That is to say, there is no intermediary between God and the Prophet's heart during this moment of intimacy but on the Day of Judgement, it is the Prophet who shall be the intermediary, as intercessor, between his community and God.

He confided in him what the Beloved confides in His beloved. The two concealed (their secret) and did not divulge their secret to anyone other than themselves. That is why He said: *Then He revealed to His slave what He revealed.* No one knows that revelation except He who revealed and him to whom it was revealed.

53:11 مَا كَذَبَ ٱلْفُؤَادُ مَا رَأَىٰٓ ﴿١١﴾

mā kadhaba'l-fu'ādu mā ra'ā

the heart[253] *belied not what it saw.*

Jaʿfar said: No one knows what he saw, except He who showed and he who saw. The Beloved came close to the beloved, a confidant for him, an intimate friend with him. God, most high, said: *We raise* [*by*] *degrees whom We will* (6:83).

53:18 لَقَدْ رَأَىٰ مِنْ ءَايَٰتِ رَبِّهِ ٱلْكُبْرَىٰٓ ﴿١٨﴾

la-qad ra'ā min āyāti Rabbihi'l-kubrā

truly he saw some of the greatest signs of his Lord.

Jaʿfar said: He witnessed such indications of love as are too great to be related.

53:32 هُوَ أَعْلَمُ بِكُمْ

huwa aʿlamu bikum

He knows you best.

Jaʿfar said: He knows you best because He created you and ordained

253 Technically *fu'ād* means 'heart' in the sense of the pericardium, while *qalb*, also 'heart', signifies the 'kernel' or interior of the heart, hence the spiritual heart. But *fu'ād* also refers to the mind or intellect and it is in this sense that some of the traditional sources understand it in this verse, for example in the *tafsīr* of the Jalālayn. See Lane at *fu'ād* under *f-'-d*.

for you [whatever] distress and felicity [is to come to you] even before your birth in being.[254] Yet you are agitated by that which has been settled upon you preveniently, of the appointed time (of death), sustenance, felicity, and distress. Works of obedience do not procure felicity nor do deeds of opposition (to God) procure distress. Rather the prevenient ordinance is what sets the seal to that which was begun.[255]

53:37 وَإِبْرَٰهِيمَ ٱلَّذِى وَفَّىٰٓ ﴿٣٧﴾

wa Ibrāhīma'lladhī waffā[256]

and Abraham who rendered fully.

Jaʿfar said: The quintessence of sincerity is faithful fulfilment in every state and in every deed.

53:44 وَأَنَّهُۥ هُوَ أَمَاتَ وَأَحْيَا ﴿٤٤﴾

wa annahu huwa amāta wa aḥyā

and that it is He who deadens and enlivens.

Jaʿfar said: He deadens through the turning away from Him; and He enlivens through spiritual knowledge of Him. He deadens souls through opposition (to Him) and He enlivens hearts with the lights of harmony (with Him).

---

254 The comment here emphasises that the final end is known before the beginning of a soul's being; in other words, in the realms beyond being.

255 As witnessed in this text, predestination is an important aspect of the Imām al-Ṣādiq's teachings. The prevenient ordinance, established in pre-eternity, in beyond being, sets the seal—it is the end. Our deeds along the way do not alter the final end, but they can affect the course the journey takes to that unalterable end.

256 *Waffā*, being the second form of the verbal root *w-f-y*, means to render fully a due or a right; to pay fully what is owed. *Wafāʾ* (faithful fulfilment).

﴾ 54 ﴿

سُورَةُ القَمَرِ

al-Qamar (The Moon)

54:55 فِي مَقْعَدِ صِدْقٍ

fī maqʿadi ṣidqin

in the seat of sincerity.

Jaʿfar said: [This is] praise of the place in which sincerity[257] is—none but the sincere ones are seated therein. It is the seat wherein God fulfils the promises [made to] His friends, in that they are permitted to look at His august face.

257 *Ṣidq* also means 'faithfulness'.

55

سُورَةُ الرَّحۡمَٰن

al-Raḥmān (The Gracious)

55:11 فِيهَا فَٰكِهَةٞ وَٱلنَّخۡلُ ذَاتُ ٱلۡأَكۡمَامِ ۝١١

fīhā fākihatun wa'l-nakhlu dhātu'l-akmām

therein is fruit and the palm tree endowed with calyces.

Jaʿfar said: The Truth has made the hearts of His friends meadows of His intimacy. He has planted in them trees of gnosis whose roots are firmly fixed in their inmost selves and whose branches stand in the divine Presence in the assembly (of witnessing). They reap the fruits of intimacy at every instant. That is [the interpretation of] the words of (God), most high: *Therein is fruit and the palm tree endowed with calyces*, that is, endowed with different varieties. Everyone harvests from it a type in keeping with the scope of his effort and (according to) the manifestations of mystical knowledge and the effects of divine friendship that are unveiled for them.

55:60 هَلۡ جَزَآءُ ٱلۡإِحۡسَٰنِ إِلَّا ٱلۡإِحۡسَٰنُ ۝٦٠

hal jazā'u'l-iḥsāni illā'l-iḥsān

is the meed of goodness aught save goodness.

Jaʿfar said: Is the meed for one to whom goodness was extended in pre-eternity aught save the preservation of the goodness upon him for all future eternity.

﴾ 56 ﴿

سُورَةُ الوَاقِعَةِ

al-Wāqiʿah (The Inevitable Event)

56:19 لَّا يُصَدَّعُونَ عَنْهَا وَلَا يُنزِفُونَ ﴿١٩﴾

lā yuṣaddaʿūna ʿanhā wa-lā yunzifūn

from which they get no headache nor are they exhausted [*by it*].

Jaʿfar said: Their intellects are not distracted from the well-springs[258] of realities [flowing] to them, nor are they absent, in any state, from the gathering of the witnessing.

56:30 وَظِلٍّ مَّمْدُودٍ ﴿٣٠﴾

wa ẓillin mamdūdin

and widespread shade.

[It is related] from Jaʿfar, concerning His [above] words, that he said: The *shade* is God's prevenient mercy to the community of Muḥammad ﷺ; and the *widespread* is His grace upon those who affirm God's unity and His justice upon deviants.

258 'Well-springs' renders the word *mawārid*, which means, among other things, 'wells, springs, the original sources'. The *mawārid* are both the source wells *in divinis* of the realities, and the flowing springs themselves. Here, the *tafsīr* refers to the continual receptivity of the inhabitants of paradise to the *ḥaqāʾiq* (the divine lights, the divine qualities), that flow to them from God.

56:33 لَّا مَقْطُوعَةٍ وَلَا مَمْنُوعَةٍ ۝٣٣

lā maqṭūʿatin wa-lā mamnūʿatin

neither cut short nor forbidden.

Jaʿfar said: Gnosis and strengthening[259] are never cut off from them—were those to be cut off from them they would perish. Nor are they forbidden from taking enjoyment in being right next to the Truth—were they forbidden that, they would be desolated.

56:73 نَحْنُ جَعَلْنَـٰهَا تَذْكِرَةً

Naḥnu jaʿalnāhā tadhkiratan

We have made it a reminder.

Jaʿfar said (glossing *reminder*): Spiritual counsel for the repentant and, for the firm sages, an instrument for bearing it.[260]

---

259 The reader should note the continuous nature of the divine influx: a continual strengthening by God, and an ongoing conferral of spiritual knowledge in the absence of which the inhabitants of the paradises would perish. This comment complements the idea expressed in the comment above; there is a constant neediness on the part of the *ʿibād* and a constant inpouring from God, serving to underline the theophanic nature of the inhabitants of the paradises that are 'next to the Truth'. By extension, all creation is also constantly and totally dependent on the Creator and Sustainer, in a way that is analogous to the constant need for sunlight and oxygen that earthly creatures have.

260 The Qurʾānic verse in full is: '*We have made it a reminder and a comfort for those in the wilderness*'. In the Qurʾānic context, the verse refers to 'the fire' mentioned in the immediately preceding verses. The comment interprets the word *tadhkirah,* 'reminder'. The reminder is spiritual counsel for the repentant and a means, for the firm sages, of bearing it. *Aqwiyāʾ* has been read as the plural of *qawīy* (firm, strong, sturdy, robust, potent). The final suffix *hu*, then, remains ambiguous. It might refer to the Qurʾān; it might refer to God. However, it would seem most likely that it refers to 'wilderness' as indicated by the word *muqwīn* ('those in the wilderness') at the end of this Qurʾānic verse; in which case it refers to the reminder that it is a means for the firm and sturdy sages to bear the wilderness

56:79 لَّا يَمَسُّهُۥٓ إِلَّا ٱلْمُطَهَّرُونَ ٧٩

lā yamassuhu illā'l-muṭahharūn

only the purified touch it [i.e., the Qurʾān].

Jaʿfar said [explaining *the purified*]: Only those who uphold its rights and who follow its commands and preserve (the sanctity) of what it has sanctified.

in which they find themselves. This comment should be read keeping in mind certain associations noted throughout the commentary. For instance, where *tadhkirah* refers to the Qurʾān; where reference is made to recollection being *tadhakkur*; where *tidhkār* is the healing reminder of God's grace and generosity; where reminder (*tadhkīr*) is mentioned alongside spiritual counsel (*mawʿiẓah*); and where *tadhkirah* refers to the Qurʾān itself and is glossed as *mawʿiẓah*.

57

سُورَةُ الحَدِيدِ

al-Ḥadīd (Iron)

57:1 سَبَّحَ لِلَّهِ مَا فِى ٱلسَّمَٰوَٰتِ

sabbaḥa li'llāhi mā fi'l-samāwāt

what(ever) is in the heavens glorifies God.

Everything—totality—praises Him while He has no need for their praise. How should that[261] attain to Him when He is the one who brings it forth and is responsible for its manifestation?

وَهُوَ ٱلْعَزِيزُ ٱلْحَكِيمُ ۝١

wa huwa'l-ʿAzīzu'l-Ḥakīm

and He is the Mighty the Wise.

Jaʿfar said: He is the one who is not grasped[262] by those who seek Him and who cannot be eluded by those who [wish to] flee from Him.

---

261 'That' most likely refers to the praise; however it might refer to totality itself, for God is responsible for manifesting both totality and the praise of totality.

262 *Lā yudrikuhu ṭālibuhu*, literally 'whose seekers do not grasp Him'. It is God who grasps the seeker. The verb *daraka,* here rendered by the verb 'to grasp', also means to know, perceive, comprehend, understand, attain to, overtake. In other words, only God knows God.

57:3 هُوَ ٱلْأَوَّلُ وَٱلْءَاخِرُ وَٱلظَّٰهِرُ وَٱلْبَاطِنُ

huwa'l-Awwalu wa'l-Ākhiru wa'l-Ẓāhiru wa'l-Bāṭin

He is the First and the Last and the Manifest and the Hidden.

Jaʿfar said: He is the one who makes first the first and makes last the last, who manifests the manifest and conceals the hidden.[263] Then these concepts fall away and there remains [only] He.

Jaʿfar [also] said: *The Hidden*—He is hidden in every place. [No place is] ever without Him, for His being was when no place was. Through His kindness, He veiled the essential nature of 'He was' while, through His power He made visible the fixedness of 'He was'. Thus He made clear to us 'He was' but He veiled from us the essential nature of 'He was'; but He disclosed to us the manifestation of the perfection of 'He was'—through the realisation of which faith is perfected.

57:10 لَا يَسْتَوِى مِنكُم مَّنْ أَنفَقَ مِن قَبْلِ ٱلْفَتْحِ وَقَٰتَلَ

lā yastawī minkum man anfaqa min qabli'l-fatḥi wa qātala

they are not equal among you, those who spent and fought [*in God's way*] *before the victory,* [*and those who did not*].

Jaʿfar said: [This is a reference to] the firm intentions and the sound faith of the emigrants, the people of the bench[264] and their *imām* and lord, the greatest sincere one, God's pleasure be upon him.[265] They are the ones

263 This translation is based on the presence, in the edition of the Arabic, of the *shaddah* over the second consonants of *a-wa-la* and *a-kha-ra*. My own preferred rendition would be without a *shaddah*: 'He is the foremost of the first, the very last of the last, the most manifest of the manifest and the most hidden of the hidden.'

264 'The people of the bench' were newly-arrived, impoverished Meccan Muslim emigrants to Madīnah, who, having nowhere to live and no means of livelihood, lived in a part of the Prophet's mosque where a stone bench was placed for their use. They endured the hardships of homelessness and poverty in order to be with the Prophet and practise their religion in peace.

265 This comment indicates the citation of a Shīʿī statement by a non-Shīʿī

who did not give preference to this world over the hereafter. Rather, they sacrificed (the world) and did not turn towards it; they relied, in that, on their Lord and sought His satisfaction and (to be in) harmony with the Messenger ﷺ. So God, glory to Him, distinguished them from among the (Muslim) community, with His words: *they are not equal...*

source. The title *al-ṣiddīq al-akbar* is used by the Shīʿah for the Imām ʿAlī b. Abī Ṭālib, on ʿAlī's own authority. However, the blessings, *raḍīya'llāhu ʿanhu* and *riḍwānu'llāhi ʿalayhi* are used for him by the Sunnīs; the Shīʿī eulogy for the Imam being *ʿalayhi'l-salām*.

《 59 》

سُورَةُ الحَشْرِ

al-Ḥashr (The Gathering)

59:23 ٱلْقُدُّوسُ

al-Quddūs

the Holy.

[It is related] from Jaʿfar b. Muḥammad, that, concerning (God's) words: *al-Quddūs; the Holy*, he said: The one who is pure of every defect and who purifies of defects whom He wills (to purify).

ٱلْمُهَيْمِنُ

al-Muhaymin

the Guardian

The one *like to whose likeness there is nothing* (42:11). The Qurʾān has been named *muhayminan* (5:48) because no other speech resembles it.[266]

---

266 *Muhaymin* is from the verb *haymana* (to say 'amen'). Hence it sets the seal on something, and comes to mean protector, guardian, or master. It seems to be in this sense of 'master', hence 'unsurpassed, unequalled' ('the last Word') that it is used in this comment.

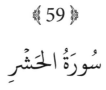

﴾ 61 ﴿

سُورَةُ الصَّفِّ

al-Ṣaff (The Ranks)

61:5 فَلَمَّا زَاغُوٓاْ أَزَاغَ ٱللَّهُ قُلُوبَهُمۡۚ

fa-lammā zāghū azāgha'llāhu qulūbahum

then when they deviated, God made their hearts deviate.

Jaʿfar said: When they abandoned the commands of service, God removed the light of faith from their hearts and He made for Satan a path to them. Thus he turned them away from the path of the Truth and made them enter the way of falsehood.

61:13 وَبَشِّرِ ٱلۡمُؤۡمِنِينَ ١٣

wa bashshiri'l-muʾminīn

and give glad-tidings to the believers.

Jaʿfar said: The good news of beholding Him[267] *in the seat of sincerity near a powerful King* (54:55).

267 *Ruʾyah* indicates the acutal visual beholding (of God), while *ruʾyā* is used for a vision.

﴾ 64 ﴿

سُورَةُ التَّغَابُنِ

al-Taghābun (Mutual Disillusion)

64:15 إِنَّمَآ أَمۡوَٰلُكُمۡ وَأَوۡلَٰدُكُمۡ فِتۡنَةٞۚ

innamā amwālukum wa awlādukum fitnatun

verily, your possessions and your children are but a trial.

Jaʿfar said: Your possessions are a trial because of your preoccupation with accumulating them improperly and misappropriating them.[268] Your children are a trial because of your preoccupation with bettering them—thus you are corrupted and they do not thrive in righteousness.[269]

---

268 *Waḍʿihā li-ghayri ahlihā* ('its placement with those to whom it does not rightly belong'); if this phrase is taken (as in the English text above) to be in apposition to *jamʿihā* and thus governed by the *bi*, then it refers to a person's misappropriation of the possessions of others in order to accumulate wealth. However, the phrase may conceivably be read in apposition to *ishtighālikum*, governed by the *li*; in which case the meaning is that the trial lies in a person's possessions being misappropriated by others.

269 Thus, as far as wealth is concerned, it is a temptation in two ways: 1) inasmuch as it becomes a preoccupation, and 2) inasmuch as it is gained improperly. Children are a temptation, not in themselves, nor in the bettering of them, but when the matter of bettering them becomes a *preoccupation* for the parents. Hence, in both parts of the comment, preoccupation is a critical part of the *fitnah*.

66

سُورَةُ التَّحْرِيمِ

al-Taḥrīm (Prohibition)

66:9 يَـٰٓأَيُّهَا ٱلنَّبِيُّ جَـٰهِدِ ٱلْكُفَّارَ وَٱلْمُنَـٰفِقِينَ

Yā ayyuhā'l-nabīyu, jāhidi'l-kuffāra wa'l-munāfiqīn

O Prophet; strive against the deniers and the hypocrites.

Jaʿfar said: Strive against the deniers[270] with the hand and against the hypocrites with the tongue.

---

270 *Al-kuffār* is translated as 'the deniers' in order to emphasise the ontological and microcosmic aspect of *kufr*. The verb *kafara* means 'to disbelieve or to deny'; it also means 'to veil or cover or obscure'. So to perform an act that veils God's light, that veils any of God's qualities (which we know, above all, through the divine names) is to perform an act of denial—of ontological *kufr*. Most people limit *kufr* to the denial of God's existence or to *shirk*. However, a formal believer may perform an act of ontological *kufr* because it is an act that obscures or veils God's light/qualities. For example, someone who professes to believe in God may perpetrate an act of violence—which deeply obscures the flow of God's Peace. Such an act denies God who is Peace itself (al-Salām). This is ontological *kufr*. To strive against such *kufr* 'with the hand' means to strive through action—that is to say, to strive against violence with active Peace, against intolerance with active tolerance (for God is the Very Patient, al-Ṣabūr, the Forbearing, al-Ḥalīm), against hatred with active love (for God is the Loving, al-Wadūd). To strive against the hypocrites (those who say they affirm God but in their behaviour deny God's qualities) 'with the tongue' is to say: strive by word, by informing or praying for them. On the intra-microcosmic level such striving begins against the *kufr* and hypocrisy (*nifāq*) present in a person's own behaviour, as part of Marwah's service (*khidmah*).

66:9 وَٱغْلُظْ عَلَيْهِمْ ۚ

wa'ghluẓ ʿalayhim

and be hard on them.

(God) commanded him ﷺ to be hard on them in order to vent His anger upon them despite the insignificance of their claims while He commanded Moses ﷺ to be gentle with Pharaoh despite his high claims.[271]

271 This comment draws attention to the sometimes unexpected manner of God's dealings with His creatures, as noted in the comments on 27:50 and 85:13.

﴾ 67 ﴿

سُورَةُ المُلْكِ

al-Mulk (Sovereignty)

67:1 تَبَٰرَكَ ٱلَّذِى بِيَدِهِ ٱلْمُلْكُ

tabāraka'lladhī bi-yadihi'l-mulk

blessed is He in whose hand is the sovereignty.

Jaʿfar said: *Blessed*, that is, He is the one who sends down blessings upon the one who is detached (from all else, dedicated) to Him [alone] or is for Him.

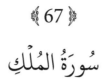

68

سُورَةُ القَلَمِ

al-Qalam (The Pen)

68:1 نٓۚ وَٱلْقَلَمِ

nūn; wa'l-qalam

nūn; by the pen.

Jaʿfar said: *Nūn* is the light of pre-eternity from which He produced all beings. He made that for Muḥammad ﷺ. That is why it was said of him: *and verily you are in possession of a tremendous nature* (68:4), that is, in possession of the light by which you were distinguished in pre-eternity.

68:4 وَإِنَّكَ لَعَلَىٰ خُلُقٍ عَظِيمٍ ۝٤

wa innaka la-ʿalā khuluqin ʿaẓīmin

and verily you are in possession of a tremendous nature.

Jaʿfar said [concerning *the tremendous nature*]: It is untaintedness of faith and the reality of the oneness of God.

68:34 إِنَّ لِلْمُتَّقِينَ عِندَ رَبِّهِمْ جَنَّٰتِ ٱلنَّعِيمِ ۝٣٤

inna li'l-muttaqīna ʿinda Rabbihim jannāti'l-naʿīm

verily, for the God-aware, there are gardens of bliss in the presence of their Lord.

Jaʿfar said: The abode of the person who is wary of sins is the gardens of bliss. As for the person who is aware of God, most high, (God) raises from him the coverings and veils so that he sees the Truth in all states.

68:42 يَوْمَ يُكْشَفُ عَن سَاقٍ وَيُدْعَوْنَ إِلَى ٱلسُّجُودِ

yawma yukshafu ʿan sāqin[272] wa yudʿawna ilā'l-sujūd

on the day when the shank is disclosed and they are summoned to prostration.

Jaʿfar al-Ṣādiq said: *On the day when the shank is disclosed*, '(When) terrors and calamities and the (narrow) bridge (across the abyss of hell) and the reckoning (are disclosed), [on that day] My believing slave to whom My care and My mercy have already been granted, shall be safe and secure from those terrors and calamities—he shall know nothing of that day's calamities and terrors.' Everyone to whom the care of God, most high, has already been given prostrates themselves before Him, (completely) in need of Him. But he to whom the justice of God, most high, has preceded will be unable to prostrate (himself); his back shall be like an inflexible rock, not yielding to the prostration to the Lord of the worlds.

Jaʿfar [also] said about His words, *on the day when the shank is disclosed:* When the Friend/friend meets the friend/Friend[273] calamities are removed from him.[274]

---

272 The phrase *yukshafu ʿan sāqin* is idiomatic, referring to the uncovering of the shanks when a man rolled up his trousers in preparation to meet a difficulty—hence the connotation of a time of difficulty and hardship.

273 The linguistic play touches on the word *walī*, which is both one of the divine names (al-Walī, the Patron, the Friend), and the Islamic word for a saint, *walīyu'llāh*, a 'friend of God'. This phrase might have been rendered as follows: 'when the (divine) Friend meets the (human) friend'; or 'when (God) the Friend meets the (creature His) friend'.

274 This comment exemplifies semi-inverse interpretation, based on the verb *ka-sh-fa*, which means to disclose, uncover, unveil, expose, to remove the veil on. In the Qurʾānic phrase the passive of the first form is used; in the comment the passive seventh form of the verb is used. The comment plays with the idiom, so that instead of calamities being disclosed by the removal of the veil upon them, the calamities themselves are removed.

﴾ 69 ﴿

سُورَةُ الحَاقَّةِ

al-Ḥāqqah (The Revealing Reality)

69:38–39 فَلَآ أُقْسِمُ بِمَا تُبْصِرُونَ ﴿٣٨﴾ وَمَا لَا تُبْصِرُونَ ﴿٣٩﴾

falā uqsimu bimā tubṣirūn. Wa mā lā tubṣirūn

nay but I swear by that which you see. And that which you do not see.

Jaʿfar said: *By that which you see* of My handiwork in My kingdom; *and that which you do not see* of My beneficence to My friends.

69:48 وَإِنَّهُۥ لَتَذْكِرَةٌ لِّلْمُتَّقِينَ ﴿٤٨﴾

wa innahu la-tadhkiratun li'l-muttaqīn

and verily it is indeed a reminder for the God-aware.

Jaʿfar said: (It is) spiritual counsel for those who have certainty.

﴾71﴿

سُورَةُ نُوحٍ

Nūḥ (Noah)

71:12 وَيَجْعَل لَّكُمْ جَنَّٰتٍ وَيَجْعَل لَّكُمْ أَنْهَٰرًا ﴿١٢﴾

wa yajʿal lakum jannātin wa yajʿal lakum anhāran

and He will grant you gardens and He will grant you rivers.

Jaʿfar said: He will adorn your external (aspect) with the adornment of service and your internal (aspect) with the lights of faith.

﴾ 73 ﴿

سُورَةُ المُزَّمِّلِ

al-Muzzamil (The Enwrapped One)

73:20 فَٱقۡرَءُواْ مَا تَيَسَّرَ مِنۡهُۚ

fa'qraʾū mā tayassara mina'l-Qurʾān

so recite what is made easy (for you) of the Qurʾān.

Jaʿfar b. Muḥammad said: *What is made easy* for you in it is humility of heart and purity of inmost self.[275]

275 In other words, the teachings of the Qurʾān facilitate humility of heart and purity/serenity of inmost self; thus its recitation should produce these things in the reciter. If the alternative reading noted by Nwyia is taken into consideration, there would be a *min* instead of *fīhi* and the comment would read: '*What is made easy* for you of humility of heart and purity of inmost self.'

76

سُورَةُ الإنسَانِ

al-Insān (Mankind)

76:1 هَلۡ أَتَىٰ عَلَى ٱلۡإِنسَٰنِ حِينٞ مِّنَ ٱلدَّهۡرِ لَمۡ يَكُن شَيۡـٔٗا مَّذۡكُورًا ﴿١﴾

hal atā ʿalāʾl-insāni ḥīnun minaʾl-dahri lam yakun shayʾan madhkūran

has there come upon man any time (in which) he was not a thing remembered?

Jaʿfar said: Has there ever come upon you, O Man, [even] an instant in which God did not remember you?

76:21 وَسَقَىٰهُمۡ رَبُّهُمۡ شَرَابٗا طَهُورًا ﴿٢١﴾

wa saqāhum Rabbuhum sharāban ṭahūran

and their Lord gives them a purifying drink to drink.

Jaʿfar said: He gives them the divine unity to drink in the inmost self, and they are totally lost to all other than Him.[276] They do not regain their senses except at the eye-to-eye seeing and the veil on that which

276 To take this highly mystical and subtle comment step by step: 1) With the drink, there is the absorption of the consciousness into the divine unity through the inmost self which is the differentiated divine spirit, the *ḥaqīqah*: in other words, the duality of differentiated consciousness is effaced in the undifferentiated Self-consciousness; 2) Then 'duality' of consciousness re-emerges as the individuated spirit in the realm of non-differentiation, at the eye-to-eye seeing, which is the seeing of the one Identity by its individuated identity. Thus the 'duality' of individuated divine consciousness re-emerges, only to be obliterated in the Self-seeing of the unindividuated Sole-identity.

is between them and Him is raised. The drink is taken in what is taken from him [i.e., from the drinker]; and no remnant of him remains in it [i.e., in what is taken from him].[277] And He draws him forth[278] into the arena of blissful joy and the divine Presence, and the divine clasp [of God's embrace].

Jaʿfar [also] said, about His words, *a purifying drink*: He purifies them, through the drink, of everything other than Him, since he is not pure who is contaminated by anything pertaining to beings.[279]

---

277 The drink of divine unity is drunk by the differentiated, individuated spirit, the *ḥaqīqah*. It is the *ḥaqīqah* that is taken out of the incarnate human being, and there is naught in the *ḥaqīqah* other than al-Ḥaqq. The extracted *ḥaqīqah* is drawn forth into the undifferentiated unity of the divine Presence and clasped therein. To express it thus: a small living inscription of the divine name is clasped by the divine named One; God clasps His living image; this living image is the aspect that is 'in the image of God', it has nothing to do with the creature, just as sunlight entering a room has nothing to do with the room that it shines into. Yet the bliss of the individuated *ḥaqīqah* is experienced by *it*. When the one God multi-manifests, He experiences things through all the vantage points of His manifestations.

278 The verb is *ḥaṣṣala*, the second form of the root *ḥ-ṣ-l*. Its use here is highly evocative as it means 'to extract, draw forth . . . gold from rock, or the kernel from the shell . . .' See Lane at *ḥ-ṣ-l*. The annihilation and union described in this comment are the highest *fanāʾ* and *jamʿ* of the Sufis.

279 The second comment provides further elucidation; we are told that the drink means that the divine aspect is purged of all contamination by that which is not divine. So the 'he' that drinks and is drawn forth from the microcosm is the uncontaminated divine aspect. Here we have entered the realm of God alone who contains and transcends all being; He who is totally beyond form and manifestation, yet manifests within the cosmos, else the cosmos would not be, for the being of the cosmos is derived directly from the beyond-being Self-existence of God. Now, He who manifests within the macrocosm also manifests within the microcosm. Just as there is a microcosmic *walī* and a microcosmic *nabī*, there is a microcosmic Ḥaqq. The microcosmic Ḥaqq is the divine Presence in the spiritual heart, transmitted there by the gaze of God, and who, in turn, transmits the gaze of God to the heart and enlivens therewith the microcosmic Ṣafā. The microcosmic Ḥaqq is the *rasūl-safīr* to the human microcosm from the abolutely transcendent Divinity. The microcosmic Ṣafā is the *rasūl-safīr* to the soul from the theophany in the heart. Ṣafā is a theophany of the microcosmic Ḥaqq who is a theophany of the absolute God. With this comment the portrait of the human microcosm presented

78

سُورَةُ النَّبَإِ

al-Nabāʾ (The Tidings)

78:35 لَّا يَسۡمَعُونَ فِيهَا لَغۡوٗا وَلَا كِذَّٰبٗا ﴿٣٥﴾

lā yasmaʿuna fīhā laghwan wa-lā kidhdhāban

therein they hear no vain talk nor any untruth.

Jaʿfar said: For God, most high, strengthens [such a one] with God-given success so that, in the world, no vain talk flows from him about Him, nor yet is any vain talk heard from him in the divine Presence. *Vain talk* is the mention of any mentionable thing, except for Him. *Nor any untruth*, that is, nor any word except for the truthful word in the attestation of His onliness, prior eternity, and singularity.

78:36 جَزَآءٗ مِّن رَّبِّكَ عَطَآءً حِسَابٗا ﴿٣٦﴾

jazāʾan min Rabbika ʿaṭāʾan ḥisāban

recompense from your Lord, a gift of generous reckoning.[280]

Jaʿfar said: The gift from God, most high, is twofold: [first] in the beginning there is (the gift) of faith and submission (to Him) (given) without request; [second] at the end, there is the gift of His disregarding lapses, negligence, and acts of disobedience. The slave's entry into paradise is by His mercy through His gifts. Even so is the gazing upon His august face.

---

by the *tafsīr* is complete.

280 *Ḥisāb* ('reckoning, settlement, consideration'), but also 'gift' or 'generous gift'. See Lane at *ḥisāb* under *ḥ-ṣ-b*.

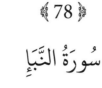

80

سُورَةُ عَبَسَ

ʿAbasa (He Frowned)

80:7 وَمَا عَلَيْكَ أَلَّا يَزَّكَّىٰ ۞

wa mā ʿalayka allā yazzakkā

yet it is not upon you if he grow not in purity.

Jaʿfar said: You will not dignify through your attention the one whom He has not dignified with guidance and whom He has not adorned with gnosis.

82

سُورَةُ الانفِطَارِ

al-Infiṭār (The Cleaving)

82:6 يَٰٓأَيُّهَا ٱلۡإِنسَٰنُ مَا غَرَّكَ بِرَبِّكَ ٱلۡكَرِيمِ ٦

Yā ayyuhā'l-insānu mā gharraka bi-Rabbika'l-Karīm

O Man; what deceives you against your generous Lord?

Jaʿfar said: What keeps you back from the service of your Patron?

82:13–14 إِنَّ ٱلۡأَبۡرَارَ لَفِي نَعِيمٖ ١٣ وَإِنَّ ٱلۡفُجَّارَ لَفِي جَحِيمٖ ١٤

inna'l-abrāra lafī naʿīmin.
Wa inna'l-fujjāra lafī jaḥīmin

verily, the godly ones will be in bliss. While the wicked, sinful ones will be in hellfire.

Jaʿfar said: *The bliss* is gnosis and the witnessing (of God); and *hellfire* is souls,[281] for they shall have fires[282] that burn.

281 Wicked, sinful souls are themselves hellfire. As well as an external, macrocosmic situation, *jaḥīm* here is an infernal, microcosmic station of the soul, penetrating it through and through; the complete inverse of a soul permeated with bliss.

282 There is an evocative play on the word *nīrān* here. As the plural of *nār* it means 'fires'; as the multiple plural of *nīr* (as in *nīru'l-faddān*) it means 'yokes'. See Lane at *nīr* under *n-y-r*. The impression thus is of 'fiery yokes that burn'.

83

سُورَةُ المُطَفِّفِينَ

al-Muṭaffifīn (The Defrauders)

83:24 تَعۡرِفُ فِي وُجُوهِهِمۡ نَضۡرَةَ ٱلنَّعِيمِ ﴿٢٤﴾

taʿrifu fī wujūhihim naḍrata'l-naʿīm

you will recognise the radiance of bliss in their faces.

Jaʿfar said: When they return to their dwelling places after visiting God, most high, there is a shining like that of the sun in their faces because of the enduring rapture of the gazing (at God).[283]

283 When reading this comment, the reader should bear in mind that the word *wajh* refers to both 'face' and 'essence'. The face reveals the identity of an individual. In the subtle realm of spiritual forms, the face reveals the state of the essence much more clearly than the corporeal face in the physical realm does. The 'shining' mentioned in this comment is a reference to the radiance of the light of God shining through the angelic nature, the perfect inner *ʿubūdīyah*—for when they gaze at God they are effaced and God's light shines through them clearly. There is a dual application of this comment. Since the gazing at God takes place in the spiritual realm, the shining face pertains in the first instance to the spiritual body (the angel within), and in the second instance to the corporeal body. On the spiritual level, when the differentiated spirits of the inhabitants of the paradises gaze at God, in that gazing they are totally reabsorbed into His undifferentiated spirit/light—for they are made of His differentiated light. Then, when they are returned, by God, to the differentiated state, the faces of their spiritual bodies shine like the sun due to the enduring rapture of their *fanāʾ fī'llāh*: this is the *fanāʾ fī'llāh* and *baqāʾ bi'llāh* in the spiritual realm. The face of an archangel appears like a radiant solar disc, brilliant white-gold in colour. On the level of the *dunyā*, if the spirit is still attached to a corporeal body, then this light of inner effacement in God (the result of the spirit gazing upon God) manifests as a non-physical radiance within the corporeal face when they return to their

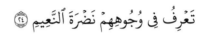

83:27 وَمِزَاجُهُۥ مِن تَسۡنِيمٍ ﴿٢٧﴾

wa mizājuhu min Tasnīmin

and its blend is from Tasnīm.[284]

Jaʿfar said: Chalices blended with intimacy from which they inhale the fragrance of closeness (to God).[285]

---

physical bodies, having been, in spirit, in God's Presence. The face of a saint, whose *ḥaqīqah* is not veiled, is suffused with ineffable light.

284 One of the springs of paradise, the others being Kāfūr and Salsabīl. For more on the springs of paradise see Sirāj ad-Dīn, *Book of Certainty*.

285 The comment refers to the drink of pure wine, sealed with musk and blended with a draught from Tasnīm, mentioned in verses 25–27 of this *sūrah*.

85

سُورَةُ البُرُوجِ

al-Burūj (The Great Constellations)

85:13 إِنَّهُۥ هُوَ يُبْدِئُ وَيُعِيدُ ١٣

innahu huwa yubdiʾu wa yuʿīd[286]

verily it is He who brings forth and restores.

Jaʿfar said: *He who brings forth*, thus He annihilates [them] from all other than Him; then *restores*, thus He preserves [them] through His maintaining [them].[287]

Jaʿfar al-Ṣādiq [also] said: *Verily it is He who brings forth and restores*, that is, He dons the garment of the friends for the enemies so that it may be a gradual advancement for them. And He dons the garment of the enemies for the friends, lest they be conceited about their souls.[288] Then He restores them, at death, [to their true state].[289]

286 *Yuʿīd* means to renew, reproduce, repeat, bring back, take back, cause to return, restore to, re-establish, etc. Al-Muʿīd, the Restorer, is one of the divine names.

287 This comment should be read in conjunction with the comments at 42:9, 53:44 and 76:21 and their notes. God annihilates a soul, effacing from it everything other than Himself, thus bringing it forth from the *daran* of its *mukhālafah* and restoring it to the theophanic state of *muwāfaqah bi'llāh*; and then He preserves the soul in that state, maintaining its harmony with God. We have here again the concepts that became famous among the Sufis as *fanāʾ fi'llāh* and *baqāʾ bi'llāh*, extinction in God and subsistence through God.

288 The clear implication is that God's wisdom is at work in both the comfortable and the uncomfortable aspects of the spiritual life.

289 Initially this comment may seem counterintuitive; but the spiritual message is a universal one: gentle persuasion of those who need it and precaution against self-satisfaction and pride for those well-advanced on

90

سُورَةُ البَلَدِ

al-Balad (The Land)

90:4 لَقَدۡ خَلَقۡنَا ٱلۡإِنسَٰنَ فِي كَبَدٍ ۝٤

la-qad khalaqnā'l-insān fī kabadin

verily We have created mankind for difficulty.[290]

Jaʿfar said: For trials and hardship.[291]

His way. Though not exactly the same, the principle here is not totally dissimilar to that which makes Grace hold the fallen one close to the divine breast. In any case, this comment describes a possible aspect of the interaction between God and creature, that may or may not manifest as God journeys with the creature, bringing him/her back to Himself.

290 The primary meanings of *kabad* are toil, hardship, pain, distress, difficulty, and trial. However, Lane (at *kabad* under *k-b-d*) cites an interpretation of this verse whereby '*fī kabadin*' is understood to mean 'in a right and just state; in an errect state; in just proportion'. Asad renders this verse as: 'Verily We have created man into [a life of] pain, toil and trial'; while Pickthall has, 'We verily have created man in an atmosphere' adding in a note 'or "in affliction"'. Our translation keeps in mind that *fī* can mean 'for' and takes into account the comment that indicates how the verse was understood.

291 'Trials and hardships' serve the purpose, among others, of providing opportunities for Marwah to help Ṣafā overcome the lower soul, the *nafs al-ammārah bi'l-sūʾ*.

90:15 يَتِيمًا ذَا مَقْرَبَةٍ ﴿١٥﴾

yatīman dhā maqrabatin

an orphan who is a close relative.

Jaʿfar said: It is that by which you draw closer to your Lord in the support of orphans and in checking on them.

93

سُورَةُ الضُّحَىٰ

al-Ḍuḥā (The Bright Morning Hours)

93:7 وَوَجَدَكَ ضَآلًّا فَهَدَىٰ ﴿٧﴾

wa wajadaka ḍāllan fa-hadā

and (did He not) find you wandering lost and guide you?

Jaʿfar said: You were straying away from My love for you in pre-eternity; so I bestowed upon you spiritual knowledge of Me.

93:9–10 فَأَمَّا ٱلْيَتِيمَ فَلَا تَقْهَرْ ﴿٩﴾ وَأَمَّا ٱلسَّآئِلَ فَلَا تَنْهَرْ ﴿١٠﴾

fa ammāʾl-yatīma falā taqhar. Wa ammāʾl-sāʾila falā tanhar

so, as for the orphan, do not oppress (them). And as for the questioner, do not rebuff (them).

Jaʿfar said: *The orphan* is one who is deprived of the honourable robe of guidance—do not make him despair of My mercy, for I am able to clothe him with the garment of guidance. As for the questioner, when he questions you about Me, direct him to Me with the most gracious/subtlest direction, for I am indeed near, responsive.[292]

292 The choice of words in this comment brings to mind two other verses from the Qurʾān, at 2:186, *And when My slaves question you about Me I am indeed near; I answer the call of the caller when he calls Me; then let them respond to Me and let them believe in Me that they may be rightly-guided.'* And the second, at 39:53, *Say O My slaves who have transgressed against yourselves, do not despair of God's mercy, verily God forgives all sins, indeed He, He is the Forgiving, the Merciful.'*

93:11 وَأَمَّا بِنِعْمَةِ رَبِّكَ فَحَدِّثْ ﴿١١﴾

wa ammā bi-niʿmati Rabbika fa-ḥaddith

and as for the blessing of your Lord, speak [*of it*].

Jaʿfar said: Inform creation of that with which I have blessed them through you and your position.

94

سُورَةُ الشَّرْحِ

al-Sharḥ (The Opening Up)

al-Inshirāḥ (The Expansion)

94:1 أَلَمْ نَشْرَحْ لَكَ صَدْرَكَ ①

a-lam nashraḥ laka ṣadraka

have We not opened up your breast for you?

Jaʿfar said: *Have We not opened up your breast for you,* for witnessing Me and beholding Me?

94:4 وَرَفَعْنَا لَكَ ذِكْرَكَ ④

wa rafaʿnā laka dhikraka

and (have not) We raised high your mention?

Jaʿfar said: No one mentions you (in connection with) the messengership without mentioning Me (in connection with) the Lordship.

94:7 فَإِذَا فَرَغْتَ فَٱنصَبْ ⑦

fa-idhā faraghta fa'nṣab

then when you are free, exert yourself.

Jaʿfar said: Remember your Lord, while you are empty of everything other than Him.

﴾ 95 ﴿

سُورَةُ التِّينِ

al-Tīn (The Fig)

95:4 لَقَدْ خَلَقْنَا ٱلْإِنسَٰنَ فِىٓ أَحْسَنِ تَقْوِيمٍ ﴿٤﴾

la-qad khalaqna'l-insāna fī aḥsani taqwīmin

We have surely created mankind in the best form.

Jaʿfar said: In the best image.

98

سُورَةُ البَيِّنَةِ

al-Bayyinah (The Clear Proof)

98:8 رَّضِيَ ٱللَّهُ عَنْهُمْ وَرَضُوا۟ عَنْهُ ۚ

raḍiya'llāhu 'anhum wa raḍū 'anhu

God is pleased with them and they are pleased with Him.

Al-Ṣādiq ﵇ said: *God is pleased with them* in that the divine care and God-given success have already proceeded from God to them; *and they are pleased with Him* in that He blessed them with their following His Messenger and (with) accepting what he brought; and (with) expending their wealth and the best of their efforts[293] [in the service] of the Messenger of God ﷺ.[294]

293 *Muhaj*, singular *muhjah*, has as one of its meanings: 'the best of one's self, one's efforts, endeavours, and energy'. See Lane at *muhjah* under *m-h-j*. Other meanings include 'life, heart, innermost self, core, soul, heartblood' (see Wehr).

294 *Bayna yadayhi*, literally: 'between his hands'. The meaning is that they placed their wealth and efforts at the Messenger's service.

104

سُورَةُ الهُمَزَةِ

al-Humazah (The Slanderer)

104:6–7 نَارُ ٱللَّهِ ٱلْمُوقَدَةُ ۝٦ ٱلَّتِى تَطَّلِعُ عَلَى ٱلْأَفْـِٔدَةِ ۝٧

nāru'llāhi'l-mūqadah. Allatī taṭṭaliʿu ʿalā'l-afʾidah

the kindled fire of God. Which rises up, overwhelming hearts.

[It is related] from Jaʿfar b. Muḥammad [that] he said, concerning [the above] words (of God) ﷻ: The fires are diverse, varied. Among them is the fire of love and gnosis burning in the hearts of the monotheists; while the fires of hell burn in the hearts of the disbelievers. When the fires of love ignite in the heart of the believer, they burn up every eagerness for (what is) other than God, and every remembrance other than His remembrance.[295]

295 Note again the blissful obliteration that is the impact of the blazing presence of the divine qualities. The fires of love/care are to be understood as light, in keeping with the comment at 28:29, where it is said of Moses that he saw a fire; at 27:34, when the conquering King comes in, the town is destroyed of its native (read 'fallen') nature; and as the unveiled vision of God would consume Moses, even so the fires of divine love burn all other than the divine Subject/Object/Content of love.

﴿ 108 ﴾

سُورَةُ الكَوثَرِ

al-Kawthar (Abundance)

108:1 إِنَّآ أَعۡطَيۡنَٰكَ ٱلۡكَوۡثَرَ ١

innā āʿṭaynākaʾl-kawthar[296]

verily We have given you abundance.

Jaʿfar al-Ṣādiq said: That is, a light in your heart which leads you to Me and cuts you off from what is other than Me.

He also said [again interpreting the word *kawthar, abundance*]: (It is) intercession for your community.

296 *Kawthar* is the name of the supreme river in paradise, source of all paradisal rivers. See Sirāj ad-Dīn, *Book of Certainty*, p. 7.

112

سُورَةُ الإِخْلَاصِ

al-Ikhlāṣ (Faithfulness)

al-Tawḥīd (The Unity)

112:2 ٱللَّهُ ٱلصَّمَدُ ﴿٢﴾

Allāhu'l-Ṣamad[297]

God, the everlasting, self-sufficient, besought Lord.

Jaʿfar said: *The everlasting, self-sufficient, besought Lord* who gave to His creation from His knowledge only the Name and the quality.[298]

Jaʿfar [also] said: *al-Ṣamad* [contains] five letters: The *alif* indicates His indivisible oneness (*aḥadīyah*). The *lām* indicates His divinity (*ulūhīyah*). These two letters are assimilated, they do not manifest upon the tongue (in the uttered word) but do manifest in writing. This shows that His indivisible unity and His divinity are hidden, not known through the senses; and that He cannot be compared to people. The concealment (of these two letters) in the spoken word is an indication that the intelligence cannot perceive Him nor yet comprehend Him through knowledge. While the manifestation (of these two letters) in writing is an indication that He manifests in the hearts of the sages

297 *Ṣamad* (a lord whom people and things repair to, turn to, resort to, betake themselves to). Also, a lord to whom obedience is due, and being that continues everlastingly. See Lane at *ṣamad* under *ṣ-m-d*. The word occurs but once in the Qurʾān and it is applied to God alone.

298 *Ṣifah* (plural *ṣifāt*) is often used with reference to the divine attributes or qualities which are directly linked with the divine names; for example, the divine names al-Raḥmān and al-Raḥīm express the divine quality of *raḥmah* (mercy); and the divine name al-Qādir expresses the divine quality of *qudrah* (power).

and that He appears to the eyes of the lovers in the Abode of Peace.

The *ṣād* is an indication that He is truthful in what He promises: His act is sincerity (*ṣidq*), His speech is sincerity (*ṣidq*), and He summons His slaves to sincerity (*ṣidq*). The *mīm* is an indication of His sovereignty (*mulk*) for He is the Sovereign King (*malik*) in reality. The *dāl* is the mark of His permanence (*dawām*) in His eternal future and His eternal past—although there is neither past-eternity nor future-eternity for they are but terms which are used among His slaves according to the [perspective of] temporal variation.[299]

112:3 لَمْ يَلِدْ وَلَمْ يُولَدْ ۝٣

lam yalid wa-lam yūlad

He did not beget nor was He begotten.

Jaʿfar said: Majestic is our Lord (beyond) that delusive imaginations, intelligences, or sciences should perceive Him. Rather He is as He described Himself—and the modality[300] of His description is not

---

299 Physical time pertains to the realm of dense matter. In the spiritual realm there is a subtler form of duration (which encompasses dense time), with a greater flexibility and easier directional movement. In the higher echelons of the subtle realm, and of being as a whole, duration is ever more purified, ever more supple, and ever more still. Within beyond being, at the level of non-individuation, the differences of temporal direction and movement disappear completely in the totally pure, absolute stillness of God's unindividuated Self. The Presence of the absolutely still Self is every 'where', all the 'time'. This still Self of God is present through all levels of beyond being and being, through all levels of existence/creation. Not only does God encompass and transcend all duration and location, He permeates them. Wherever, whenever, in His essential Self, He transcends the terms of time. *Wheresoever you turn*, temporally or spatially, *there is the face/identity/self of God.*

300 *Wa'l-kayfiyyah ʿan waṣfihi ghayru maʿqūlah* might also be rendered: 'and (to pose the question of) "how?" concerning His description is absurd'. *Kayfiyyah* became an important point in the anthropomorphist (*tashbīh*) / deanthropomorphist (*tanzīh*) debate in Islamic theology. Ibn Ḥanbal used the phrase *bilā kayf* (literally, 'without asking how') to mean that God's description of Himself in the Qurʾān should be accepted without any questions. Later Ḥanbalīs such as Ibn Ḥanbal's own son, were more

intellectually perceivable. Glory to Him (beyond) that understandings or intelligences should attain to His modality! *everything is perishing save for His Face/Essence* (28:88). To Him belongs eternal subsistence, beginningless and endless eternity, eternal future, onliness, will and power;[301] blessed and most high is He!

قُلْ هُوَ ٱللَّهُ أَحَدٌ ﴿١﴾ ٱللَّهُ ٱلصَّمَدُ ﴿٢﴾ لَمْ يَلِدْ وَلَمْ يُولَدْ ﴿٣﴾

112:1–4 وَلَمْ يَكُن لَّهُۥ كُفُوًا أَحَدٌۢ ﴿٤﴾

qul: huwa'llāhu aḥad. Allāhu'l-Ṣamad. Lam yalid wa-lam yūlad. Wa-lam yakun lahu kufuwan aḥad

say: He, God, is one. God, the everlasting, self-sufficient, besought Lord. He does not beget nor is He begotten. And there is nothing equal or comparable to Him.[302]

[It is related] from Jaʿfar b. Muḥammad concerning His (above) words:

---

anthropomorphist, almost corporealists. Abū al-Ḥasan al-Ashʿarī's attitude of *bilā kayf* was somewhat different and was based on the equation of *kayfiyyah* with *tashbīh* (anthropomorphism). For al-Ashʿarī, *bilā kayf* meant that one affirmed the divine attributes or qualities without equating them with human attributes or qualities. This principle was known as *al-ithbāt bi-ghayri tashbīh* (affirmation without anthropomorphism). (Thanks are due to Toby Mayer for help with this note.)

301 That is, eternal subsistence (*baqā'*), beginningless and endless eternity (*sarmadīyah*), eternal future (*abadīyah*), onliness (*waḥdānīyah*), will (*mashī'ah*) and power (*qudrah*);

302 To pick up on the linguistic lead of this *sūrah*, God, who is the very essence of the masculine and feminine principles, contains within Himself all levels and inhabitants of creation: beyond-being and being (like the unejaculated seed is contained in the paternal loins and the unbegotton babe in the maternal womb, respectively). Never is anything outside of God—for God does not beget: the whole of undifferentiated existence is within the divine 'loins'; the whole of differentiated being is as the unborn babe in the divine 'womb'. Metaphysically speaking, God is the full androgynous parent. Nothing encompasses Him, nor is He begotton from another for there is no existence nor existent other than God's unique Self-existence. God is sui generic. The first verse of *Sūrat al-Ikhlāṣ* is

This means: He has manifested what the souls desire in the written form of the letters. For the deepest realities are well-guarded from being attained by delusive imagination or understanding. The manifestation of that in letters is so that he be rightly guided who *gives ear* (5:37); it is an allusion to the Unseen. The letter *hāʾ* (of the word *huwa*) tells of the immutable reality[303] [of God] while the (letter) *waw* is an allusion to that which is hidden from the senses.

---

a statement of oneness, *aḥadīyah*; it pertains to the level of the *kunh*, beyond beyond-being, which encompasses, but also transcends, beyond-being. With the use of the name *al-Ṣamad*, the second verse states both the Self-sufficiency of the one Divinity/Existence, but also introduces duality through this same name which also means 'the Lord to whom others resort to'; this duality pertains to both beyond-being (through indviduation) and to being (through differentiation). In graphic and easily comprehensible terms, the third verse describes, first, the condition of duality as being contained within the Oneness, not outside of it; and second, the condition of the Oneness not being outside anything else that it might have issued from. The fourth verse sums this up in a statement of the utter uniqueness of the One, all-encompassing Divinity, and rejoins the first verse through the oneness. The *sūrah* provides a divinely succinct and comprehensive metaphysical description.

303 *Maʿnā thābit*. The word *thābit* (fixed, established, constant) is a specific term in later Islamic philosophy that denotes 'ontological subsistence'. Likewise, the word *maʿnā* (meaning, reality, mental image, idea), in Islamic philosophical discourse, is used specifically for an idea/concept as opposed to a material entity. In Lane, the *maʿnā* of something is said to be termed *māhīyah* if it is the response to the question *mā huwa*? (what is it?); *huwīyah* if the subject is being distinguished from others; and *ḥaqīqah* when the subject is being considered as objectively existing. Perhaps we have here the earliest extant use of this phrase as precursor of later philosophical terms.

Al-Aḥad (the One), is the sole one (*al-fard*) who has no equivalent, for He is the one who unifies the (multiple) individuations (*al-āḥād*).[304]

وَٱلْحَمْدُ لِلَّهِ رَبِّ ٱلْعَالَمِينَ وَبِهِ نَسْتَعِينُ آمِين

304 This last comment is a marvellous, pithy explanation of the indivisible unity of God. Initially it is seemingly paradoxical: God is the indivisible One (*al-Aḥad*), yet 'He is the one who unifies the multiple individuations'. But it is not contradictory; rather it is an affirmation of two facts: 'simplexity' and complexity. His unity contains multiplicity within itself. God as a totality is indivisible; a segment or part of Him cannot be detached from Him and set apart from Him. But within His sole one Self, He contains the whole multiplicity of individuated and differentiated creation, of multiple levels of existence and being.

Glossary

ʿabd, pl. *ʿibād*: slave; a being that is absolutely and totally receptive to the Lord (*Rabb*) and to His influx
abad: future eternity
abadīyah: future eternity; God's eternal future
al-Aḥad: the One (divine name); *al-āḥād*: multiple individuations
aḥadīyah: (God's) unity, His unindividuated oneness; total oneness
ʿahd: pledge
ahwāʾ, sing. *hawan:* desires, whims, passions, longings, inclinations
ajal: the appointed time, moment of death, deadline
akhlāq: moral qualities; innate characteristics
akwān, sing. *kawn*: beings
ālāʾ, sing. *ilan*: divine favours
albāb, sing. *lubb:* spiritual minds, inmost spiritual consciousness
amānī, sing. *umniya:* desirous demands, longings
amr: command (particularly the divine command)
ʿaql: intellect
ʿarsh: throne, specifically the divine throne
aṣfiyāʾ: see *ṣafīy*
ʿaṭf: compassion
awṣāf, sing. *waṣf*: attributes, qualities, characteristics
āyah, pl. *āyāt*: sign, verse of the Qurʾān
ʿayn: eye, essence, core, fountain, spring
pl. *aʿyun*: eyes (*bi aʿyuninā*: under Our eye (of God))
pl. *aʿyān*: essences
pl. *ʿuyūn*: springs, fountains
azal: pre-eternity, beyond being
azalīyah: prior eternity; God's eternal past
ʿaẓamah: the divine sublimity
bahāʾ: (God's) brilliance
al-Barr: the Beneficient (divine name)
baqāʾ: eternal subsistence
bāqin: subsistent
al-Bāqī: the Eternally Subsistent (divine name)
baṣīrah: the faculty of spiritual sight, of subtle seeing/vision
bāṭil: falsehood
bāṭin: the inward, concealed dimension; *Bāṭin*, the Hidden One (God), the unseen
birr: beneficence

ḍamīr, pl. *ḍamāyir/ḍamāʾir:* conscience
darak: attainment
daran: dirt
daran al-mukhālafah/āt: the spiritual dirt or pollution of op-posing God or of being in disharmony with the divine qualities
dawām: permanence; continuity
daymūmīyah: (the divine) permanence
Dhāt: essence, specifically, the divine essence
dhawq: taste; actual personal experience of something
dhikr: remembrance, recollection
dhikru'llāh: the remembrance of God, the practice of invoking God's name/s
dhikrā: recollection or remembrance due to being reminded
dīn: religion
al-dunyā: the lowest (i.e. physical) world; worldliness
faḍl: (God's) Grace
fahm: understanding, comprehension
fanāʾ / *fanā fī'llāh:* extinction, annihilation, effacement in God: of the soul and of all other than God
fānin: transient
faqr: neediness (to God)
faqīr, pl. *fuqarāʾ*: the person who is needy to God and empty for Him
fardanīyah: (the divine) uniqueness, singularity
fawāʾid, sing. *fāʾidah:* benefits, advantages, profits, good, knowledge
fitnah: temptation
fuʾād, pl. *afʾidah*: mind, heart
futūwah: chivalry, nobleness, honourableness, generosity
ḥāl, pl. *aḥwāl*: state (esp. spiritual); condition
ḥamd: praise
al-Ḥaqq: God the Truth, the Reality, the Fact
ḥaqīqah, pl. *ḥaqāʾiq*: reality, truth, specifically, the deepest Truth/Reality in the human, the manifestation of the divine lights at the core of the spiritual heart; the level of interpretation pertinent to the holy content of the spiritual heart
ḥayāʾ: shame
ḥayāh: life
haybah: awe, awesomeness
ḥayrah: bewilderment
ḥifẓ al-qalb: protection of the heart
ḥikmah: wisdom
hudā: right guidance
ḥukm: ordinance, ruling, decree, judgement; specifically, the divine ordinance
ḥurmah: sacredness, sanctity, dignity, honour, inviolability; respect, reverence, veneration

huwīyah: the divine Identity or Ipseity
ḥuwah: a state of fortunateness, nearness to the heart, being beloved
ʿibārah: literal expression, the literal text
idrāk: perception
iftiqār: neediness (to God)
iḥāṭah: encompassment; the realised knowledge of being totally encompassed by God
iḥsān: goodness
ījād: birth in being
ikhlāṣ: faithfulness
ikhtiṣāṣ: distinction; specifically, being chosen for divinely conferred spiritual privileges
ʿilal, sing. *ʿillah:* causes, weaknesses, deficiencies
ʿilm, pl. *ʿulūm*: knowledge
ʿilm al-ḥurūf: knowledge of the esoteric significance of letters
ʿilm ladunī: knowledge bestowed by God directly
īmān: faith, belief in God
ʿināyah: God's pre-eternal, continual loving care for His creatures
infiṣāl: detachment
iqtirāb: drawing close
irādah, pl. *irādāt*: wish, desire, intention, volition, decree, specifically, the potent divine intention
ishārah, pl. *ishārāt*: allusion, indication; the level of interpretation pertinent to the distinguished/elite (*khawāṣṣ*)
ʿishq: passionate love
islām: submission/surrender to God; receptivity to the influx of the divine qualities
ʿiṣmah: infallibility, impeccability, purity, divine-preservation from sin and error, innocence
iṣṭifāʾīyah: pre-election by God, being chosen by God
istiqāmah: integrity
istikānah: quiescence, quietude, submissiveness
istitār: the divine Self-veiling
ithbāt: affirmation, specifically the affirmation of 'except God' after the negation in the testimonial of faith: 'there is no God except God'
iṭṭilāʿ: beholding
iṭṭiṣāl: attachment, conjunction, attaining to union
ʿiwaḍ: replacement, specifically the replacement of the human qualities by the divine ones; recompense
ʿiyān: eye-witnessing, seeing with one's own eyes
  muʿāyin: one who views or sees
iẓhār: manifestation, to make clear, to make apparent
jafr: the esoteric interpretation of letters
jaḥīm: hellfire

Jalāl: the divine majesty
jannah, pl. *jannāt*: a paradisal garden
kāfir, pl. *kuffār, kāfirūn*: one who denies God by veiling the divine lights with the darkness of his sins
kalām: speech
kalām Allāh: the speech or Word of God, the Qurʾān
karam: generosity
karāmah: munificence, favour, mark of honour
pl. *karāmāt*: specifically miracles that are vouchsafed to saints
kawn: being
kayfīyah: modality, nature
khabar, pl. *akhbār*: reported sayings from the Prophet and the Imams
khalwah: solitude with God
khawf: fear
khawāṣṣ, sing. *khāṣṣ*: distinguished people; elite
khayrāt, sing. *khayrah:* good deeds, blessings
khidmah: service
khidmat Allāh: the service of God (to serve God)
khiṭāb: God's direct oration to the heart
khushūʿ: humility
kibriyāʾ: (divine) magnificence
kufr: disbelief in God, to deny God, to veil or obscure (God's light)
kullīyah: totality, 'allness'
kunh: core, essential nature, substance; the unindividuated essence of God.
kursī: (the divine) seat, chair
al-Laṭīf: the Kind (divine name)
laṭīfah, pl. *laṭāʾif*: subtlety; the level of interpretation pertinent to sanctity of soul, with reference to the subtle realm
ladhdhah: rapture, joy, delight
lawḥ: the heavenly tablet
lubb: see *albāb*
luṭf: kindness
maḥabbah: love
maʿānī/maʿānin, sing. *maʿnā/maʿnan*: significances, meanings, concepts, good characteristics, qualities
maḥall: locus, place
al-maḥall al-adnā: the place of closest proximity
māʾīyah: quiddity, quintessence, sap, juice
majd: (God's) glory
malak, pl. *malāʾikāt*: angel
al-Mālik: the Sovereign King (divine name)
maqām, pl. *maqāmāt*: station, rank, standing position; tone (sound), musical mode
marḍāt: gratification

maʿrifah: gnosis, spiritual knowledge, mystical knowledge, realisatory knowledge
Marwah: a hill in Mecca; symbol of the heroic soul
mashhad: the place of the assembly of witnessing; assembly, meeting
mashīʾah: will, wish; specifically, the divine will
mawaddah: devoted love, friendship
mawʿiẓah: spiritual counsel
mawāqif, sing. *mawqif:* way stations, stopping places, stands
miʿrāj: specifically, the Prophet's spiritual/mystical (re-)ascent to God, riding through the seven heavens on the spiritual steed named Burāq, accompanied by Gabriel upto the furthest boundary; the (re-)ascending spiritual journey of the soul/spirit to God
mīthāq: covenant
    al-mīthāq al-awwal: the first covenant; the primordial covenant made between God, Lord of all, and all humanity in potentia: 'Am I not your Lord? (*A-lastu bi-Rabbikum*)', 'Indeed you are (*Balā*)!'
muʿāyanah: eye to eye
muhjah, pl. *muhaj*: best effort, energy, life blood, innermost self, core, heart
mukhālafah, pl. *mukhālafāt*: opposition/contrast (to God)
al-Muʿīd: the Restorer (divine name)
mulāḥaẓah: perception
mulk: authority, sovereignty, power, dominion
munājah, pl. *munājāt:* secret converse with God
al-Munʿim: the Bestower (divine name)
murūwah: heroic valor/virtues, chivalry, knightly behaviour
muṣḥaf, pl. *maṣāḥif:* copy or edition of the Qurʾān
mushāhadah: witnessing by seeing or being present or by personal experience
muṭālaʿah: beholding
muwāfaqah (bi'llāh): to be in harmony (with God)
nabī, pl. *anbiyāʾ*: prophet
nafī: negation, specifically the negation in the Islamic testimonial of faith (see *ithbāt* above)
nafs, pl. *nufūs/anfus*: soul, specifically lower soul; ego
nahī: prohibition
naḥīzah: natural disposition
naʿīm: bliss
naʿt, pl. *nuʿūt*: qualities, characteristics, description
naẓar: (God's) gaze; seeing; perception
al-naẓar ilā'llāh: the gazing at God; looking at God
    al-naẓar bi nūri'l-ʿilm: perception through the light of knowledge
nifāq: hypocrisy
niʿmah, pl. *niʿam:* blessing
nubūwah: prophethood, prophecy
nūr: Light

qabḍah: the divine grasp
qaḍāʾ: the divine decree; fate
qadar, pl. *aqdār*: destiny; rank
al-Qadīm: the Pre-existent One (divine name)
al-Qahhār: the Irresistible (divine name)
qalb: heart, specifically the spiritual heart
qawl: word/s, speech
qanāʿah: temperance
qanūʿ, pl. *qunuʿ:* to be content, temperate
qudrah: the divine power
qurb / *qurbah*: closeness/proximity (to God)
qūwah: strength, power, potency
raḥmah: the divine mercy
al-Raḥmān: the Gracious (divine name)
al-Raḥīm: the Merciful (divine name)
rajāʾ: hope
rasūl, pl. *rusul*: Messenger (of God)
riʿāyah: (divine) care/charge (for His creatures)
riḍāʾ/ riḍā: satisfaction, pleasure, delight, contentment
riḍwān: God's pleasure
risālah: message; messengership, prophetic mission
rubūbīyah: the divine Lordship; the Divinity
rūḥ: Spirit;
pl. *arwāḥ*: spirits; individuations of the One Spirit
ruʾyah: seeing, beholding
ruʾyāʾ: a vision in the sense of apparition or mental vision
saʿādah: felicity, happiness, bliss
sabab, pl. *asbāb:* cause, means, link
ṣabr: patience
ṣādiq, pl. *ṣādiqūn*: truthful, faithful, sincere, veracious ones
Ṣafā: a hill in Mecca; symbol of the individuated, differentiated spirit
ṣafāʾ: serenity, purity
ṣafīy, pl. *aṣfiyāʾ*: bosom friend, intimate companion
safīr: ambassador (of God)
sakhāʾ: liberality, munificence, generosity
al-Sakīnah: the Peace of the Presence of God
al-Salām: Peace (divine name)
sālik: traveller, specifically the spiritual aspirant; an exact equivalent of the ʿjourneyman' of the alchemists
al-Ṣamad: the Everlasting, Self-sufficient, besought Lord (divine name)
ṣamadīyah: the absolute Self-sufficiency of God
sanāʾ: (God's) resplendence
sarāyir/Sarāʾir, sing. *sarīrah:* secret reaches of the soul, secret thoughts; mind/s, soul/s

sarmadīyah: beginningless and endless eternity of God
shabḥun: a bodily, corporeal form; an apparition, indistinct shape, ghost, phantom
shafāʿah: intercession
shafaqah: compassion, sympathy, loving care, solicitude
shahādah: testimony; the Islamic testimonial of faith: *lā ilāha illā'llāh,* 'there is no God except God'.
shaqāwah: misery, misfortune, distress
sharīʿah, pl. *sharāʾiʿ:* revealed ʿlaws' i.e. guiding prinicples for way of life
shawq: yearning
ṣiddīq, pl. *ṣiddiqūn*: truthful, honest, sincere, veracious, loyal
ṣidq: sincerity, truthfulness, veracity, faithfulness
ṣifah, pl. *ṣifāt*: quality, attribute, description
sirr, pl. *asrār:* secret, specifically, the divine secret embedded in the human; the inmost self; in the text, *sirr* is almost synonymous with *ḥaqīqah*
sukūn: peace, clam, tranquillity
Sunnah: custom/s of the Prophet; norm or convention
surūr: joy
tadhakkur: recollection
tafsīr: explanation, exposition, interpretation, commentary (esp. scriptural)
tafwīḍ: entrustment (of one's affairs to God); to give God full power over one's affairs
taḥqīq bi'l-Ḥaqq: realisation of the Truth, God-realisation
tajallī: divine Self-disclosure; theophany, divine manifestation
taslīm: consent, surrender, acceptance
taṭbīq: the interpretive method of analogous correspondences
tawāḍuʿ: humility
tawakkul: trusting reliance upon God
tawfiq: God-given success (in goodness)
tawḥīd: God's oneness, belief in and affirmation of it; monotheism
taʾwīl: a method of symbolic interpretation through associated meanings based on the constituent letters of words and their verbal roots
tawlīyah: governance
thiqqah bi'llāh: confidence in God
ṭumaʾnīnah: tranquillity, serenity, equanimity, the composure that comes through confidence (in God)
ʿubūdīyah: slavehood, the creature's receptivity towards the Lord
ʿujb: self-admiration, pride, vanity, conceit
ulfah: intimate love
ulūhīyah: Godhood; divinity
ummu'l-kitāb: literally, the 'Mother of the Book', the original source of scripture; the archetype of all revealed books
uns: intimacy
wafāʾ: faithful fulfillment

waḥdanīyah: onliness of God; His uniqueness
al-Wāḥid*:* the Only (divine name)
wāḥidīyah: (God's) singularity and onliness; the fact that He is alone and unique
walah: rapture
walāyah: divine friendship, sanctity
athār al-walāyah—the effects/traces of sanctitiy/divine friendship
waqār: dignity
walī (ref. to God): protecting friend, patron
walīyu'llāh / *walī* pl. *awliyā'*: friend of God, saint
wuṣlah: means of attachment (to God)
yaqīn: certainty
Ẓāhir: the Manifest One (God), the outward, external dimension, the literal, the obvious, visible aspect
ẓālim: sinner, one who produces darkness in his soul
zulfah: intimate closeness
ẓulm: darkness, sin; the darkness of sin in the soul
zūr: 'falsehood' in a general sense; specifically, something false that is taken as lord or worshipped in place of God

Select Bibliography

ʿAbd al-Bāqī, Fuʾād. *Al-muʿjam al-mufahris li-alfaẓ al-Qurʾān al-karīm*. Cairo: Dār al-Ḥadīth, 1988.

Abul Quasem, M. *The Recitation and Interpretation of the Quran: al-Ghazzālī's Theory.* London/Boston: Kegan Paul International, 1982.

Ali, Abudullah Yusuf. *The Meaning of the Glorious Qur'an*. London: Nadim and Co., 1983.

Arberry, A. J. (ed. and trans.). *The Mawāqif and Mukhātabāt of Muḥammad b. ʿAbdi 'l-Jabbār al-Niffarī*. Cambridge: Gibb Memorial Trust, (reprint) 1978.

Asad, Muhammad. *The Message of the Qurʾān*. Gibralter: Dar al-Andalus, 1984.

Ayoub, Mahmoud, *The Qurʾān and Its Interpreters.* Albany: State University of New York Press, 1984.

al-ʿAyyāshī, Abū al-Naḍr M. b. Maṣʿūd al-Samarqandī. *Kitāb al-Tafsīr*. Qum: Chāpkhāna-yi ʿIlmīyah, 1961–2.

Böwering, Gerhard. *The Minor Qurʾān Commentary of Abū ʿAbd ar-Raḥmān Muḥammad b. al-Ḥusayn as-Sulamī (d. 412/1021)*. Beirut: Dār al-Mashriq, 1997.

——. 'The Qurʾān Commentary of al-Sulamī.' In *Islamic Studies presented to Charles J. Adams*. Leiden: Brill, 1991.

Chittick, William. *A Shiʿite Anthology*. London: Muhammadi Trust, 1980.

Crow, Douglas. *The Teaching of Jaʿfar al-Ṣādiq, with Reference to his Place in Early Shīʿism*. Thesis, McGill University, Montreal, 1980.

Daftary, F. *Ismāʿīlīs in Medieval Muslim Societies*. London: I.B.Tauris and the Institute of Ismaili Studies, 2005.

Danner, Victor. 'The Early Development of Sufism.' In *Islamic Spirituality: Foundations*, pp. 239–264. London: SCM Press Ltd., 1989.

Ernst, Carl. *Words of Ecstasy in Sufism*. Albany: State University of New York Press, 1985.

Godwin, J. *Harmonies of Heaven and Earth: The Spiritual Dimension of Music from Antiquity to the Avant-Garde*. London: Thames & Hudson, 1987.

Grill, Denis. 'Adab and Revelation.' In *Muhyiddin b. ʿArabi, A Commemorative Volume*, edited by Stephen Hirtenstein and Michael Tiernan, pp. 228–63. Rockport, MA: Element Books, 1993.

Habil, Abdurrahman. 'Traditional Esoteric Commentaries on the Quran.' In *Islamic Spirituality: Foundations*, pp. 24–47. London: SCM Press Ltd., 1989.

Hamza, F., S. Rizvi, and F. Mayer (eds.). *An Anthology of Qur'anic Commentaries*, vol. 1: *On the Nature of the Divine*. London: Oxford University Press and the Institute of Ismaili Studies, 2008.

Hodgson, M. G. S. *The Venture of Islam*. Chicago: University of Chicago Press, 1974.

Ibn ʿInabah, Jamāl al-Dīn Aḥmad b. ʿĀlī. *ʿUmdat al-ṭālib*. Najaf: Manshūrāt al-Maṭbaʿah al-Ḥaydarīyah, 1961.

Imam Jaʿfar al-Sadiq. *The Lantern of the Path*. Translated by M Bilgrami. Dorset, UK: Element Books/ Zahra Publications, 1989.

al-Kūfī, Furāt b. Furāt. *Tafsīr*. Beirut: Muʿassasat al-Nuʿmān, 1992.

al-Kulaynī, Abū Jaʿfar M. b. Yaʿqūb. *al-Uṣūl min al-kāfī*. Tehran: Dār al-Kutub al-Islāmīyah, 1968.

Lane, E. W. *Arabic-English Lexicon*. Cambridge, UK: Islamic Texts Society, 1984.

Lings, Martin. *Muhammad: His Life based on Earliest Sources*. Rochester, VT: Inner Traditions, 1983.

Massignon, Louis. *Essai sur les origines du lexique technique de la mystique musulmane*. Paris: J. Vrin, 1954.

———. 'La méditation coranique et les origines du lexique soufi.' *Actes Congress International Histoire des Religions* 2 (1923), pp. 412–414.

McCarthy, R. J. *Al-Ghazali: Deliverance From Error*. Louisville, KY: Fons Vitae, 2004.

Meri, Josef (ed.). *Medieval Islamic Civilisation*. New York: Routledge, 2006.

Mojaddedi, Jawid. *The Biographical Tradition in Sufism*. Surrey, UK: Curzon Press, 2001.

Momen, Moojan. *An Introduction to Shiʿi Islam*. Oxford: George Ronald Publishers, 1985.

al-Nuʿmān, Abū Ḥanīfah b. Muḥammad al-Tamīmī al-Maghribī. *Sharḥ al-akhbār fī faḍāʾil al-aʾimma al-athār*. Qum: Muʾassasat al-Nashr al-Islāmī, n. d.

———. *Daʿāʾim al-islām*. Translated by A. A. Fyzee and I. K. Poonawala as *The Pillars of Islam*. Oxford: Oxford University Press, 2002.

Nwyia, Paul. '*Le Tafsīr Mystique*, attribué à Gaʿfar Ṣādiq.' In *Mélanges de l'Université Saint-Joseph* 43, pp. 179–230. Beirut: Imprimerie Catholique, 1968.

———. *Exégèse coranique et langage mystique*. Beirut: Librairie Orientale, 1970.

Pearce, Stewart. *The Alchemy of Voice*. London: Hodder Mobius, 2005.

Pickthall, Muhammad. *The Glorious Koran*. London: George Allen and Unwin, 1980.

Qāshānī, ʿAbd al-Razzāq. *Tafsīr al-Qurʾān al-karīm li'l Shaykh al-akbar Ibn ʿArabī*. Beirut: Dār al-Andalūs, 1981.

———. *Iṣṭilāḥāt al-Ṣūfīyah*. Translated by Nabil Safwat as *A Glossary of Sufi Technical Terms*. London: Octagon Press Ltd., 1991.

Qummī, ʿAbbās b. M. Riḍā. *al-Anwār al-bahīyah fī tawārīkh al-ḥujaj al-ilāhīyah*. Qum: Muʾassasat al-Nashr al-Islāmī, 1996–97.

al-Qummī, ʿAlī b. Ibrāhīm. *Tafsīr*. Beirut: Muʾassasat al-Aʿlamī li'l-Maṭbuʿāt, 1991.

Richard, Yann. *Shi'ite Islam: Polity, Ideology, and Creed.* Translated by Antonia Nevill. Oxford, UK: Blackwell, 1995.

Sachedina, A. A. 'The Significance of Kāshī's *Rijāl*'. *Logos Islamikos.* Toronto: Pontifical Institute of Mediaeval Studies, 1984.

Savoury, R. M. and D. Agius (eds). *Logos Islamikos, Studia Islamica.* Toronto: Pontifical Institute of Mediaeval Studies, 1984.

Sells, Michael. *Early Islamic Mysticism.* New York: Paulist Press, 1996.

Shahrastānī, ʿAbd al-Karīm. *Kitāb al-milal wa'l-nihal.* Translated by A. K. Kazi and J. G. Flynn as *Muslim Sects and Divisions.* London: Kegan Paul International, 1984.

Sirāj ad-Dīn, Abū Bakr. *The Book of Certainty.* Cambridge: Islamic Texts Society, 1992.

Ṭabāṭabāʾī, Muḥammad Ḥusayn. *Shiʿite Islam.* Translated by Seyyed Hossein Nasr. Albany: State University of New York Press, 1977.

Taylor, John. 'Jaʿfar al-Ṣādiq: Spiritual Forbear of the Ṣūfīs'. *Islamic Culture* 40, no. 2, 1966. pp. 97–113.

Wehr, Hans. *A Dictionary of Modern Written Arabic.* Edited by J. Milton Cowan. Beirut: Librairie du Liban, 1980.

Index of Qurʾānic Verses

General Index

Lordship (*rubūbīyah*), li, 22, 23, 26, 27, 29, 37, 38, 116, 139, 187
lote tree, li, 38
love, xvi, xix, xxiii, xxiv, xxxix, xl, xlii, xliii, xlv, xlvii, xlviii, xlix, l, li, lix, lxiv, lxv, 19, 22, 23, 30, 39, 41, 49, 54, 55, 56, 59, 60, 64, 66, 70, 71, 76, 98, 102, 105, 109, 113, 114, 124, 128, 134, 135, 148, 152, 154, 167, 185, 190
lower soul, xxi, xxxiv, xxxv, xxxvi, xxxvii, lvii, 62, 63, 65, 83, 103, 104, 110, 122, 183
lowest world, 41, 68, 150
lubb (pl. *albāb*; kernal, essence, innermost), 60

maʿānī (sing. *maʿnan*; qualities), xxiii, 38, 79
maʿnā (meaning, reality), 195
macrocosm, xxxi, xxxii, xxxv, xlvii, l, li, lv, 62, 89, 114, 124, 151, 176, 179
madhhab, xiv
maḥabbah (*maḥabbat*; love), xvi, xxiv, xlii, lxiv, lxv, 76
maḥall (locus), xxiv, 61
maḥall al-mushāhadah, 149
māhīyah (quiddity), xxiii, 5, 195
māʾīyah (quiddity, quintessence), xxiii, 5
majd (glory), xxxiv, 5
malak (angel), xxxvi, xli, xlv
malakīyah (angelic), xlvii
Mālik b. Anas, xv
Manifest (al-Ẓāhir; name of God), 162
manifestation, xlvi, l, lii, lxi, 89, 94, 101, 116, 161, 162, 176, 192, 195
mansions, of the heart, lxv, 102
mansions (verse), xxiv, lxiii, lxiv, lxv, 14, 102
maqām (pl. maqāmat; stations), xxiv, lxiii, 11, 72, 74, 88
maʿrifah (gnosis, spiritual knowledge), xvi, xxi, xxiv, lxiv, 7, 8, 9, 69, 75, 76
Marwah, xxxi, xxxii, xxxiv, xxxvii, xxxviii, xxxix, xl, xliv, xlix, lvii, 11, 12, 115, 134, 167, 183
Mary, lii, liii, 83, 84
mashhad (witnessing), xvi, 85
mashīʾah (will), 31, 194
Massignon, Louis, xxiv, xxvi, xxix, 17
mawaddah (devoted love), 70, 134
mawḍiʿ (rank, position, location), xlv
mayyit (dying, dead), 127
Merciful (al-Raḥīm; name of God), xxv, xxxiii, 1, 3, 5, 6, 8, 91
message, xlv, l, liii, 10, 28, 32, 38, 67, 88, 137, 182
Messenger (of God), xvii, l, 29, 32, 43, 48, 50, 100, 101, 121, 135, 140, 163, 189
microcosm, xxxi, xxxiv, xxxv, xlvii, l, lii, lv, 7, 38, 62, 89, 95, 114, 124, 167, 176, 179
Mighty (ʿAzīz; name of God), 161
Mīkāʾīl (Michael), 98
miracles, 6, 70, 112, 127
miʿrāj (ascent), xlvii, xlviii, lix, 74
mīthāq (covenant), 22
modality, xxxvi, 193, 194
Moses, xli, xliii, xliv, xlv, xlvi, xlix, li, lii, liii, lix, lx, 36, 37, 38, 39, 40, 53, 76, 77, 81, 86, 87, 88, 111, 112, 190
muhājirūn (emigrants), 49
Muḥammad, Prophet, xlvii, l, li, lii, liii, liv, lix, 19, 29, 30, 38, 65, 69, 140, 145, 150, 170
al-Muʿīd (Restorer; name of God), 182
muʿjizah (miracle), 70

RECTIFICATIF

Une erreur s'est glissée dans nos pages de titre. Nous nous en excusons auprès de nos lecteurs.

Chaque tome nouveau des *Mélanges de l'Université Saint-Joseph* présente les mémoires et articles rédigés pendant l'année précédente.

Publié en 1968 ce tome XLIII devrait donc porter le millésime de 1967.

Nous prions nos lecteurs de bien vouloir rectifier eux-mêmes pour qu'il n'y ait pas de discordance entre la tomaison et le millésime.

La Direction

MÉLANGES DE L'UNIVERSITÉ SAINT - JOSEPH

TOME XLIII FASC. 4

PAUL NWYIA, S. J.

LE TAFSĪR MYSTIQUE

ATTRIBUÉ A ĞA'FAR ṢĀDIQ

Édition critique

BEYROUTH
IMPRIMERIE CATHOLIQUE
196~~8~~7

LE *TAFSĪR* MYSTIQUE

attribué à Ǧa'far Ṣādiq

Édition critique

Comme pour tant d'autres textes mystiques anciens, l'importance du *Tafsīr* mystique attribué par les soufis sunnites à l'Imām Ǧa'far Ṣādiq (m. 148/765) a été soulignée pour la première fois par L. Massignon dans son *Essai sur le lexique technique de la mystique musulmane* (pp. 201-206). A la même époque, J.F. Ruska consacrait à Ǧa'far une monographie (1) dans laquelle il examinait la mystérieuse question des rapports entre Ǧābir Ibn Ḥayyān et Ǧa'far dont les historiens arabes disent qu'il s'occupa d'alchimie et qui aurait été, au témoignage d'Ibn al-Nadīm lui-même, le maître en sciences occultes de Ǧābir (2). Dans la première partie de son travail, Ruska passe en revue les divers ouvrages attribués à l'Imām Ǧa'far, mais il semble ignorer l'activité exégétique de ce VIe Imām chiite ou la laisse en dehors du champ de ses investigations.

L. Massignon, par contre, centre toute son étude sur le « problème littéraire » que pose l'attribution à Ǧa'far par les milieux soufis sunnites d'un commentaire mystique du Coran. Ce commentaire nous est parvenu dans l'importante compilation de Sulamī intitulée *Ḥaqā'iq al-tafsīr*, et Sulamī lui-même indique, dans son Introduction, qu'il en reproduit la recension établie par Ibn 'Aṭā (m. 309/921). Examinant la question de l'authenticité de ce commentaire, Massignon émet l'opinion suivante: « On ne peut a priori rejeter absolument l'attribution de sentences de ce *tafsīr* mystique

(1) *Arabische Alchemisten*, II, *Ǧa'far al-Ṣādiq, der sechste Imām*, 1924.

(2) V. *Fihrist*, p. 355.

à Ǧa'far, vu les coïncidences doctrinales remarquables que l'on rencontre entre certaines d'entre elles et les fragments de Ǧa'far invoqués de façon indépendante par les Imāmites orthodoxes et par les *ġulāt* (Nuṣayris et Druzes). »

Cette opinion contient deux affirmations majeures que Massignon n'a malheureusement pas pris la peine d'étayer par des preuves. En effet, on aurait aimé savoir ce que sont ces « coïncidences doctrinales » entre le *tafsīr* conservé et transmis par Sulamī et les « fragments » circulant dans les milieux imāmites sous le nom de Ǧa'far Ṣādiq. D'autre part, il eut été nécessaire de faire la preuve de l'indépendance réciproque de ces deux traditions. Car si, dans les milieux chiites, on a pu conserver, de façon indépendante des soufis sunnites, des *ḥadīṯ* donnant le commentaire du VIe Imām sur le Coran, le contraire n'est pas de soi évident. Par contre, il est de plus en plus manifeste que les soufis ont été très ouverts aux idées venant du Chiisme, et rien ne s'oppose à ce qu'ils aient emprunté à quelques sources chiites leur propre recension du commentaire qu'ils attribuent à l'Imām Ǧa'far. Massignon ne met-il pas lui-même en doute la valeur de l'*isnād* de Ḏu-l-Nūn Miṣrī faisant remonter ce *tafsīr* à Ǧa'far *via* Mālik?

L'authenticité de ce *tafsīr* mystique, attribué à Ǧa'far par les soufis, nous renvoie donc aux problèmes fort complexes et encore mal étudiés que soulève l'immense littérature attribuée par les chiites à leurs premiers Imāms.

En ce qui concerne l'Imām Ǧa'far lui-même, il existe par bonheur tout un commentaire du Coran compilé sous son nom par Muḥammad b. Ibrāhīm al-Nu'mānī qui fut disciple de Kulaynī (m. 329/940). Ce commentaire dont une copie existe à la bibliothèque de Bankipore (1) peut être considéré comme le pendant chiite de la recension que nous éditons ici et qui est la recension connue dans les milieux sunnites. La comparaison entre ces deux recensions révèle en fait plus que les « coïncidences doctrinales » dont faisait mention L. Massignon. Nous sommes en présence d'une même

(1) No 1460, 232 folios. Nous remercions vivement notre ami le P. Hambye qui a bien voulu prendre la peine de nous le microfilmer.

œuvre, ayant même inspiration, même style et même contenu spirituel. Bien plus, de part et d'autre, nous retrouvons des sentences qui sont littéralement les mêmes, avec, cependant, des variantes importantes qui indiquent deux sources de transmission différentes. Cette constatation, pour importante qu'elle soit, ne résoud évidemment pas le problème de savoir ce qui, réellement, dans ces *Riwāyāt*, soit sunnites soit chiites, provient de l'Imām Ǧa'far.

Un fait est certain, en ce qui regarde l'histoire du soufisme, et c'est sur ce fait que nous voudrions ici attirer l'attention: quelle que soit l'origine historique de ce *tafsīr* attribué à Ǧa'far, son entrée dans les milieux soufis se situe au moment où se forme la doctrine mystique sunnite et où, possédant un vocabulaire technique varié et précis, les soufis du IIIe siècle tentent de traduire par écrit le développement de leur expérience spirituelle. C'est dire que ce *tafsīr* est un document primordial pour l'étude de la formation du langage technique mystique en Islam. Dans un ouvrage qui est en préparation, nous montrerons en détail tout ce que les grands soufis du siècle d'or doivent à ce commentaire. Massignon y a fait quelques sondages en ce qui concerne l'influence subie par Ḥallāǧ, mais cette influence déborde Ḥallāǧ, puisque le *tafsīr* attribué à Ǧa'far contient les structures mêmes qui seront celles de l'itinéraire mystique suivi par tous les soufis à qui il a fourni aussi les termes techniques les plus importants. Mentionnons ici, à titre d'exemples, la célèbre classification des étapes mystiques en *maqāmāt* et *aḥwāl*. L'opposition entre ces deux concepts n'est certes pas dans les textes que nous éditons, encore que les deux termes soient fréquemment utilisés, mais le *tafsīr* donne à plusieurs reprises une nomenclature des états mystiques où il faut voir la toute première ébauche des listes de *maqāmāt* et *aḥwāl* devenues classiques après le IIIe siècle. Faut-il rappeler aussi les éléments du *ǧafr* — sens ésotérique des lettres de l'alphabet — que le *tafsīr* contient et qui seront repris par les soufis? Soulignons aussi les très importants passages du *tafsīr* qui analysent l'expérience religieuse des personnages bibliques comme Abraham ou Moïse, passages qui donnent le prototype de ce que sera la méditation des soufis sur les versets coraniques touchant ces mêmes personnages bibliques.

Pour toutes ces raisons il importait que ce document exceptionnel ne reste pas plus longtemps ignoré de ceux qui s'intéressent au soufisme. Son édition n'était pourtant pas aisée car, comme nous l'avons dit, nous ne connaissons ce commentaire que par les citations qu'en a faites Sulamī (m. 412/1021) dans ses *Ḥaqā'iq al-tafsīr*. Il fallut tout d'abord les repérer dans une masse d'autres citations, puisque les *Ḥaqā'iq* sont une vaste compilation de textes soufis anciens. Une fois ce travail achevé sur un seul manuscrit, il fallut de nouveau se livrer au même repérage dans deux autres manuscrits afin d'établir une édition critique.

Celle-ci a été, en effet, effectuée d'après trois manuscrits provenant tous les trois des bibliothèques d'Istanbul:

F = Fatih 260 (164 folios). Manuscrit sans date, copié avec soin, d'une écriture très fine, parfois difficile à lire. Nous l'avons adopté comme manuscrit de base et nous n'avons eu que très rarement à nous écarter de ses lectures.

B = Bašir Aġa 36 (338 folios), daté de 1091/1680. Œuvre d'un calligraphe fort distrait qui saute des lignes entières et qui connaît mal son arabe, ce manuscrit est utile surtout pour confirmer la lecture des deux autres manuscrits, écrits beaucoup moins lisiblement. Ses variantes sont rarement intéressantes.

Y = Yeni Cami 43 (384 folios), manuscrit sans date, mais portant attestation de lecture datée de 771/1369; écriture négligée, souvent sans points diacritiques; mais, copié avec soin par un lettré familiarisé avec les termes techniques soufis, le texte en est excellent, parfois même meilleur que Fatih 260.

On sait qu'il existe un grand nombre de manuscrits des *Ḥaqā'iq al-tafsīr* de Sulamī; nous en avons, nous-même, examiné dix dans les seules bibliothèques d'Istanbul et un au British Museum (Or. 9433). Fallait-il collationner tous ces manuscrits avant d'éditer notre texte? Autant dire qu'il ne serait jamais édité! Encouragé par l'exemple de Massignon qui a publié, à partir de quelques manuscrits, les sentences de Ḥallāǧ citées par Sulamī, nous avons pensé que trois manuscrits offraient des garanties suffisantes pour obtenir un texte fidèle autant que possible à l'original.

Le Bouchet-en-Brenne, 22 août 1967

1, CVIII « انا اعطيناك الكوثر » . قال جعفر الصادق : اي نورًا في قلبك دلّك عليّ وقطعك عما سواي .

وقال ايضاً : الشفاعة لأمتك .

2, CXII « الله الصمد » . قال جعفر : الصمد الذي لم يعط لخلقه مــن معرفته الا الاسم والصفة .

وقال جعفر : الصمد خمسة احرف : الالف دليل على احديته . واللام دليل على الوهيته . وهما مدغمان لا يظهران على اللسان ويظهران في الكتابة . فدل ذلك على ان احديته والوهيته خفية لا تدرك بالحواس وانه لا يقاس بالناس . فخفاؤه في اللفظ دليل على ان العقول لا تدركه ولا تحيط به علماً . واظهاره في الكتابة دليل على انه يظهر على قلوب العارفين ويبدو لاعين المحبين في دار السلام .

والصاد دليل على[1] انه صادق فيما وعد ، فعله صدق وكلامه صدق ودعا عباده الى الصدق — والميم دليل على ملكه فهو الملك على الحقيقة — والدال علامة دوامه في ابديته وازليته ، وان كان لا ازل ولا ابد لانهما ألفاظ تجري على العوادي في عباده .

3, CXII « لم يلد ولم يولد » . قال جعفر : جل ربنا عن ان تدركه الاوهام والعقول والعلوم بل هو كما وصف نفسه والكيفية عن وصفه غير معقولة . سبحانه ان تصل الفهوم والعقول الى كيفيته . « كل شيء هالك الا وجهه » . له البقــاء والسرمدية والابدية والوحدانية والمشيئة والقدرة تبارك وتعالى .

4-1, CXII عن جعفر بن محمد في قوله « قل هو الله احد الخ... » . قال : يعني أظهر ما تريده النفوس بتأليف الحروف . فان الحقائق مصونة عن ان يبلغه وهم او فهم . واظهار ذلك بالحروف ليهتدي بها من « القى السمع » وهو اشارة الى غائب . والهاء هو تنبيه على معنى ثابت والواو اشارة الى الغائب عن الحواس و « الاحد » الفرد الذي لا نظير له لانه هو الذي احّد الآحاد[2] .

1) F : — دليل على || 2) B : — وقال جعفر... الذي احد الآحاد .

4, xc « لقد خلقنا الانسان في كبد » . قال جعفر : في بلاء وشدة .

15, xc « يتيماً ذا مقربة » . قال جعفر . هو ما تتقرب به الى ربك في تعهد الايتام وتفقدهم .

7, xciii « ووجدك ضالاً فهدى » . قال جعفر : كنت ضالاً عن محبتي لك في الازل فمننت عليك بمعرفتي .

10-9, xciii « فاما اليتيم فلا تقهر واما السائل فلا تنهر » . قال جعفر : اليتيم العاري عن خلعة الهداية لا تقنطه من رحمتي فاني قادر ان ألبسه لباس الهداية . والسائل اذا سألك عني فدله عليّ بألطف دلالة فاني قريب مجيب .

11, xciii « واما بنعمة ربك فحدث » . قال جعفر : أخبر الخلق بما انعمت عليهم بك[1] وبمكانك .

1, xciv قال جعفر : « الم نشرح لك صدرك » لمشاهدتي ومطالعتي .

4, xciv « ورفعنا لك ذكرك » . قال جعفر : لا يذكرك احد بالرسالة الاّ ذكرني بالربوبية .

7, xciv « فاذا فرغت فانصب » . قال جعفر : اذكر ربك على فراغ منك عن كل ما دونه .

4, xcv « لقد خلقنا الانسان في احسن تقويم » . قال جعفر : احسن صورة .

8, xcviii « رضي الله عنهم ورضوا عنه » . قال الصادق رضي الله عنه : رضي الله عنهم بما سبق لهم من الله العناية والتوفيق . ورضوا عنه بما منّ عليهم بمتابعتهم لرسوله وقبول ما جاء به وانفاقهم الاموال والمهج بين يدي رسول الله صلعم .

7-6, civ عن جعفر بن محمد قال في قوله عز وجل « نار الله الموقدة التي تطلع على الافئدة » قال : النيران شتى مختلفة : فمنها[2] نار المحبة والمعرفة تتقد[3] في افئدة الموحدين . ونيران جهنم تتقد[3] في أفئدة الكافرين . ونيران المحبة اذا اتقدت في قلب المؤمن احترقت[4] كل همة لغير[5] الله وكل ذكر سوى ذكره .

1) F : — بك || 2) F : — فنها || 3) B : تنفذ || 4) Y : تحرق || 5) Y : غير ||

35,LXXVIII لا يسمعون فيها لغواً ولا كذاباً ». قال جعفر : لان الله تعالى ايده[1] بتوفيقه[2] فلا يجرى منه في الدنيا عليه لغو ولا يسمع منه في الحضرة لغو . واللغو ذكر كل مذكور سواه . « ولا كذابا » اي ولا قولا الا القول الصادق بالشهادة على وحدانيته وازليته وفردانيته .

36,LXXVIII « جزاءً من ربك عطاءً حساباً ». قال جعفر : العطاء من الله تعالى على وجهين : في الابتداء الايمان والاسلام من غير مسئلة . والعطاء في الانتهاء[3] التجاوز عن الزلّات والغفلات والمعاصي . ودخول العبد في الجنة برحمته من عطاياه . وكذلك النظر الى وجهه الكريم .

7, LXXX « وما عليك الا يزكى ». قال جعفر : لم تكرم بالاقبال على[4] من لم يكرمه بالهداية ولم يزينه بالمعرفة .

6, LXXXII « يا ايها الانسان ما غرك بربك الكريم ». قال جعفر : ما الذي اقعدك عن خدمة مولاك .

14-13,LXXXII « ان الابرار لفي نعيم وان الفجّار لفي جحيم ». قال جعفر : النعيم المعرفة والمشاهدة والجحيم النفوس فان لها نيران تتقد[5] .

24,LXXXIII « تعرف في وجوههم نضرة النعيم ». قال جعفر : ببقاء[6] لذة النظر يتلألأ مثل الشمس في وجوههم اذا رجعوا من زيارة الله تعالى الى اوطانهم .

27,LXXXIII « ومزاجه من تسنيم ». قال جعفر : كؤوساً مزجت بالأنس فتنسموا منها رائحة القرب .

13, LXXXV « انه هو يبدي ويعيد ». قال جعفر : يبدي فيفني عما سواه ثم يعيد فيبقي بابقائه . وقال جعفر الصادق : «انه هو يبدي ويعيد» اي يلبس لباس الاولياء للاعداء حتى يكون لهم استدراجاً . ويلبس لباس الاعداء للاولياء لئلا يعجبوا بانفسهم ثم يعيد عند الموت[7] .

---

1) B : + في الدنيا ‖ 2) YB : + وعصمته ‖ 3) Y : الآخرة ‖ 4) F : + عليه (؟) ‖ 5) B : والجحيم الجهل والحجاب ‖ 6) Y : يبقى ‖ 7) YB : – وقال... الموت ‖

له عنايتي ورحمتي[1] سالم من تلك الاهوال والشدائد ولا يكون له علم بشدائدها واهوالها . وكل من سبق له من الله تعالى العناية يسجد بين يديه مفتقرًا اليه . ومن سبق له من الله تعالى العدل لا يقدر ان يسجد وكان ظهره كالحجر لا يلين للسجود لرب العالمين. وقال جعفر في قوله « يوم يكشف عن ساق » قال : اذا التقى الولي مع الولي انكشف عنه الشدائد .

39-38, LXIX « فلا اقسم بما تبصرون وما لا تبصرون » . قال جعفر : بما تبصرون من صنعي في ملكي وما لا تبصرون من برّي الى اوليائي[2] .

48, LXIX « وانه لتذكرة للمتقين » . قال جعفر : موعظة للموقنين[3] .

12, LXXI « ويجعل لكم جنات ويجعل لكم انهارا » . قال جعفر : يزين ظاهركم بزينة الخدمة وباطنكم بانوار الايمان .

20, LXXIII « فاقرأوا ما تيسّر من القرآن » . قال جعفر بن محمد : ما تيسر لكم فيه[4] خشوع القلب وصفاء السر[5] .

1, LXXVI « هل اتى على الانسان ... » . قال جعفر : هل اتى عليك يا انسان وقت لم يكن الله لك ذاكرًا فيه .

21, LXXVI « وسقاهم ربهم شرابًا طهورًا » . قال جعفر : سقاهم التوحيد في السرّ فتاهوا عن جميع ما سواه فلم يفيقوا الا عند المعاينة ورفع الحجاب فيما بينهم وبينه واخذ الشراب في ما اخذ عنه[6] فلم يبقَ عليه منه[7] باقيـة وحصله في ميدان السرور والحضور والقبضة[8] .

وقال جعفر في قوله « شرابًا طهورًا : طهرهم به عن كل شيء سواه اذ لا طاهر من[9] تدنس[10] بشيء من الاكوان .

---

1) B : المومن من سبقت له من الله العناية والرحمة || 2) B : لأوليائي || 3) YB : للموفقين || 4) Y : من || 5) B : – قال جعفر... وصفاء السر || 6) B : – واخذ ... عنه || 7) B : منهم || 8) B : – وحصله... والقبضة || 9) B : طهر لمن || 10) F : + الطاهر لم يتدنس ||

5, LXI « فلما زاغوا أزاغ الله قلوبهم » . قال جعفر : لما تركوا اوامر الخدمة نزع الله من قلوبهم نور الايمان وجعل للشيطان اليهم طريقاً فأزاغهم عن طريق الحق وادخلهم في سبيل[1] الباطل .

13, LXI « وبشّر المومنين » . قال جعفر : بشارة برويته « في مقعد صدق عند مليك مقتدر » (55,LIV) .

15, LXIV « انما اموالكم واولادكم فتنة » . قال جعفر : اموالكم فتنة لاشتغالكم بجمعها من غير وجهها ووضعها في غير اهلها واولادكم فتنة لاشتغالكم باصلاحهم فتفسدون انتم ولا يصلحون هم .

9, LXVI « يا ايها النبي جاهد الكفار والمنافقين » . قال جعفر : جاهد الكفار باليد والمنافقين باللسان . « واغلظ عليهم » : أمره بالغلظة عليهم ليشفي غيظه منهم مع قلة دعاويهم وأمر موسى عليه السلام باللين مع فرعون مع علوّ دعاويه[2] .

1, LXVII « تبارك الذي بيده الملك » . قال جعفر : تبارك اي هو المبارك على من انقطع اليه او كان له[3] .

1, LXVIII « ن والقلم » . قال جعفر : نون هو نور الازلية الذي اخترع منه الاكوان كلها فجعل ذلك لمحمد صلعم . فلذلك قيل له « وانك لعلى خلق عظيم» (4,LXVIII) اي على النور الذي خصصت به في الازل .

4, LXVIII « وانك لعلى خلق عظيم » . قال جعفر : هو صرف الايمان وحقيقة التوحيد .

34, LXVIII « ان للمتقين عند ربهم جنات النعيم » . قال جعفر : من اتقى الذنوب كان مأواه جنات النعيم ومن اتقى الله[4] تعالى كشف عنه الغطاء والحجب حتى يشاهد الحق في جميع الاحوال .

42, LXVIII « يوم يكشف عن ساق ويدعون الى السجود » . قال جعفر الصادق : يوم يكشف عن ساق ، عن الاهوال والشدائد والصراط والحساب وعبدي المومن الذي سبقت

---

1) Y : مسالك || 2) YB : دعواه || 3) B : – قال ... كان له || 4) B : السوى ||

33, LVI « لا مقطوعة ولا ممنوعة » . قال جعفر : لم يقطع عنهم المعرفة والتأييد ولو قطع ذلك عنهم لهلكوا ولا يمنعوا (sic) من التلذذ بمجاورة الحق ولو منعوا عن ذلك لاستوحشوا .

73, LVI « نحن جعلناها تذكرة » . قال جعفر : موعظة للتائبين وآلة للاقوياء من العارفين في حمله .

79, LVI « لا يمسّه الا المطهرون » . قال جعفر : الا القائمون بحقوقه والمتبعون اوامره والحافظون حرماته .

1, LVII « سبح لله ما في السموات » . قال جعفر : سبح له الكل وهو غني عن تسبيحهم . كيف يصل اليه ذلك وهو الذي اخرجه وتولى اظهاره .

« وهو العزيز الحكيم » . قال جعفر : هو الذي لا يدركه طالبوه ولا يعجزه هاربوه .

3, LVII « وهو الاول والاخر... » . قال جعفر : هو الذي اوّل الاول وأخّر الآخر واظهر الظاهر وأبطن الباطن . فسقطت هذه المعاني وبقي هو .

وقال جعفر : «الباطن» هو باطن في كل مكان لم يخلُ منه اذ كان كونه[1] ولا مكان فحجب بلطفه كنه الكان وأبدى بقدرته تمكين الكان[2] فبآن لنا الكان واحتجب عنا كنه الكان وتجلى لنا ظهور كمال الكان الذي بتحقيقه يتم الايمان .

10, LVII « لا يستوي منكم من انفق من قبل الفتح وقاتل » . قال جعفر : الارادات القوية والايمان السليم للمهاجرين واهل الصفة وامامهم وسيدهم الصديق الاكبر رضوان الله عليه . وهم الذين لم يوثروا الدنيا على الآخرة بل بذلوها ولم يعرجوا عليها واعتمدوا في ذلك على ربهم وطلبوا رضاه وموافقة الرسول صلعم فخصهم الله سبحانه من بين الامة بقوله « لا يستوي... » .

23, LIX عن جعفر بن محمد قال في قوله « القدوس » الطاهر من كل عيب وطهر من شاء من العيوب و « المهيمن » الذي ليس كمثله شيء وسمى القرآن مهيمناً[3] لانه لا يشبه غيره من الكلام[4] .

---

1) Y : كانه || 2) FB : المكان || 3) V 48, || 4) B : – عن جعفر... الكلام ||

18, LIII « لقد رأى من آيات ربه الكبرى » . قال جعفر : شاهد من علامات المحبة ما كبر عن الاخبار عنها .

32, LIII « هو اعلم بكم » . قال جعفر : اعلم بكم لانه خلقكم وقدر عليكم الشقاوة والسعادة قبل ايجادكم . فانتم متقلبون فيما اجرى عليكم في السبق من الاجل والرزق والسعادة والشقاوة ولا تستجلب الطاعات سعادة ولا المخالفات شقاوة ولكن سابق المقدور هو الذي يختم بما بدى .

37, LIII « وابراهيم الذي وفّى » . قال جعفر : مائية الصدق الوفاء في كل حال وفعل .

44, LIII « وانه هو امات واحيا » . قال جعفر : يميت بالاعراض عنه ويحيي بالمعرفة به . وامات النفوس بالمخالفة واحيا القلوب بانوار الموافقة .

55, LIV « في مقعد صدق » . قال جعفر : مدح المكان الذي فيه الصدق فلا يقعد فيه الا اهل الصدق وهو المقعد الذي يصدق الله فيه مواعيد اوليائه بان يبيح لهم[1] النظر الى وجهه الكريم .

11, LV « فيها فاكهة والنخل ذات الاكمام » . قال جعفر : جعل الحق قلوب اوليائه رياض أنسه فغرس فيها اشجار المعرفة اصولها ثابتة في اسرارهم وفروعها قايمة بالحضرة في المشهد . فهم يجنون ثمار الأنس في كل أوان . وهو قوله تعالى « فيها فاكهة والنخل ذات الاكمام » اي ذات الالوان كل يجني منه لوناً على قدر سعيه وما كشف له من بوادي المعرفة وآثار الولاية .

60, LV « هل جزاء الاحسان الا الاحسان » . قال جعفر : هل جزاء من احسنت اليه في الازل الا حفظ الاحسان عليه الى الابد .

19, LVI « لا يصدعون عنها » . قال جعفر : لا تذهل عقولهم عن موارد الحقائق عليهم ولا يغيبون عن مجلس المشاهدة بحال .

30, LVI عن جعفر في قوله « وظل ممدود » قال : الظل رحمة الله التي سبقت لامة محمد صلعم والممدود فضله على الموحدين وعدله على الملحدين .

---

1) F : يبيحهم ||

وقال : النجم قلب محمد « اذا هوى » ، اذا انقطع عن جميع ما سوى الله .

2, LIII « ما ضلّ صاحبكم وما غوى » . قال جعفر : ما ضل عن قربه طرفة عين .

3, LIII « وما ينطبق عن الهوى » . قال جعفر : كيف ينطق عن الهوى من هو ناطق باظهار التوحيد واتمام الشريعة وآداب[1] الامر والنهي . بل ما نطق الا بأمر وما سكت الا بأمر . أمر فكان أمره قربة عن الحق ونهى فكان نهيه ادباراً وزجرا .

8, LIII « ثم دنا فتدلى » . قال جعفر : انقطعت الكيفية عن الدنو . الا ترى ان الله تعالى حجب جبريل عن دنوه ودنو ربه منه .

وقال ايضاً : دنا محمد صلعم الى ما اودع في قلبه من المعرفة والايمان فتدلى بسكون قلبه الى ما أدناه وزال عن قلبه الشك والارتياب .

9, LIII « فكان قاب قوسين او ادنى » . قال جعفر : ادناه منه حتى كان منه كقاب قوسين . والدنو من الله تعالى لا حد له والدنو من العبد بالحدود .

10, LIII « فاوحى الى عبده ما اوحى » . قال جعفر : بلا واسطة فيما بينه وبينه سرًا الى قلبه لا يعلم به احد سواه بلا واسطة الا في العقبى حين[2] يعطيه الشفاعة لأمته .

وقال الصادق في قوله « دنا فتدلى » : لما قرب الحبيب من الحبيب بغاية القرب نالته غاية الهيبة . فلاطفه الحق بغاية اللطف لانه لا تحمل غاية الهيبة الا غاية اللطف . وذلك قوله « فاوحى الى عبده ما اوحى » اي كان ما كان وجرى ما جرى وقال الحبيب ما يقول الحبيب لحبيبه وألطف له الطاف الحبيب لحبيبه واسر اليه ما يسر الحبيب الى حبيبه . فأخفيا ولم يطلعا على سرهما احدًا سواهما . فلذلك قال « فاوحى الى عبده ما اوحى » ولا يعلم احد ذلك الوحي الا[3] الذي اوحى والذي أوحي اليه .

11, LIII « ما كذب الفؤاد ما رأى » . قال جعفر : لا يعلم احد ما الذي رأى الا الذي أرى والذي رأى . صار الحبيب من الحبيب قريباً وله نجيًّا[4] وبه انيساً . قال الله تعالى : « نرفع درجات من نشاء » (83,VI) .

---

1) B : وايجاب || 2) F : حتى || 3) Y : + الله || 4) B : محباً ||

قدرة القادر الباري في نفسه وملكوته وارضه وسمائه فاستدل بها على وحدانيته وقدرته ومشيئته.

قال جعفر في قوله تعالى : « ضيف ابراهيم المكرمين »[1] مكرمين[2] حيث انزلهم اكرم 24, LI
الخليقة واظهرهم فتوة واشرفهم نفساً واعلاهم همة ، الخليل صلوات الله وسلامه عليه .

« ومن كل شيء خلقنا زوجين لعلكم تذكرون » . قال جعفر : لينظر الموحد الى 49, LI
الاغيار[3] فيراها ازواجاً مثاني واربعاً فيفرّ منها ويرجع الى الواحد الاحد ليصح له التوحيد بذلك .

« وذكر فان الذكرى تنفع المؤمنين » . قال جعفر الصادق رضي الله عنه : يعني 55, LI
يا محمد ذكّر عبادي جودي وكرمي وآلائي ونعماي وما سبق من رحمتي لأمتك خاصة . والذكرى التي تنفع المؤمنين ذكر الله تعالى للعبد وما سبق من العناية القديمة بالايمان والمعرفة والتوفيق للطاعة والعصمة عن المعاصي .

وقال جعفر : كل من ذكر الله تعالى فاذا نسي ذكره كان مجهولاً عن ذكره . والله تعالى ذكره[4] احديته وازليته ومشيئته وقدرته وعلمه . ولا يقع عليه النسيان والجهل لانهما من صفات البشرية . وكل من ذكر الله تعالى فبذكره له يذكره .

قال جعفر في قوله « وما خلقت الجن والانس الا ليعبدوني » قال : الا ليعرفوني 56, LI
ثم يعبدوني على بساط المعرفة ليتبرءوا من الرياء والسمعة .

« والطور » . قال جعفر : ما يطرأ على قلب احبائي من الانس بذكري والالتذاذ 1, LII
بحبي « وكتاب مسطور » ، وما كتب الحق على نفسه لهم من الاقتراب والقربة .

« فاصبر لحكم ربك فانك بأعيننا » . قال جعفر : عند هذا الخطاب سهل عليه 48, LII
معالجة الصبر واحتمال مؤنته . وكذلك كل حال يرد على العبد في محل المشاهدة .

« والنجم اذا هوى » . قال جعفر : هو محل التجلي والاستتار من قلوب اهل المعرفة . 1, LIII
عن جعفر بن محمد في قوله تعالى « والنجم اذا هوى » قال : النجم محمد صلعم اذا هوى انسرح منه الانوار .

---

1) B : + صاروا || 2) F : – مكرمين || 3) B : الى الاشياء بعين الاعتبار ||
4) Y : ذكر ||

9, XLVI «ما كنتُ بدعاً من الرسل». قال جعفر في هذه الآية: لم يكن لي في نبوّتي شيء. انما هو شيء اعطيته لا بي[1] بل بفضل من عند الله حيث اهلني لرسالته ووصفني في كتب الانبياء السالفة صلوات الله عليهم اجمعين.

13, XLVI «ان الذين قالوا ربنا الله ثم استقاموا». قال جعفر: استقاموا مع الله تعالى بحركات القلوب مع مشاهدات التوحيد.

30, XLVI «يهدي الى الحق والى طريق مستقيم». قال جعفر: يدل على طريق الحق بالخروج من المعلومات والمرسومات والتحقيق بالحق وهو الصراط المستقيم.

3, XLVII «الذين كفروا اتبعوا الباطل». قال جعفر: لا يوفق لسلوك طريق الحق من لم يُحكم مبادي احواله مع الحق ومن اهمل مبادي الاحوال كيف يرجى له التناهي فيها.

19, XLVII وقال جعفر في قوله «انه لا إله الاّ الله»: ازال العلل عن الربوبية ونزه الحق عن الدرك.

2, XLVIII «ويتم نعمته عليك». قال جعفر: من تمام النعمة على نبيّه صلعم ان جعله حبيبه واقسم بحياته ونسخ به شرائع الرسل اجمع وعرج به الى المحل الادنى وحفظه في المعراج حتى «ما زاغ» «وما طغى» وبعثه الى الاسود والابيض واحل له ولأمته الغنائم وجعله شفيعاً مشفعاً وجعله سيد ولد آدم وقرن ذكره بذكره ورضاه برضاه وجعله أحد ركني التوحيد. فهذا وامثاله من تمام النعمة عليه وعلى امته به وبمكانه.

26, XLVIII «حمية الجاهلية». قال جعفر: الحمية المذمومة التخطي من الحدود الى التشفّي.

13, XLIX «ان اكرمكم عند الله اتقاكم». قال جعفر: الكريم هو المتقي على الحقيقة والمتقي المنقطع عن الاكوان الى الله.

7, L قال جعفر في قوله «لمن كان له قلب»: يعني قلباً يسمع ويعقل ويبصر. فكلما سمع خطاب الله تعالى بلا واسطة فيما بينه وبين الحق عقل ما منّ عليه بالايمان والاسلام من غير مسئلة ولا شفيع ولا وسيلة كانت له عند الله في الازل وابصر

1) F: بشيء ||

66, XL « وأمرتُ ان اسلم لرب العالمين » . قال جعفر : لا ألتجي الا اليه ولا اذل الا له لان الالجاء اليه محل الفرح والتذلل له معدن العزة .

12, XLI « وزينا السماء الدنيا بمصابيح » . قال جعفر : زينا جوارح المؤمنين بالخدمة .

31, XLI « نحن اولياؤكم في الحياة الدنيا » . قال جعفر : من لاحظ في اعماله الثواب والاعواض كانت الملائكة اولياءه . ومن تحقق في افعاله وَعَمِلَها على مشاهدة امرها فهو وليّه لانه يقول الله تعالى « الله ولي الذين آمنوا » (257,II) .

44, XLI « قل هو للذين آمنوا هدى وشفاء » . قال جعفر : القرآن شفاء لمن كان في ظل العصمة وعمى على من كان في ظلمة الخذلان .

9, XLII « وهو يحيي الموتى » . قال جعفر : يحيي نفوس المؤمنين بخدمته ويميت نفوس المنافقين بمخالفته[1] .

23, XLII « قل لا اسألكم عليه اجرًا الا المودة » . قال جعفر : الا ان تتوددوا اليّ من الاعمال ما يقربكم الى ربكم .

68, XLIII « لا خوف عليكم ولا انتم تحزنون » . قال جعفر رضي الله عنه : لا خوف على من اطاعني في الاوامر والفرائض واتبع الرسول فيما سنّ[2] .

وقال ايضاً : لا خوف في الآخرة على من خافني في الدنيا[3] . ولا خوف على من احبني وازال عن قلبه محبة الاغيار . ولا خوف على من صان وديعتي عنده وهو الايمان والمعرفة . ولا خوف على من احسن ظنه بي فاني اعطيه مأموله . والخوف يكون على الجوارح والحزن على القلب من مخافة القطيعة .

71, XLIII « وفيها ما تشتهي الانفس وتلذ الاعين » . قال جعفر : شتان بين ما تشتهي الانفس وبين ما تلذ الاعين . لان جميع ما في الجنة من النعيم والشهوات واللذات في جنب ما تلذ الاعين كاصبع تغمس في البحر . لان شهوات الجنة لها حد ونهاية لانها مخلوقة ولا تلذ الاعين في الدار الباقية الا بالنظر الى الباقي جلّ وعلا . ولا حد لذلك ولا صفة ولا نهاية .

1) B : قال ... بمخالفته || 2) B : في السنن || 3) B : – لا خوف... في الدنيا ||

والاحزان والخوف العظيم حتى لحق بربه . فهذه وان كانت المواقعة فيها تتسع فان عاقبتها عظمت وجلت وعلت لان الله قد اعطاه بذلك الزلفى والحظوة .

35,XXXVIII قال جعفر : « هب لي ملكاً » اي القنوع بقسمتك حتى لا يكون لي مع اختيارك اختيار .

78,XXXVIII « وان عليك لعنتي الى يوم الدين » . قال جعفر : سخطي الذي لم يزل مني جارية (sic) عليك وواصلة (sic) اليك في اوقاتك المقدرة وايامك الماضية[1] .

29, XXXIX « الحمد لله ، بل اكثرهم لا يعلمون » . قال جعفر : لا يعلمون ان احداً من عباد الله لم يبلغ الواجب في حمده وما يستحق من الحمد على عباد الله بنعمه وان احداً لم يحمده حق حمده الا حمده لنفسه .

30, XXXIX « انك ميّت وانهم ميتون » . قال جعفر : انك ميت عما هم فيه من الاشتغال بانفسهم واولادهم ودنياهم وانهم ميتون اي مبعدون عما خصصت به من انواع الكرامات .

65, XXXIX « لئن اشركت ليحبطن عملك » . قال جعفر : لئن نظرت الى سواه لتحرمن في الآخرة لقاه .

74, XXXIX قال جعفر[2] : « الحمد لله الذي صدقنا وعده » هو حمد العارفين الذين استقروا في دار القرار مع الله تعالى . وقوله « الحمد لله الذي اذهب عنا الحزن » (34,XXXV) حمد الواصلين .

16, XL « لمن الملك اليوم » . قال جعفر : اخرس المكونات ذوات الارواح عن جواب سؤاله في قوله « لمن الملك » فلم يجسر احد على الاجابة وما كان بحقيق ان يجيب سؤاله سواه . فلما سكنت الانس عن الجواب اجاب نفسه بما كان يستحق من الجواب فقال « لله الواحد القهار » .

51, XL « اننا لننصر رسلنا والذين آمنوا » . قال جعفر[3] : ننصر رسلنا بالمومنين ظاهراً وننصر المومنين بالرسل باطناً .

---

1) B : – قال... الماضية || 2) YB : + الصادق || 3) B : + بن محمد ||

الى نفسه تفضلاً منه وكرما ؛ ثم قال « اصطفينا » جعلهم كلهم اصفيا مع علمه بتفاوت مقاماتهم[1] ثم جمعهم في آخر الآية بدخول الجنة فقال « جنات عدن يدخلونها » ثم بدأ بالظالمين اخبارًا انه لا يتقرب اليــه الا بصرف كرمه . فان[2] الظلم لا يؤثر في الاصطفائية . ثم ثنّى بالمقتصدين لانهم بين الخوف والرجاء . ثم ختم بالسابقين لئلا يامن احد مكره . وكلهم في الجنة بحرمة كلمة واحدة يعني كلمة الاخلاص .

وقال جعفر : النفس ظالمة والقلب مقتصد والروح سابق .

وقال ايضاً[3] : من نظر بنفسه الى الدنيا فهو ظالم ومن نظر بقلبه الى الآخرة فهو مقتصد ومن نظر بروحه الى الحق فهو سابق .

1, xxxvi « يس » . قال جعفر الصادق رضي الله عنه في قوله « يس » اي يا سيد ، مخاطباً لنبيه صلعم . لذلك قال النبي عليه السلام : انا سيدكم[4] ولم يمدح بذلك نفسه ولكنه اخبر عن معنى مخاطبة الحق اياه بقوله « يس » .

103, xxxvii « فلما اسلما » . قال جعفر : اخرج ابراهيم من قلبه محبة ابنه[5] واخرج اسمعيل من قلبه محبة الحياة .

164, xxxvii « وما منا الا له مقام معلوم » . قال جعفر : الخلق مع الله على مقامات شتى . من يجاوز حدّه هلك . فللانبياء مقام المشاهدة وللرسول[6] مقام العيان وللملائكة مقام الهيبة وللمؤمنين مقام الدنو والخدمة وللعصاة مقام التوبة وللكفار مقام الطرد والغفلة . هذا بمعنى قوله تعالى « وما منا الا له مقام معلوم » .

20, xxxviii « وآتيناه الحكمة وفصل الخطاب » . قال جعفر : صدق القول وصحة العقد والثبات في الامور .

25, xxxviii « وظن داود انما فتناه فاستغفر ربه » . قال جعفر : ومن ذلك ما ذكره الله تعالى من فتنه داود وبلواه ومحنته[7] وما خرج اليه من عظيم التنصّل[8] والاعتذار ودوام البكاء

1) YB : معاملاتهم || 2) B : وان || 3) B : — وقال ايضاً || 4) Y : انا سيد ولد آدم ولا فخر || 5) Y : + اسمعيل || 6) YB : والرسل || 7) B : ومحبته || 8) B : التنقيل ||

17, xxx « فسبحان الله حين تمسون وحين تصبحون » . قال جعفر : بالله فابدأ في صباحك
وبه فاختم مساك . فمن كان به ابتداؤه واليه انتهاؤه لا يشقى فيما بينهما .

40, xxx « الله الذي خلقكم ثم رزقكم... » . قال جعفر : « خلقكم ثم رزقكم » ، حرككم
الى اظهار اثار الربوبية فيكم « ثم يميتكم ثم يحييكم » بالاستتار والتجلي[1] .

53, xxx « وما انت بهادي العمى » . قال جعفر : اظهار آيات رسالاتك على من أظهر
الحق عليه في الازل آيات السعادة وحلاه بحلية الاختصاص فيكون دعاؤك له دعاء
تذكير وموعظة لا دعاء ابتداء . لانه من لم تجر له السعادة في الازل لم يمكنك ان
توصله الى محل السعادة . انت الداعي والمنذر والله الهادي . الا تراه يقول : « وما انت
بهادي العمى » .

16, xxxii « يدعون ربهم خوفاً وطمعاً » . قال جعفر : خوفاً منه وطمعاً فيه .

35, xxxiii « ... والصادقين والصادقات... » . قال جعفر : الصادق من يصف لك خير الآخرة
لا خير الدنيا ويدلك على حسن الاخلاق لا على سيّئها ويعطيك قلبه لا جوارحه .

46, xxxiii « وداعياً الى الله باذنه وسراجاً منيرًا » . قال جعفر : داعياً الى الله لا الى نفسه افتخر
بالعبودية ولم يفتخر بالنبوة ليصح له بذلك الدعاء الى سيده . فمن اجاب دعوته صارت
الدعوة له سراجاً منيرًا يدله على سبيل الرشد ويبصره عيوب النفس وغيّها[2] .

10, xxxiv « ولقد آتينا داود منا فضلاً » . قال جعفر : « فضلاً » ، ثقة بالله تعالى[3] وتوكلاً عليه .

1, xxxv « يزيد في الخلق ما يشاء » . قال جعفر : صحة النحيزة وقوة البصيرة .

28, xxxv « انما يخشى الله من عباده العلماء » . قال جعفر : خشية العلماء من ترك الحرمة
في العبادات وترك الحرمة في الاخبار عن الحق وترك الحرمة في متابعة الرسول صلعم
وترك الحرمة في خدمة الاولياء والصديقين .

32, xxxv قال جعفر في قوله تعالى « فمنهم ظالم لنفسه ومنهم مقتصد ومنهم سابق بالخيرات »
قال : فرق الله تعالى المومنين ثلاث فرق سماهم مومنين اولاً ثم سماهم عبادنا فاضافهم

1) B : — قال... والتجلي || 2) B : وغيرها || 3) B : تقرباً الى الله ||

22, xxviii « فلما توجه تلقاء مدين » . قال جعفر : توجه بوجهه الى ناحية مدين وتوجه بقلبه الى ربه طالباً منه سبيل الهداية فأكرمه الله تعالى بالكلام . وكل من اقبل على الله تعالى بالكلية فان الله تعالى يبلغه[1] مأموله .

24, xxviii « اني لما انزلت الي من خير فقير » . قال جعفر : فقير اليك طالب منك زيادة الفقر اليك[2] لاني لم استغن عنك بشيء سواك .

وقال ايضاً : فقير في جميع الاوقات غير راجع الى الكرامات والآيات دون الفقر اليك والاقبال عليك .

29, xxviii « أنس من جانب الطور ناراً » . قال جعفر : ابصر ناراً دالة على الانوار لانه رأى النور على هيئة النار . فلما دنا منها شملته انوار القدس واحاطت به جلابيب الانس فخوطب بألطف خطاب وأستُدعي منه احسنُ جواب . فصار بذلك ملكاً شريفاً مقرباً . اعطي ما سأل وامن[3] مما خاف. وكذلك قوله « انس من جانب الطور ناراً » .

35, xxviii « ونجعل لكما سلطاناً » . قال جعفر : هيبةً في قلوب الاعداء ومحبة في قلوب الاولياء .

21, xxix « يعذب من يشاء ويرحم من يشاء » . قال جعفر : يعذب من يشاء بشتات الهم ويرحم من يشاء بجمعها له .

45, xxix « ان الصلاة تنهى عن الفحشاء والمنكر » . قال جعفر : الصلاة اذا كانت مقبولة فانها تنهى عن مطالعات[4] الاعمال وطلب الاعواض .

69, xxix « والذين جاهدوا فينا » . قال جعفر : المجاهدة صدق الافتقار وهو انفصال العبد من نفسه واتصاله بربه . والمجاهدة تبري العبد من جميع ما اتصل به[5] والمجاهدة بذل الروح في رضاء الحق .

وقال ايضاً : من جاهد بنفسه لنفسه وصل الى كرامة ربه ومن جاهد بنفسه لربه وصل الى ربه .

---

1) Y : + الى || 2) F : – اليك || 3) Y : وأومن || 4) B : مطالعة || 5) B : – والمجاهدة تبري... اتصل به ||

127, xxvi « وما اسألكم عليه من اجر » . قال جعفر : ازيلت الاطاع عن الرسل اجمع لدناءتها .
فاخبر كل رسول عن نفسه بقوله : « وما اسألكم عليه من أجر » .

212, xxvi « انهم عن السمع لمعزولون » . قال جعفر : هو ان يسمع المواعظ ولا يتعظ بها .

220, xxvi « انه هو السميع العليم » . قال جعفر[1] : السميع من يسمع مناجات الاسرار والعليم
من يعلم ارادات الضماير .

21, xxvii « لاعذبنه عذاباً شديدًا » . قال جعفر : لابلينه بشتات السر .

34, xxvii « ان الملوك اذا دخلوا قرية افسدوها » . قال جعفر[2] : اشار الى قلوب المومنين .
ان المعرفة اذا دخلت القلوب زال عنها الاماني والمرادات اجمع . فلا يكون في القلب
محل لغير الله تعالى .

36, xxvii « بل انتم بهديتكم تفرحون » . قال جعفر : الدنيا اصغر عند الله وعند انبيائه واوليائه
من ان يفرحوا بها او يحزنوا عليها .

50, xxvii « ومكروا مكرًا ومكرنا مكرًا » . قال جعفر[3] : مكر الله اخفى من دبيب النمل
على الصخرة السوداء في الليلة الظلماء .

61, xxvii قال جعفر في قوله « أم من جعل الارض قرارًا » اي من جعل[4] قلوب اوليائه مستقر
معرفته وجعل فيها انهار الزوايد من بره في كل نفس واثبتها بجبال التوكل وزينها بانوار
الاخلاص واليقين والمحبة « وجعل بين البحرين حاجزًا » اي بين القلب والنفس لئلا
تغلب النفس القلب بظلماتها فتظلمها (sic) فجعل الحاجز بينهما التوفيق والعقل .

88, xxvii « وترى الجبال تحسبها جامدة » . قال جعفر : ترى النفس جامدة عند خروج الروح .
والروح تسري في الفردوس[5] لتأوى الى مكانها من تحت العرش .
وقال جعفر : نور قلوب الموحدين وانزعاج انين المشتاقين تمرّ مرّ السحاب حتى
يشاهدوا الحق فيسكنون .

10, xxviii « واصبح فؤاد ام موسى فارغاً... لولا ان ربطنا على قلبها » .
قال جعفر[6] : الصدر معدن التسليم والقلب معدن اليقين والفؤاد معدن النظر والضمير
معدن السر والنفس مأوى كل حسنة وسيئة .

1) B : + الصادق || 2) B : + الصادق || 3) B : + الصادق || 4) Y : + قرار ||
5) YB : القدس || 6) B : + الصادق ||

صلاح القلب كما ان الاثني عشر برجاً من الحمل والثور الى آخر العدد بها صلاح الدار الفانية[1] واهلها .

63, xxv قال جعفر : « الذين يمشون على الارض هوناً » بلا فخر ولا خيلاء ولا تبختر بل بتواضع وسكينة ووقار وطمانينة وحسن خلق وبشر وجه كما وصف النبي صلعم المومنين فقال : « هينون ليّنون كالجمل الانف ان قيد انقاد وان انيخ على صخرة استناخ » . وذلك لما طالعوا من تعظيم الحق وهيبته وشاهدوا من كبريائه وجلاله خشعت لذلك ارواحهم وخضعت نفوسهم فالزمهم ذلك التواضع والتخشّع .

71, xxv « يتوب الى الله متاباً » . قال جعفر : لم يرجع الى الحق من له مرجع الى سواه . حتى يكون رجوعه ظاهراً وباطناً اليه دون غيره حينئذ يكون تائباً اليه .

72, xxv « الذين لا يشهدون الزور » . قال جعفر : الزور اماني النفس ومتابعة هواها .

74, xxv « هب لنا من ازواجنا وذرياتنا قرة أعين » . قال جعفر : هب لنا من ازواجنا معاونة على طاعتك ومن اولادنا برهم حتى تقر اعيننا بهم .

50, xxvi « قالوا لا ضير انا الى ربنا منقلبون » . قال جعفر : من احسّ بالبلاء في المحبة لم يكن محباً بل من شاهد البلاء فيه لم يكن محباً[2] . بل من لم يتلذذ بالبلاء في المحبة لم يكن محباً . الا ترى السحرة لما وردت عليهم شواهد اوائل المحبة كيف زالت عنهم حظوظهم وهانت عليهم بذل ارواحهم في مشاهدة محبوبهم فقالوا « لا ضير » .

62, xxvi « قال كلا ان معي ربي سيهديني » . قال جعفر[3] : من كان في رعاية الحق وكلايته لا يؤثر عليه شيء من الاسباب ولا يهوله مخوفات الموارد لانه في وقاية الحق وقبضته . ومن كان في المشاهدة والحضرة كيف يؤثر عليه ما منه يصدر واليه يرد . الا ترى كيف حكى الله تعالى عن الكليم قوله « ان معي ربي سيهديني » .

80, xxvi « واذا مرضت فهو يشفيني » . قال جعفر : اذا مرضت بروية افعالي واحوالي شفاني بتذكار الفضل والكرم .

114, xxvi « وما انا بطارد المومنين » . قال جعفر : ما انا بمكذب الصادقين .

1) B : دار الفناء || 2) Y : – بل من شاهد... محباً || 3) B : + رحمه الله ||

39, XXIV « والذين كفروا اعمالهم كسراب » . قال جعفر : اظلتهم ظلم صحبة الاغيار فكانت على قلوبهم مثل السراب لم تغن عنهم شيئاً ولم تدلهم على حق . ولو وجدوا السبيل الى الله تعالى لأضآءت سرايرهم فكانت كما قال الله تعالى « نور على نور » .

63, XXIV « لا تجعلوا دعاء الرسول بينكم كدعاء بعضكم بعضاً » . قال جعفر : الحرمات تتبع بعضها بعضاً . من ضيع حرمة الخلق فقد ضيع حرمة المومنين . ومن ضيع حرمة المومنين فقد ضيع حرمة الاولياء . ومن ضيع حرمة الاولياء فقد ضيع حرمة الرسول . ومن ضيع حرمة الرسول فقد ضيع حرمة الله . ومن ضيع حرمة الله تعالى فقد دخل في ديوان الاشقياء . وافضل الاخلاق حفظ الحرمات . ومن اسقط عن قلبه الحرمات تهاون بالفرائض والسنن .

7, XXV « ما لهذا الرسول يأكل الطعام ويمشي في الاسواق » . قال جعفر : عيّروا الرسل بالتواضع والانبساط ولم يعلموا ان ذلك اتم لهيبتهم واشد في بيان الاحترام لهم . وذلك انهم لم يشاهدوا منهم الا ظاهر الخلقة . ولو شاهدوا منهم خصائص الاختصاص لالهاهم ذلك عن قولهم « ما لهذا الرسول... » .

20, XXV « وما ارسلنا قبلك من المرسلين الا انهم لـيأكلون الطعام... » . قال جعفر : ذلك ان الله تعالى لم يبعث رسولاً الا اباح ظاهره للخلق بالكون معهم على شرط البشرية ومنع سره عن ملاحظاتهم والاشتغال بهم لان اسرار الانبياء في القبضة لا تفارق المشاهدة بحال .

61, XXV عن جعفر بن محمد في قوله عز وجل « تبارك الذي جعل في السماء بروجاً » قال : سمي السماء سماء لرفعتها والقلب سماء لانه يسمو بالايمان والمعرفة بلا حد ولا نهاية . كما ان المعروف لا حد له كذلك المعرفة به لا حد لها . وبروج السماء مجاري الشمس والقمر وهم الحمل والثور والجوزاء والسرطان والاسد والسنبلة والميزان والعقرب والقوس والجدي والدلو والحوت . وفي القلب بروج وهو برج الايمان وبرج المعرفة وبرج العقل وبرج اليقين وبرج الاسلام وبرج الاحسان وبرج التوكل وبرج الخوف وبرج الرجاء وبرج المحبة وبرج الشوق وبرج الوله . فهذه اثنا عشر برجاً بها دوام

الاحاطة ثم نور الهيبة ثم نور الحيرة ثم نور الحياة ثم نور الانس ثم نور الاستقامة ثم نور الاستكانة ثم نور الطمأنينة ثم نور العظمة ثم نور الجلال ثم نور القدرة[1] ثم نور الجلال[2] ثم نور الالوهية ثم نور الوحدانية ثم نور الفردانية ثم نور الابدية ثم نور السرمدية ثم نور الديمومية ثم نور الازلية ثم نور البقاء[3] ثم نور الكلية ثم نور الهوية . ولكل واحد من هذه الانوار اهل وله حال ومحل وكلها من انوار الحق التي ذكر الله تعالى في قوله « الله نور السموات والارض » ولكل عبد من عبيده مشرب من نور[4] هذه الانوار وربما كان له حظ من نورين ومن ثلاثة . ولن تتم هذه الانوار لاحد الاّ للمصطفى صلوات الله عليه وسلامه لانه القائم مع الله تعالى بشرط تصحيح العبودية والمحبة . فهو نور وهو من ربه على نور .

عن جعفر بن محمد الصادق في هذه الآية قال : نور السموات بنور الكواكب والشمس والقمر ونور الارضين بنور النبات الاحمر والابيض والاصفر وغير ذلك ونور قلب المؤمن بنور الايمان والاسلام . ونور الطرق الى الله بنور ابي بكر وعمر وعثمان وعلي رضي الله عنهم . فمن اجل ذلك قال النبي صلعم : اصحابي كالنجوم بايّهم اقتديتم اهتديتم .

وقال ايضاً في هذه الآية : نور السموات بأربع : بجبرئيل وميكائيل واسرافيل وعزرائيل عليهم السلام . ونور الارض بابي بكر وعمر وعثمان وعلي رضوان الله عليهم اجمعين .

35, XXIV « لا شرقية ولا غربية » . قال جعفر في هذه الآية : لا خوف يوجب القنوط ولا رجاء يجلب الانبساط . فيكون واقفاً بين الخوف والرجاء .

37, XXIV « رجال لا تلهيهم تجارة ... » . قال جعفر : هم الرجال من بين الرجال على الحقيقة لان الله تعالى حفظ اسرارهم[6] عن الرجوع الى ما سواه وملاحظات غيره[7] . فــلا تشغلهم تجارات الدنيا ونعيمها وزهرتها ولا الآخرة وثوابها عن الله تعالى[8] لانهم في بساتين الانس ورياض الذكر .

1) Y : ثم نور الحول || 2) Y : ثم نور القوة || 3) Y : البقائية || 4) Y : — نور ||
5) B : — الله نور ... اجمعين || 6) Y : سرائرهم || 7) B : — وملاحظات غيره ||
8) B : عن الذكر ||

26, XXII عن جعفر بن محمد في قوله « وطهّر بيتي للطائفين » قال : طهّر نفسك عن مخالطة المخالفين والاختلاط بغير الحق « والقائمين » مع فؤاد العارفين المقيمين معه على بساط الانس والخدمة « والركع السجود »[1] الأئمة السادة الذين رجعوا الى البداية عن تناهي النهاية .

28, XXII « ليشهدوا منافع لهم » . قال جعفر : هو ما يشهدونه في ذلك المشهد من برّ الحق بان وفقهم لشهود ذلك المشهد العظيم . ثم منافعهم ما وعد لهم عليه من الزيادات والبركات والاجابات .

34, XXII عن جعفر بن محمد في قوله « وبشر المخبتين » قال : من اطاعني ثم خافني في طاعته وتواضع لاجلي وبشر من اضطرب قلبُه شوقاً الى لقائي وبشر من ذكرني بالنزول في جواري وبشر من دمعت عيناه خوفاً من هجري . بشرهم ان رحمتي سبقت غضبي .
وقال ايضاً : الملك بالشفاعة .

وقال ايضاً : بشر المشتاقين الى النظر الى وجهي .

وقال ايضاً : المخبت في التواضع كالارض تحمل كل قذر وتواري كل نجس وخبث .

78, XXII « فنعم المولى ونعم النصير » . قال جعفر : نعم المعين (sic) لمن استعان به « ونعم النصير » لمن استنصره .

30, XXIV « قل للمؤمنين يغضوا من ابصارهم » . قال جعفر الصادق في هذه الآية : الغض عن المحارم وعما لا يليق بالحق فرض على العباد . وفرض الفرض غض الخاطر عن كل ما يستحله[2] العبد ومعناه حفظ القلب وخواطره عن النظر الى الكون لئلا يكون به طريداً غافلاً محجوباً وان كان ذلك مباحاً في الظاهر .

35, XXIV « الله نور السموات والارض ... » . قال جعفر بن محمد : الانوار مختلفة اولها نور حفظ القلب ثم نور الخوف ثم نور الرجاء[3] ثم نور التذكر ثم النظر بنور العلم ثم نور الحياء ثم نور حلاوة الايمان ثم نور الاسلام ثم نور الاحسان ثم نور النعمة ثم نور الفضل ثم نور الآلاء ثم نور الكرم ثم نور العطف ثم نور القلب ثم نور

1) B : + هم ‖ 2) B : يستحليه ‖ 3) Y : + ثم نور الحب ثم نور التفكر ثم نور اليقين ‖

في حال فنسينا واشتغل بالجنة فابتلي بارتكاب النهي وذاك انه ألهاه النعيم عن المنعم فوقع من النعمة بالبلية فاخرج من النعيم والجنة ليعلم ان النعيم هو مجاورة المنعم لا الالتذاذ بالاكل والشرب .

121, xx « وعصى آدم ربه فغوى » . قال جعفر : طالع الجنان ونعيمها بعينه فنودي عليه الى يوم القيامة « وعصى آدم ربه » . ولو طالعها بقلبه لنودي عليه بالهجران ابد الابد . ثم عطف عليه ورحمه بقوله « ثم اجتباه ربه فتاب عليه وهدى » (122,XX) .

124, xx « ومن اعرض عن ذكري » . قال جعفر في هذه الآية : لو عرفوني ما اعرضوا عني ومن اعرض عني رددته الى الاقبال على ما يليق به من الاجناس والاكوان .

83, xxi « وايوب اذ نادى ربه انى مسني الضر وانت ارحم الراحمين » . قال جعفر : خرج منه هذا القول على المناجاة مستدعياً للجواب من الحق ليسكن اليه لا على حد الشكوى. وقال جعفر : لما سلط الله البلاء على ايوب وطال به الامر اتاه الشيطان فقال: ان اردت ان تتخلص من هذا البلاء فاسجد لي سجدة . فلما سمع ذلك قال مسني الشيطان بنصب و « مسني الضر » حين[1] طمع الشيطان في ان أسجد له .

وقال ايضاً : لما تناهى ايوب في البلاء واستعذبه صار البلاء وطناً له . فلما إطمأنت اليه نفسه وسكن عند البلاء شكره الناس على صبره ومدحوه . فقال « مسني الضر » لفقد الصبر .

عن جعفر في قوله « مسني الضر » قال : حبس الوحي عنه اربعون يوماً فخشي الهجران من ربه والقطيعة فقال « مسني الضر » [2] .

89, xxi « وزكريا اذ نادى ربه ربِّ لا تذرني فردًا » . قال جعفر : لا تجعلني ممن لا سبيل له الى مناجاتك والتزين بزينة خدمتك .

وقال جعفر : « فردًا » عنك لا يكون لي سبيل اليك .

2, xxii « وترى الناس سكارى » . قال جعفر : اسكرهم ما شهدوا من بساط العز وسلطان الجبروت وسرادق الكبرياء حتى ألجأ النبيين الى ان قالوا نفسي نفسي .

1) B : حتى || 2) B : – عن جعفر... مسني الضر ||

12-11, xx « فلما أتاها نودي يا موسى اني انا ربك ». قال جعفر : قيل لموسى عليه السلام كيف عرفت ان النداء هو نداء الحق ؟ فقال : لانه افناني وشملني وكأنّ كل شعرة مني كانت مخاطباً بنداء من جميع الجهات وكأنها تعبر من نفسها بجواب . فلما شملتني انوار الهيبة واحاطت بي انوار العزة والجبروت علمت اني مخاطب من جهة الحق . ولما كان اول الخطاب « اني » ثم بعده « انا » علمت انه ليس لاحد ان يخبر عن نفسه باللفظتين جميعاً متتابعاً الا الحق . فادهشتُ وهو كان محل الفناء . فقلت انت انت الذي لم تزل ولا تزال ليس لموسى معك مقام ولا له جرأة الكلام الا ان تبقيه ببقائك وتنعته بنعتك فتكون انت المخاطِب والمخاطَب جميعاً . فقال : لا يحمل خطابي غيري ولا يجيبني سواي وانا المتكلم وانا المكلَّم وانت في الوسط شبح يقع بك محل الخطاب .

12, xx « فاخلع نعليك ». قال جعفر : اقطع عنك العلائق فانك باعيننا .

18, xx « ولي فيها مآرب اخرى ». قال جعفر : منافع شتى واكبر منفعة لي فيها خطابك اياي بقولك « وما تلك بيمينك يا موسى » (17,XX) .

27, xx « واحلل عقدة من لساني ». قال جعفر : لما كلم الله موسى عقد لسان موسى عن مكالمة غيره . فلما امره بالذهاب الى فرعون ناجاه بسره فقال « واحلل عقدة من لساني » لاكون قايماً بالامر على اتم مقام .

33, xx «كي نسبحك كثيرًا » . قال جعفر : قيل لموسى استكثرت تسبيحك وتهليلك وتكبيرك ونسيت بدايات فضلنا عليك في حفظك في اليم وردك الى امك وتربيتك في حجر عدوك . واكثر من هـذا كله خطابنا معك وكلامنا اياك . واكثر منـه اخبارنا باصطناعنا لك .

82, xx قال جعفر : « واني غفار لمن تاب » لمن رجع اليّ في مهماته ولم يرجع الى غيري « وآمن » وشاهدني ولم يشهد معي سواي « وعمل صالحاً » واخلص قلبه لي « ثم اهتدى » ثم لم يخالف سنّة النبي صلعم .

115, xx « ولقد عهدنا الى آدم من قبل فنسي ». قال جعفر : عهدنا الى آدم ان لا ينسانا

101, xviii « وكانوا لا يستطيعون سمعاً » . قال جعفر الصادق : لا يستطيعون سماع كلام الحق ولا سماع سنن المصطفى صلعم ولا سماع سير[1] الهداة الصالحين من الانبياء والصديقين لانهم لم يجعلوا[2] من اهل القبول للحق فمنعوا عن سماع خطاب الحق .

110, xviii « ولا يشرك بعبادة ربه احداً » . قال جعفر : لا يرى في وقت وقوفه بين يدي ربه غيره ولا يكون في همه وهمته غيره .

6, xix « واجعله ربِّ رضياً » . قال جعفر : رضياً اي راضياً بما يبدو له وعليه .

8, xix « قال ربِّ انى يكون لي غلام » . قال جعفر : استقبل النعمة بالشكر قبل حلولها «انى يكون لي غلام» وبأي بر واي عمل واي طاعة استوجب منك هذه الاجابة وهذا التفضل والكرم الا بسابق تفضلك[3] ونعمك على عبادك في جميع الاحوال فاني ان ايست من عملي فلا آيس من فضلك .

23, xix « يا ليتني متّ قبل هذا » . قال جعفر : لما لم ترَ في قومها موفقاً ولا رشيداً ولا صاحب فراسة يبريها من قولهم قالت « يا ليتني مت قبل » ان ارى في قومي ما ارى .
وقال جعفر : « يا ليتني مت قبل » ان ارى لقلبي متعلقاً دون الله .

52, xix « وقربناه نجيّاً » . قال جعفر : للمقرّب من الله تعالى ثلاث علامات : اذا افاده الله علماً رزقه العمل به واذا رفعه الله للعمل به اعطاه الاخلاص في عمله واذا اقامه لصحبة[4] المسلمين رزقه في قلبه حرمة لهم ويعلم ان حرمة المؤمنين من حرمة الله تعالى .

85, xix « يوم نحشر المتقين » . قال جعفر : المتقي الذي اتقى كل شيء سوى الله والمتقي الذي اتقى متابعة هواه . فمن كان بهذا الوصف فان الله يحمله الى حضرة المشاهدة على تجانب[5] النور ليعرف اهل المشهد محله فيهم .

93, xix « الا اتى الرحمن عبداً » . عن جعفر بن محمد في قوله « الا اتى الرحمن عبداً » قال: فقيراً ذليلاً باوصافه او عزيزاً دالاً باوصاف الحق .

3, xx « الا تذكرة لمن يخشى » . قال جعفر : انزل الله القرآن موعظة للخائفين ورحمة للمؤمنين وأنساً للمحبين فقال « ما انزلنا عليك القرآن لتشقى الا تذكرة لمن يخشى » .

1) B : سنن الهداية || 2) B : — لم يجعلوا || 3) Y : فضلك || 4) B : لنصيحة || 5) B : جنايب ||

17, XVIII « ذات اليمين... ذات الشمال ». قال جعفر : يمين المرء قلبه وشماله نفسه . والرعاية تدور عليها ولولا ذاك لهلك .

18, XVIII « لو اطلعت عليهم لوليت منهم فرارًا ». قال جعفر : لو اطلعت عليهم من حيث انت لوليت منهم فرارًا ولو اطلعت عليهم من حيث الحق لشاهدت فيهم معـــاني الوحدانية والربانية .

وقال جعفر : لو اطلعت على ما بهم من اثار قدرتنا ورعايتنا لهم وتولية حياطتهم لوليت منهم فرارًا اي ما قدرت على الثبات لمشاهدة ما بهم من هيبتنا . فيكون حقيقة الفرار منا لا منهم لان ما بدا عليهم منّا .

وقال ايضاً : لو اطلعت عليهم من حيث انت لفررت ولو اطلعت عليهم من حيث انا لوقفت . وذلك ان الولي له مع الله احوال لا يقدر على مشاهدته من نظر اليه من عند نفسه من ضعف البشرية يفر من رؤيته . وقد فر النبي صلعم من الكفار .

24, XVIII « واذكر ربك اذا نسيت ». قال جعفر : اذا نسيت الاغيار فتقرب الي بالاذكار .

30, XVIII « انّا لا نضيع اجر من احسن عملاً ». قال جعفر : ان الذين صدقوا الله[1] في الارزاق والكفايات[2] وطلبوا الرزق من وجهه الذي اباح الله طلبه ، فان الله لا يضيع سعيهم في طلب مرضاته ويسهل عليهم سبيل التوكل ليستغنوا بذلك عن الطلب والحركة ويخرجهم من ضيق الطلب الى فسحة التوكل .

46, XVIII قال جعفر الصادق : « الباقيات الصالحات » هو تفريد التوحيد فانه باق ببقاء الموحد.

67, XVIII « قال انك لن تستطيع معي صبرًا ». قال جعفر[3] : لن تصبر مع من هو دونك فكيف تصبر مع من هو فوقك .

84, XVIII « وآتيناه من كل شيء سبباً ». قال جعفر : ان الله تعالى جعل لكل شيء سبباً وجعل الاسباب معاني الوجود[4] . فمن شهد السبب انقطع عن المسبب ومن شهد صنع المسبب امتلأ قلبه من ريب الاسباب . واذا امتلأ قلبه من الريبة حال بينه وبين الملاحظة وحجبه عن المشاهدة .

1) B : — الله || 2) F : + الذين || 3) B : ابو حفص || 4) B : الوجوه ||

65, XVII « وكفى بربك وكيلاً » . قال جعفر : كفى بربك وكيلاً لمن توكّل عليه وفوض امره اليه .

70, XVII « ولقد كرمنا بني آدم » . قال جعفر : كرمنا بني آدم بالمعرفة .

80, XVII عن جعفر بن محمد[1] في قوله « ادخلني مدخل صدق » قال : ادخلني فيها على حد الرضا « واخرجني » عنها وانت عني راض .

وقال ايضاً : واخرجني من القبر[2] الى الوقوف بين يديك على طريق الصدق مع الصادقين .

وقال جعفر : طلب التولية ان يكون هو المتولي له اي ادخلني[3] ميـــدان معرفتك واخرجني من مشاهدة المعرفة الى مشاهدة الذات .

80, XVII « واجعل لي من لدنك سلطاناً » قال جعفر : قوة لي في الدين يوجب لي بها المحبة .

101, XVII « ولقد آتينا موسى تسع آيات » قال جعفر : من الآيات التي خصه الله بها الاصطناع والقاء المحبة عليه والكلام والثبات في محل الخطاب والحفظ في اليم واليد البيضاء واعطاء الالواح .

105, XVII « وبالحق انزلناه وبالحق نزل » . قال جعفر : الحق انزل على قلوب خواصه من مكنون فوايده وعجايب بره ولطايف صنعه ما نور به اسرارهم وطهر به قلوبهم وزين به خوارجهم وبالحق نزل عليهم هذه اللطائف .

14, XVIII « وربطنا على قلوبهم اذ قاموا » . قال جعفر : اذ قاموا اي قاموا واخلصوا في دعائنا . وقال جعفر : قاموا الى الحق بالحق قيام ادب ونادوه نداء صدق واظهروا له صحة الفقر ولجأوا اليه احسن لجاء وقالوا « ربنا رب السموات والارض » افتخاراً به وتعظيماً له فكافأهم الحق على قيامهم[4] الاجابة عن ندائهم بأحسن جواب وألطف خطاب واظهر عليهم من الآيات ما تعجب منه الرسل حين[5] قال : « لو أطلعت عليهم لوليت منهم فراراً » (18,XVIII).

1) B : + الصادق || 2) B : النفس || 3) B : + في || 4) B : فنائهم || 5) F : حتى ||

87, xv « ولقد آتيناك سبعاً من المثاني » . عن جعفر[1] في هذه الآية قال : اكرمناك وانزلنا اليك[2] وارسلناك والهمناك وهديناك وسلطناك ثم اكرمناك بسبع كرامات اولها الهدى والثاني النبوة والثالث الرحمة والرابع الشفقة والخامس المودة والالفـــة والسادس النعيم والسابع السكينة والقرآن العظيم وفيه اسم الله الاعظم .

12, xvi « وسخر لكم الليل والنهار والشمس والقمر » . قال جعفر الصادق رضي الله عنه :

سخر لك ما في السموات من الامطار وما في الارض من النبات وما في الليل والنهار من انواع الدواب وسخر لك الملائكة يسبحون لك وما في الارض من الانعام والبهايم[3] والفلك والخلق . سخر لك الكل لئلا يشغلك عنه شيء وتكون مسخرًا لمن سخر لك هذه الاشياء . فانه سخر لك كل شيء وسخر قلبك لمحبته ومعرفته وهو حظ العبد من ربه .

96, xvi « ما عندكم ينفد وما عند الله باق » . قال جعفر : ما عندكم ينفد يعني الافعال من الفرائض والنوافل وما عند الله باق من اوصافه ونعوته لان الحدث يفنى والقديم يبقى.

97, xvi « فلنحيينه حياة طيبة » . قال جعفر : الحياة الطيبة المعرفة بالله وصدق المقام مع الله وصدق الوقوف مع الله .

وقال جعفر : الحياة الطيبة ان يطيب له بان كل ذلك من الله واليه[4] .

125, xvi « ادع الى سبيل ربك بالحكمة والموعظة » . قال جعفر : الدعاء بالحكمة ان يدعوه من الله الى الله بالله والموعظة الحسنة ان يرى الخلق في أسر القدرة فيشكر من اصاب ويعذر من أبى .

127, xvi « واصبر وما صبرك الا بالله » . قال جعفر : امر الله أنبياءه بالصبر وجعل الحظ الاعلى منه للنبي صلعم حيث جعل امر صبره بالله لا بنفسه .

1, xvii قيل : جاء رجل الى جعفر بن محمد[5] فقال : صف لي المعراج ! فقال : كيف اصف لك مقاماً لم يسع فيه جبرئيل مع عظم محله !

1) B : قال جعفر || 2) B : + القرآن || 3) F : – من النبات... الارض || 4) B : – قال... واليه || 5) B : + الصادق ||

26, xiv « ومثل كلمة خبيثة كشجرة خبيثة » . قال جعفر : الشجرة الخبيثة الشهوات وارضها النفوس وماءها الامل واوراقها الكسل وثمارها المعاصي وغايتها النار .

32, xiv « وسخر لكم الفلك لتجري في البحر بأمره » . قال الصادق : سخر لكم السموات بالامطار والارض بالنبات والبحران[1] سبيلاً ومتجرًا وسخر لكم الشمس والقمر يدوران عليك ويوصلان اليك[2] منافع الثمار والزروع . وسخر قلب المؤمن لمحبته ومعرفته . وحظ الله من العباد القلوب لا غير لانه موضع نظره ومستودع امانته ومعرفة[3] اسراره .

35, xiv عن جعفر بن محمد[4] قال في قوله : « اجعل هذا البلد آمناً » يعني افئدة العارفين : اجعلهم امناء سرك وآمنين من قطيعتك .

35, xiv « واجنبني وبنيّ ان نعبد الاصنام » . قال جعفر : لا تردني الى مشاهدتي الخلة ولا ترد اولادي الى مشاهدة النبوة .

37, xiv قال جعفر : « اجعل افئدة من الناس تهوى اليهم » لان افئدتهم تهوى اليك .

52, xiv « هذا بلاغ للناس » . قال جعفر : موعظة للخلق وانذار لهم ليجتنبوا قرناء السوء ومجالسة المخالفين . فان القلوب اذا تعودت مجالسة الاضداد تنعكس وتنتكس[5] .

9, xv « انا نحن نزلنا الذكر وانا له لحافظون » . قال جعفر : « وانا له لحافظون » على من اردنا به خيرًا وذاهبون به عمن اردنا به شرًا .

28, xv « اني خالق بشرًا من صلصال » . قال جعفر : امتحنهم [الملائكة] ليحثهم على طلب الاستفهام فيزدادوا علماً بعجائب قدرته وتتلاشى عندهم نفوسهم .

42, xv « ان عبادي ليس لك عليهم سلطان » . عن جعفر الصادق في قوله « عباد الرحمان » (63,XXV) قال : جملة الخلق من جهة الخلقة لا من جهة المعرفة . و « عبادي » تخصيص في العبودية والمعرفة .

72, xv قال جعفر في قوله « لعمرك انهم لفي سكرتهم يعمهون » قال : بحياتك يا محمد ان الكل في سكرة الغفلة وحجاب البعد الا من كنتَ وسيلته ودليله الينا .

1) B : + تتخذوه || 2) B : عليكم... اليكم || 3) B : ومعدن || 4) B : جعفر الصادق || 5) B : وتتنكس ||

لتغيير اسرارهم ولا يغير عليهم احوالهم ولو وفقهم لتغيير الاسرار ومشاهدة البلوى لذلوا وافتقروا فنالوا به النجاة .

14, xiii « وما دعاء الكافرين الا في ضلال » . قال جعفر[1]: من دعا بنفسه فالى نفسه دعا وهو الكفر والضلال وذلك محل الخيانة والاسقاط من درجات اهل الامانة . فان الدواعي تختلف : داعٍ بالحق وداعٍ الى الحق وداعٍ الى طريق الحق . كل هولاء دعاة يدعون الخلق الى هذه الطرقَ لا بانفسهم . فهذه طرق الحق . وداعٍ يدعو بنفسه ،[2] فالى اي شيء دعا فهو ضلال .

27, xiii « ان الله يضل من يشاء ويهدي اليه من اناب » . قال جعفر : يضل عن ادراكه ووجوده من قصده بنفسه ويهدي اي يوصل الى حقايقه من طلبه به .

38, xiii « ولكل اجل كتاب » . قال جعفر الصادق : للروية وقت .

39, xiii عن جعفر بن محمد[3] في قوله « يمحو الله ما يشاء ويثبت » قال : يمحو الكفر ويثبت الايمان[4] ويمحو النكرة ويثبت المعرفة ويمحو الغفلة ويثبت الذكر ويمحو البغض ويثبت المحبة ويمحو الضعف ويثبت القوة ويمحو الجهل ويثبت العلم ويمحو الشك ويثبت اليقين ويمحو الهوى ويثبت العقل على هذا النسق . ودليله «كل يوم هو في شأن » (29.LV) محوًا واثباتاً .

39, xiii « وعنده ام الكتاب » . قال جعفر : الكتاب الذي قدر فيه الشقاوة والسعادة . فلا يزاد فيه ولا ينقص منه « وما يبدل القول لدي » (29,L) والاعمال اعلام . فمن قدر له بالسعادة ختم[5] له بالسعادة ومن قدر له بالشقاوة ختم له بها .

1, xiv «كتاب انزلناه اليك لتخرج الناس من الظلمات الى النور » . قال جعفر : عهد خصصت به فيه بيان هلاك[6] سالف الامم ونجاة امتك انزلناه اليك لتخرجهم به من ظلمات الكفر الى نور الايمان ومن ظلمات البدعة الى انوار السنة ومن ظلمات النفوس الى انوار القلوب .

---

1) B : قيل || 2) Y : لنفسه || 3) B : قال جعفر الصادق || 4) B : – يمحو ... الايمان || 5) B : حكم || 6) B : – هلاك ||

93, XII « اذهبوا بقميصي هذا » . عن جعفر[1] قال : كان المراد في[2] القميص أنه اتاه الهمّ[3] من قبل[4] القميص بقوله « وجاءوا على قميصه بدم كذب » (18,XII) فاحب ان يدخل السرور عليه من الجهة الذي[5] دخل الهم به عليه .

94, XII « قال ابوهم اني لا اجد ريح يوسف » . قال جعفر الصادق : يقول[6] ان ريح الصبا سأل الله تعالى فقال خصني بان ابشره بابنه . فاذن الله له في ذلك . وكان يعقوب ساجداً فرفع رأسه وقال « اني لا اجد ريح يوسف » . فقالت له اولاده « انك لفي ضلالك القديم » (95,XII) اي في محبتك القديمة . وكان[7] الريح ممزوجاً بالعناية والشفقة والرحمة والاخبار بزوال المحنة . وكذلك المومن المتحقق يجد ريح نسيم الايمان في قلبه وروح المعرفة من العناية التي سبقت له من الله في سره .

100, XII « وقد احسن بي اذ اخرجني من السجن » . قال جعفر الصادق : قال يوسف « احسن بي اذ اخرجني من السجن » ولم يقل اخرجني من الجب وهو اصعب . قال : لانه لم يرد مواجهة اخوته بانكم جفوتموني وألقيتموني في الجب بعد ان قال « لا تثريب عليكم اليوم » .

100, XII « ان ربي لطيف لما يشاء » . قال جعفر[8] الصادق : اوقف عباده تحت مشيئته ان شاء عذبهم وان شاء عفا عنهم وان شاء قربهم وان شاء بعدهم لتكون المشيئة والقدرة له لا لغيره ثم اظهر لطفه لعباده المخصوصين بالمحبة والمعرفة[9] والايمان وذلك قوله : « ان ربي لطيف لما يشاء » لعباده الذين سبقت لهم منه العناية والولاية .

111, XII « عبرة لاولي الالباب » . قال جعفر الصادق ؛ لاولي الاسرار مع الله .

9, XIII « الكبير المتعال » . قال جعفر : كبر في قلوب العارفين محله فصغر عندهم سواه وتعالى عن[10] ان يتقرب اليه الا بصرف كرمه .

11, XIII « ان الله لا يغيّر ما بقوم حتى يغيروا ما بانفسهم » . قال جعفر الصادق : لا يوفقهم

---

1) B : قال جعفر الصادق || 2) B : من || 3) Y : الحزن || 4) B : جهة || 5) YB : التي || 6) B : يقال || 7) Y : فكان || 8) Y : – جعفر || 9) Y : المغفرة || 10) YB : – عن ||

وقال جعفر : كان لله في يوسف سر مغطى عليهم ، مودع فيه حين اخرجوه من الجب فبيع بالثمن البخس . ولو شهدوا فيه ودايع اسرار الحق عنده لماتوا اجمعين في النظر[1] اليه ولم تطاوعهم[2] الالسنة بقولهم « هذا غلام » . فهو عندهم غلام وعند الحق علم من الاعلام .

30, XII « قد شغفها حبًّا » . قال جعفر : الشغاف مثل الغين[3] اظلم قلبه[4] عن التفكر في غيره والاشتغال بسواه .

30, XII « انا لنراها في ضلال مبين » . سئل جعفر بن محمد[5] عن العشق فقال : ضلال . ثم قرأ « انا لنراها في ضلال مبين » . قال : معناه في عشق ظاهر .

31, XII « فلما رأينه واكبرنه » . قال جعفر : سترت هيبة النبوة عليهن مواضع ارادتهن منه فاكبرنه .

67, XII « لا تدخلوا من باب واحد » . قال جعفر[6] : نسي يعقوب اعتماده على العصمة والقوة وان القضاء يغلب التدبير بقوله « لا تدخلوا من باب واحد » ثم استدرك عن قريب وساعده التوفيق فقال : « ما اغنى عنكم من الله من شيء » .

70, XII « ايتها العير انكم لسارقون » . قال جعفر : اضمر يوسف في امره مناديه اياهم بالسرقة ما كان منهم في قصته مع ابيهم : ان فعلكم الذي فعلتم مع ابيكم يشبه فعل السراق .

76, XII «كذلك كدنا ليوسف » . قال جعفر : اظهرنا عليه عامة بركات آبائه الصادقين بما عصمناه به في وقت الهمّ .

81, XII « ان ابنك سرق » . قال جعفر : معناه[7] ان ابنك ما[8] سرق وكيف يجوز هذه اللفظة على نبي بن نبي . وهذا من مشكلات القرآن وهو كقوله في قصة داود « خصمان بغى بعضنا على بعض » (22,XXXVIII) وما كانا خصمين وما بغيا .

92, XII « لا تثريب عليكم » . قال جعفر : لا عيب عليكم فيما عملتم لانكم كنتم مجبورين عليه وذلك في سابق القضاء عليكم .

---

1) B : حين نظروا || 2) B : ولما طاوعتهم || 3) B : الغيم || 4) B : قلبها ||
5) B : جعفر الصادق || 6) B : جعفر الصادق || 7) B : — معناه || 8) B : — ما ||

وقال ايضاً : عملت الدعوة في السراير فتحللت بها وركنت اليها[1] .

57, x « وشفاءٌ لما في الصدور » . قال جعفر : شفاء لما في الصدور اي راحة لما[2] في السراير .

وقال جعفر : لبعضهم شفاء المعرفة والصفاء ولبعضهم شفاء التسليم والرضا ولبعضهم شفاء التوبة والوفاء ولبعضهم شفاء المشاهدة واللقاء .

58, x « قل بفضل الله وبرحمته فبذلك فليفرحوا » . قال جعفر في هذه الآية : انه انتباه من غفلة او انقطاع عن ذلة والمباينة من دواعي الشهوات[3] .

وقال جعفر : فضل الله معرفته ورحمته توفيقه .

107, x « وان يمسسك الله بضرّ ... وان يردك بخير » . قال جعفر : جعل الله مسّ الضر منوطاً بصفتك وارادة الخير لك منوطاً بصفته ليكون رجاؤك اغاب من خوفك .

96, xi « ولقد ارسلنا موسى بآياتنا وسلطان مبين » . قال جعفر : الآيات هو[4] التواضع عند اولياء الله والسلطان التكبر على اعداء الله .

112, xi « فاستقم كما امرت » . قال جعفر الصادق : افتقر الى الله بصحة العزم[5] .

19, xii « قال يا بشرى هذا غلام وأسرّوه بضعةً » . قال جعفر : كان لله تعالى في يوسف سر فغطى عليهم موضع سره ولو كشف لهم عن حقيقة ما اودع فيه لماتوا . الا تراهم كيف قالوا « هذا غلام » ولو علموا اثار القدرة فيه لقالوا هذا نبي وصديق . ولما كشف للنسوة بعض الامر قلن « ما هذا بشراً ان هذا الا ملك كريم » (31,XII)

20, xii « وشروه بثمن بخس » . قال جعفر : باعوه بالبخس من الثمن لجهلهم بما اودع الله فيه من لطائف العلوم وبدايع الآيات .

وقال جعفر : انت تتعجب من بيع اخوة يوسف يوسف بالبخس من الثمن وما تفعله اعجب منه لانك تبيع حظك من الآخرة بشهوة نظرة او خطرة من الدنيا . وربما باع الرجل معرفته باخس ثمن وربما فاته حظه من ربه باقل القليل .

1) B : – قال... اليها || 2) B : – لما || 3) B : – قال... الشهوات || 4) Y : هي || 5) B : – قال... العزم ||

46, IX « ولكن كره الله انبعاثهم » . قال جعفر : طالب عباده بالحق ولم يجعلهم لذلك اهلاً ثم لم يعذرهم ولامهم على ذلك . الا تراه يقول : « وقالوا لا تنفردوا في الحرّ »[1] (81, IX).

« ولو ارادوا الخروج لاعدوا له عدة » . قال جعفر : لو عرفوا الله لاستحيوا منه ولخرجوا له عن انفسهم وارواحهم[2] واموالهم بدلاً من[3] واحد من اوامره .

91, IX « ما على المحسنين من سبيل » . قال جعفر : المحسن الذي يحسن اداب خدمة سيده .

100, IX « رضي الله عنهم ورضوا عنه » . قال جعفر : رضي الله عنهم بما كان[4] سبق لهم من الله[5] من عناية وتوفيق ورضوا عنه بما منّ عليهم بمتابعتهم لرسوله صلعم وقبول ما جاء به وانفاقهم الاموال وبذل المهج .

111, IX قال جعفر في قوله : « ان الله اشترى من المؤمنين انفسهم واموالهم » . قال : يكرمهم على لسان الحقيقة وعلى لسان المعاملة : اشترى منهم الأجساد لمواضع وقوع المحبة من قلوبهم فأحياهم بالوصلة .

116, IX « ان الله له ملك السموات والارض » . قال جعفر : الاكوان كلها له فلا يشغلنّك ما له عنه .

128, IX « لقد جاءكم رسول » : قال جعفر الصادق : علم الله عجز خلقه عن طاعته فعرفهم ذلك لكي يعلموا انهم لا ينالون الصفو[6] من خدمته فاقام بينه وبينهم مخلوقاً من جنسهم في الصورة فقال : « لقد جاءكم رسول من انفسكم عزيز عليه ما عندهم ... » فألبسه من نعته الرأفة والرحمة واخرجه الى الخلق سفيراً صادقاً وجعل طاعته طاعته وموافقته موافقته وقال : « من يطع الرسول فقد اطاع الله » (80, IV) .

13, X « لما ظلموا » . قال جعفر : لما قابلوا نعمنا بالكفران .

25, X « والله يدعو الى دار السلام » . قال جعفر : الدعوة عامة والهداية خاصة .

وقال ايضاً : ما طابت الجنة الا بالسلام وانما اختارك بهذه الخصائص لكي لا تختار عليه احداً .

1) B : – قال... الحر || 2) Y : وازواجهم || 3) Y : + أمر || 4) B : – كان || 5) B : – من الله || 6) Y : العفو ||

24, VIII « استجيبوا لله وللرسول » . قال جعفر : اجابوه الى الطاعة لتحيا بها قلوبكم[1] . « اذا دعاكم لما يحييكم » قال جعفر : الحياة هي الحياة بالله وهو المعرفة . كما قال الله تعالى : « فلنحيينه حياة طيبة » (97,XVI)[2] .

44, VIII « ليقضي الله امرًا كان مفعولا » . قال جعفر : ما قضاه في الازل يظهره في الحين بعد الحين والوقت بعد الوقت .

53, VIII « ذلك بان الله لم يكن مغيرًا نعمة... » . قال جعفر : ما دام العبد يعرف نعم الله عنده فان الله لا ينزع منه نعمة حتى اذا جهل النعمة ولم يشكر الله عليها اذ ذاك حريّ ان[3] ينزع منه .

67, VIII « تريدون عرض الدنيا والله يريد الآخرة » . قال جعفر : تريدون الدنيا والله يريد لكم الآخرة وما يريد الله لكم خير مما تريدونه لانفسكم .

69, VIII « فكلوا مما غنمتم حلالاً طيباً » . قال جعفر : الحلال ما لا يعصى الله فيه والطيب ما لا ينسى الله فيه .

25, IX « لقد نصركم الله في مواطن كثيرة » . قال جعفر : استجلاب النصر[4] في شيء واحد وهو الذلة والافتقار والعجز لقوله « لقد نصركم الله في مواطن كثيرة » لم تقوموا فيها بانفسكم ولم تشهدوا قوتكم وكثرتكم وعلمتم ان النصر لا يوجد بالقوة وان الله هو الناصر والمعين . ومتى علم العبد حقيقة ضعفه نصره الله . وحلول الخذلان بشيء واحد وهو العجب . قال الله « ويوم حنين اذ أعجبتكم كثرتكم فلم تغن عنكم شيئاً » . فلما عاينوا القوة من انفسهم دون الله رماهم الله بالهزيمة وضيق الارض عليهم . قال الله « ثم ولّيتم مدبرين » موكلين الى حولكم وقوتكم وكثرتكم .

37, IX سئل جعفر الصادق عن قوله « زين لهم سوء اعمالهم » قال : هو الرياء .

40, IX قال جعفر في قوله « وايده بجنود لم تروها » قال : ذلك جنود اليقين والثقة بالله والتوكل على الله .

---

1) B : – قال ... قلوبكم || 2) B : + وقال جعفر رضي الله عنه : حياة القلوب في المعاشرة وحياة الارواح في المحبة وحياة النفوس في المتابعة || 3) B : – اذ ... ان || 4) Y : النصرة ||

ولا قلب يصل اليه ولا عقل يعرفه . لان اصل المعرفة من الفطرة واصل المواصلة من المسافة واصل المشاهدة من المباينة .

143, VII قال جعفر في قوله « لن تراني ولكن انظر الى الجبل » : اشغله بالجبل ثم تجلى ولولا ما كان من اشغاله بالجبل لمات موسى صعقاً بلا افاقة[1] .

قال جعفر في قوله « سبحانك تبت اليك » قال : نزّه ربه واعترف اليه بالعجز وتبرأ من عقله . « تبت اليك » ، رجعت اليك من نفسي ولا اميل الى علمي . فالعلم ما علمتني والعقل ما اكرمتني به « وانا اول المومنين » انك لا ترى في الدنيا[2] .

157, VII « ويضع عنهم اصرهم والاغلال » . قال جعفر : اثقال الشرك وذل المخالفات وغلّ الاهمال[3] .

160, VII « فانبجست منه اثنتا عشرة عيناً » . عن جعفر بن محمد في هــذه الآية قال : انبجست من المعرفة اثنا عشر (sic) عينا يشرب كل اهل مرتبة في مقام من عين من تلك العيون على قدرها . **فاول** عين منها عين التوحيد . **والثاني** عين العبودية والسرور بها . **والثالث** عين الاخلاص . **والرابع** عين الصدق . **والخامس** عــين التواضع . **والسادس** عين الرضا والتفويض . **والسابع** عين السكينة والوقار . **والثامن** عين السخاء والثقة بالله . **والتاسع** عين اليقين . **والعاشر** عين العقل . **والحادي عشر** عين المحبة . **والثاني عشر** عين الانس والخلوة وهي عين المعرفة بنفسها ومنها تتفجر هذه العيون . فمن شرب من عين منها يجد حلاوتها ويطمع في العين التي هي ارفع منها[4] ، من عين الى عين حتى يصل الى الاصل . فاذا وصل الى الاصل تحقق[5] بالحق .

196, VII سئل جعفر عن الحكمة في قوله « وهو يتولى الصالحين » ونحن نعلم انه يتولى العالمين ، فقال : التولية على وجهين : تولية اقامة وابداء وتولية عناية ورعاية لاقامة الحق .

17, VIII « وليبلى المؤمنين منه بلاءً حسناً » . قال جعفر : ان يفنيهم عن نفوسهم . فاذا افناهم عن نفوسهم كان هو عوضاً لهم عن نفوسهم[6] .

---

1) B : – وقال... افاقة || 2) B : – قال... الدنيا || 3) Y : الانهماك || 4) B : + فلم يزل يشرب || 5) B : + هناك || 6) F : – فاذا ... نفوسهم ||

120, vii «والقى السحرة ساجدين». قال جعفر[1] : وجدوا نسيم رياح العناية القديمة بهم فالتجوا الى السجود شكرًا وقالوا «آمنا برب العالمين» (121, VII).

142, vii «وواعدنا موسى ثلاثين ليلة». قال جعفر : كان وعده ثلاثين ليلة فاليوم[2] على ميعاد ربه وانتهى الاجل لقدومه فاخرجه عن حده ورسمه واكرم موسى بكلامه وبان عليه شرفه خارجاً عن رسوم البشرية حتى سمع ما سمع من ربه من غير نفسهِ وعلمهِ وغيرِ وقته الذي وقّت لقومه دليلاً بذلك على ان منازل الربوبية خارج عن رسوم البشرية.

143, vii «ولما جاء موسى لميقاتنا وكلمه ربه». قال جعفر : الميقات طلب الروية[3].

وقال جعفر[4] : سمع كلاماً[5] خارجاً عن بشريته واضاف الكلام اليه وكلمه[4] من نفسية موسى وعبوديته فغاب موسى عن نفسه وفنى موسى عن صفاته[6] وكلمه ربه من حقائق معانيه فسمع موسى صفة موسى من ربه[7] ومحمد سمع من ربه صفة[8] ربه فكان احمد المحمودين عند ربه. ومن هنا كان مقام محمد صلعم سدرة[9] المنتهى ومقام موسى الطور. ومنذ كلّم الله[10] موسى على الطور افنى صفتها فلم يظهر فيها النبات ولا تمكين لاحد عليها[11].

143, vii «قال ربّ ارني انظر اليك». قال جعفر : انبسط الى ربه في معنى رويته لانه راى[12] خيال كلامه على قلبه. فبه[13] انبسط اليه. فقال له : «لن تراني» اي لا تقدر ان تراني لانك انت الفاني فكيف السبيل لفان الى باقٍ. «ولكن انظر الى الجبل». فقال[14] : وقع على الجبل علم الاطلاع فصارَ دكًّا متفرقاً، زال الجبل من ذكر اطلاع ربه وصعق موسى من روية تدكدك الجبل. فكيف له بروية ربه عياناً، معاينة روية الله لعبده والعبد فانٍ وروية العبد لربه والعبد بربه باقٍ.

وقال[15] : ثلاث من العبيد الى ربهم محال : التجلي والوصلة والمعرفة. فلا عين تراه

---

1) B : + رحمه الله || 2) B : فالتزم (؟) || 3) B : — قال ... الروية || 4) B : بعضهم || 5) YB : كلامه || 6) B : فلما كلم موسى غيب عن صفاته ونفسه || 7) B : + فكان من غير موسى || 8) B : صفات || 9) YB : — سدرة || 10) B : — الله || 11) B : ولا يمكن لاحد عليها المكث || 12) B : + في || 13) B : فيه || 14) B : — فقال || 15) Y : ثم قال ||

رضى حكمه[1] استراح وهُدي لسبيل رشده ومن سخطه فان حكمه ماض عليه[2] وله فيه السخط والهوان .

3, v « اليوم اكملت لكم دينكم » . قال جعفر بن محمد[3] : اليوم اشارة الى يوم بعث محمد رسول الله صلعم ويوم رسالته .

18, v « يغفر لمن يشاء ويعذب من يشاء » . قال جعفر : يغفر لمن يشاء فضلاً ويعذب من يشاء عدلاً .

35, v « وابتغوا اليه الوسيلة » . قال جعفر : اطلبوا منه القربة .

59, vi قال جعفر في قوله « وعنده مفاتح الغيب » قال : يفتح من القلوب الهداية ومن الهموم الرعاية ومن اللسان الرواية[4] ومن الجوارح السياسة والدلالة .

79, vi « اني وجهت وجهي » قال جعفر : يعني اسلمت قلبي للذي خلقه وانقطعت اليه من كل شاغل وشغل « للذي فطر السموات والارض » قال : الذي رفع السماء[5] بغير عمد واظهر فيها بدايع صنعه قادر على حفظ قلبي من الخواطر المذمومة والوساوس التي لا تليق بالحق .

122, vi قال جعفر في قوله « اومن كان ميتاً فاحييناه » قال: ميتاً عنّا فاحييناه بنا وجعلناه إماماً يهتدي بنوره الاجانب ويرجع اليه الضال « كمن مثله في الظلمات » كمن ترك مع شهوته وهواه فلم يؤيد بروايح القرب وموانسة الحضرة .

قال جعفر : « اومن كان ميتاً » بالاعتماد على الطاعات « فاحييناه » فجعلنا له نور التضرع والاعتذار[6] .

153, vi « وان هذا صراطي مستقيماً ». قال جعفر بن محمد[7] : طريق من القلب الى الله بالاعراض عما سواه .

31, vii « خذوا زينتكم عند كل مسجد » . قال جعفر[8] : أبعد اعضاءك من[9] ان تمس بها شيئاً بعد ان جعلها الله آلة تؤدي بها فرايض الله[10] .

1) B : بحكمه ‖ 2) B : – عليه ‖ 3) B : – بن محمد ‖ 4) B : الدراية ‖ 5) B : السموات ‖ 6) B : – قال ... والاعتذار ‖ 7) B : جعفر الصادق ‖ 8) B : + رحمه الله ‖ 9) B : عن ‖ 10) B : فرائضه ‖

عن طلب دني المنازل وسمت به الرفعة حتى يكون الحق نهايته « وان الى ربك المنتهى » (42,LIII) وسموّ همته مما خص به من الاختصاص من التعريف والالهام .

9, IV « فليتقوا الله وليقولوا قولاً سديداً » . قال جعفر بن محمد[1] : الصدق والتقوى يزيدان في الرزق ويوسعان[2] المعيشة .

59, IV « اطيعوا الله واطيعوا الرسول واولي الامر منكم » . قال جعفر الصادق : لا بد للعبد المؤمن من ثلاث سنن : سنّة الله وسنة الانبياء وسنة الاولياء . فسنة الله كتمان السر . قال الله : « عالم الغيب فلا يظهر على غيبه احداً » (26,LXXII) . وسنة الرسول صلعم مداراة الخلق وسنة الاوليا الوفاء بالعهد والصبر في البأساء والضراء .

64, IV « ولو انهم اذ ظلموا انفسهم جاءوك » . قال جعفر : من لم يجعل قصده الينا على سبيلك وسننك وهديك ضل الطريق واخطأ الرشد[3] .

80, IV « من يطع الرسول فقد اطاع الله » . قال جعفر بن محمد : من عرفك بالرسالة والنبوة فقد عرفني بالربوبية والالهية[4] .

125, IV عن جعفر بن محمد[5] في قوله « اتخذ الله ابراهيم خليلاً » قال : اظهر اسم الخلة لابراهيم لان الخليل ظاهر في المعنى واخفى اسم المحبة لمحمد صلعم لتمام حاله . اذ لا يحب الحبيب اظهار حال حبيبه بل يحب اخفاءه وستره لئلاّ يطلع عليه سواه ولا يدخل احد فيما بينهما . وقال لنبيّه وصفيّه محمد صلعم لما اظهر له حال المحبة « قل ان كنتم تحبون الله فاتبعوني » (31,III) اي ليس الطريق الى محبة الله الا باتباع حبيبه ولا يتوسل الى الحبيب بشيء احسن من مبايعة[6] حبيبة وطلب رضائه[7] .

1, V قال جعفر بن محمد في قوله « يا ايها الذين آمنوا » قال : فيه اربع خصال : نداء وكناية واشارة وشهادة : **يا** نداء **واي** خصوص نداء — **وها** كناية — **والذين** اشارة — **وآمنوا** شهادة .

1, V « ان الله يحكم ما يريد » . قال جعفر : حكم بما اراد وامضى ارادته ومشيئته . فمن

1) B : جعفر الصادق || 2) B : + في || 3) B : الرشيد || 4) B : — قال ... والالهية || 5) B : جعفر الصادق || 6) V : متابعة || 7) B : — ولا يتوسل... رضائه ||

وقال جعفر : لن يصلوا الى الحق حتى ينفصلوا عما دونه[1] .

97, III قال جعفر في قوله « من دخله كان آمناً » قال : من دخل الايمان قلبه كان آمناً من الكفر[2] .

101, III « ومن يعتصم بالله فقد هدي الى صراط مستقيم » . قال جعفر[3] في هذه الآية : من عرفه استغنى به عن جميع الانام .

102, III « اتقوا الله حق تقاته » . قال جعفر : التقوى ان لا ترى في قلبك شيئاً سواه .

110, III قال جعفر الصادق : « يأمرون بالمعروف » والمعروف هو موافقة الكتاب والسنّة[4] .

138, III « هذا بيان للناس » . قال جعفر : أظهر البيان للناس ولكن لا يتبينه الا من أيّد منه[5] بنور اليقين[6] وطهارة السرّ . الا تراه يقول : «وهدى وموعظة للمتقين » . ألا[7] ان الاهتداء بهدى البيان والاتعاظ به للمتقين الذين اتقوا كل شيء سواه .

150, III « بل الله مولاكم » . قال جعفر : متولي اموركم بدئاً وعاقبةً[8] .

159, III « فاذا عزمت فتوكل على الله » . قال جعفر : أمر باستقامة الظاهر مع الخلق وبتجريد باطنه للحق . الا تراه يقول : « فاذا عزمت... »

191, III « الذين يذكرون الله قياماً وقعوداً وعلى جنوبهم » . قال جعفر : يذكرون الله قياماً في مشاهدات الربوبية وقعوداً في اقامة الخدمة وعلى جنوبهم في روية الزلف[9] .

200, III « اصبروا وصابروا ورابطوا واتقوا الله لعلكم تفلحون » . قال جعفر : اصبروا عن المعاصي وصابروا على الطاعات ورابطوا الارواح بالمشاهدة واتقوا الله اي تجنبوا[10] الانبساط مع الحق « لعلكم تفلحون » ، تبلغون مواقف اهل الصدق فانه محل الفلاح.

1, IV قال جعفر في قوله « يا ايها الناس » اي كونوا من الناس الذين هم الناس ولا تغفلوا عن الله . فمن عرف انه من الانسان الذي خص خلقته بما خص به كبرت همته

---

1) B : لن ينالوا الحق حتى ينفصلوا عن الخلق || 2) B : — قال... الكفر || 3) B : ابو جعفر (؟) || 4) B : — قال... والسنة || 5) Y : — منه || 6) B : التوفيق || 7) B : اي || 8) B : — قال... وعاقبة || 9) B : الزلفى ؛ Y : الزلفة || 10) B : اجتنبوا ||

35, III « اني نذرت لك ما في بطني محررًا » قال جعفر : عتيقاً من رق الدنيا واهلها[1] . وقال جعفر : « محررًا » اي عبدًا لك خالصاً لا يستعبده شيء من الاكوان .

37, III « فتقبلها ربها » قال جعفر : تقبلها حتى يعجب الانبياء مع علو اقدارهم في عظم شأنها عند الله . الا ترى ان زكريا قال لها « انى لك هذا ؟ قالت هو من عند الله » اي من عند من تقبلني .

39, III « وسيدًا وحصورًا » . قال جعفر : السيد المباين عن الخلق وصفاً وحالاً وخلقاً .

61, III « فمن حاجّك فيه من بعد ما جاءك من العلم » . قال جعفر : هذه اشارة في اظهار المدعين لاهل الحقائق ليفتضحوا في دعاويهم عند اظهار اثار انوار التحقيق وبطلان ظلمات الدعاوي الكاذبة .

68, III « ان اولى الناس بابراهيم لـلّـذين اتبعوه وهذا النبي » . قال جعفر : لـلّـذين اتبعوه في شرايعهم ومناسكهم « وهذا النبي » لقرب حال ابراهيم من حال النبي صلى الله عليهما وشريعته من شريعته دون ساير الانبياء وساير الشرايع ، « والذين آمنوا » لقرب حالهم من حال ابراهيم . « والله ولي المومنين » في تشريفهم[2] الى بلوغ مقام الخليل عليه السلام اذ[3] القرب منه من[4] درجة المحبة بقوله : « ويحبهم ويحبونه » (54, V) .

76, III « بلى من اوفى بعهده واتقى فان الله يحب المتقين » . قال جعفر : من أوفى بالعهد الجاري عليه في الميثاق الاول « واتقى» وطهر ذلك العهد وذلك الميثاق من تدنسه بباطل . والوفاء بالعهد الكون[5] معه بقطع ما سواه . لذلك قال النبي صلعم : « اصدق كلمة تكلم بها العرب قول لبيد : الا كل شيء ما خلا الله باطل » . ومن وفى بالعهد سمي محباً[6] والله يحب المتقين .

79, III قال جعفر « كونوا ربانيين » قال : مستمعين بسمع القلوب ناظرين باعين الغيوب .

92, III قال جعفر : بانفاق المهج يصل العبد[7] الى بر حبيبه وقرب مولاه . قال الله : « لن تنالوا البر حتى تنفقوا مما تحبون » .

---

1) B : — قال جعفر ... واهلها ‖ 2) B : تشريكهم ‖ 3) Y : او ‖ 4) YB : في ‖ 5) Y : ان يكون ‖ 6) Y : متقياً ‖ 7) B : المحب ‖

توكلوا على الله في جميع امورهم ونبذوا تدابيرهم وراء ظهورهم واعرضوا عنها وهم الفقراء الصبّر الراضون .

222, II « ان الله يحب التوابين » . قال جعفر : يحب التوابين من سوالاتهم ويحب « المتطهرين » من اراداتهم .

284, II قال جعفر : « لله ما في السماوات وما في الارض » : من اشتغل بهما قطعاه عن الله عز وجل، ومن اقبل على الله وتركهما ملكهما الله اياه .

= « وان تبدوا ما في انفسكم » . قال جعفر : الاسلام . « او تخفوه » الايمان .

1, III « الم » . قال جعفر : الحروف المقطوعة[1] في القرآن اشارات الى الوحدانية والفردانية والديمومية وقيام الحق بنفسه بالاستغناء عما سواه .

5, III قال جعفر في قوله « ان الله لا يخفى عليه شيء » قال : لا يطلعنّ عليك فيرى في قلبك سواه فيمقتك .

18, III قال جعفر[2] في قوله « شهد الله » قال : شهد الله بوحدانيته واحديته وصمديته « وشهد الملائكة واولو العلم » له بتصديق ما شهد هو لنفسه .

وسُئل جعفر[3] عن حقيقة هذه الشهادة ما هي فقال : هي مبنية على اربعة اركان . اولها اتباع الامر والثاني اجتناب النهي والثالث القناعة والرابع الرضا .

19, III قال جعفر[4] « ان الدين عند الله الاسلام » قال : هو ما سلم عليه صاحبه من وساوس الشيطان وهواجس النفس وعذاب الآخرة .

28, III قال جعفر : « ويحذركم الله نفسه » ان تشهد لنفسك بالصلاح لان من كانت له سابقة ظهرت سابقته في خاتمته[5] .

31, III قال جعفر في قوله « قل ان كنتم تحبون الله فاتبعوني » قال : قيّد اسرار الصديقين بمتابعة محمد صلعم لكي يعلموا انهم وان علت احوالهم وارتفعت مراتبهم لا يقدرون مجاوزته ولا اللحوق به .

1) YB : المقطعة || 2) B : + الصادق || 3) B : الشبلي || 4) B : + الصادق || 5) B : – قال جعفر ... خاتمته ||

7, I قال جعفر : « آمين » اي قاصدين نحوك وانت اكرم من ان تخيب قاصداً[1] .

32, II « سبحانك لا علم لنا » . قال جعفر[2] : لما باهوا باعمالهم وتسبيحهم وتقديسهم ضربهم كلهم بالجهل حتى قالوا « لا علم لنا » .

125, II « واذ جعلنا البيت مثابة للناس » . عن جعفر بن محمد[3] قال : البيت هاهنا محمد . فمن آمن به وصدق برسالته دخل في ميادين الامن والامان « مقام ابراهيم » مقام القبلة . جعل قلبك مقام المعرفة ولسانك مقام الشهادة وبدنك مقام الطاعة . فمن حفظها فانه مستجاب الدعاء البتة[4] .

128, II « ربنا واجعلنا مسلمين لك » . قال جعفر : اجعلنا مسلمين لك اي احفظني واهل بيتي كي نسلم انفسنا وقلوبنا اليك ولا نختار الا ما اخترته لنا . وقال ايضاً[5] : اجعلنا مقيمين معك لك .

158, II « ان الصفا والمروة من شعائر الله » : عن جعفر بن محمد[6] قال : الصفا[7] الروح لصفايها عن درن المخالفات ، والمروة النفس لاستعمالها المروة في القيام بخدمة سيدها . وقال : الصفا صفاء[8] المعرفة والمروة مروة العارف .

201, II « ربنا آتنا في الدنيا حسنة » . قال جعفر[9] : صحبة الصالحين .

210, II « هل ينظرون الا ان يأتيهم الله في ظلل من الغمام » . قال جعفر : هل ينظرون الا اقبال الله عليهم بالعصمة والتوفيق فيكشف عنهم أستار الغفلة فيشهدون برّه ولطفه بل يشهدون البار اللطيف .

210, II « وقضي الامر » . قال جعفر[10] : وقضي الامر[11] وكشف عن حقيقة الامر ومغيبه .

212, II « زين للذين كفروا الحياة الدنيا » . قال جعفر : زين للذين جحدوا التوكلَ زينة الحياة الدنيا حتى جمعوها وافتخروا بها « ويسخرون من الذين آمنوا » اي من الذين

1) Y : قاصدك || 2) B : + الصادق || 3) E : عن الرضا... عن جده ؛ Y : – بن محمد || 4) YB : – مقام ابراهيم... البتة || 5) Y : بعضهم || 6) Y : سمعت منصورا يقول سمعت ابا القسم يقول سمعت ابا جعفر عن علي بن موسى الرضا عن ابيه عن جعفر || 7) B : + عبارة عن || 8) Y : – صفاء || 9) B : + الصادق || 10) B : + الصادق || 11) B : + اي ||

1,1 عن الرضا عن ابيه عن جده[1] في قوله « الرحمن الرحيم » قال : هو واقع على المريدين والمرادين . فاسم الرحمن للمرادين لاستغراقهم في الانوار والحقــائق والرحيم للمريدين لبقائهم مع انفسهم واشتغالهم باصلاح الظواهر . والرحمن المنتهي بكرامته الى ما لا غاية له لانه قد اوصل الرحمة بالازل وهو غاية الكرامة ومنتهاه بدءٌ وعاقبة . والرحيم وصل رحمته بالياء والميم وهو ما يتصل به من رحمة الدنيا والعوافي والارزاق[2] .

2,1 ذكر عن جعفر الصادق في قوله « الحمد لله » قال : من حمده[3] بصفاته كما وصف نفسه فقد حمده . لان الحمد حاء وميم ودال . فالحاء من الوحدانية والميم من الملك والدال من الديمومية . فمن عرفه بالوحدانية والديمومية والملك فقد عرفه .

2,1 سئل جعفر بن محمد[4] عن قوله « الحمد لله رب العالمين » قال : معناه الشكر لله وهو المنعم بجميع نعمائه[5] على خلقه وحسن صنعه[6] وجميل بلائه[7] . وألف[8] الحمد من آلائه وهو الواحد . فبآلائه انقذ اهل معرفته من سخطه وسوء قضائه . واللام من لطفه وهو الواحد . فبلطفه اذاقهم حلاوة عطفه وسقاهم كأس برّه[9] . والحاء فمن حمده وهو السابق بحمد نفسه قبل خلقه . فبسابق حمده استقرت النعم على خلقه وقدروا على حمده . والميم فمن مجده . فبجلال مجده زينهم بنور قدسه . والدال من دينه الاسلام . فهو السلام ودينه الاسلام[10] وداره السلام وتحيتهم فيها سلام لاهل الاسلام في دار السلام .

3,1 عن جعفر بن محمد الصادق[11] قال : «الرحمن» الذي يرزق الخلائق[12] ظاهرًا وباطناً . فرزق الظاهر الاقوات من المأكولات والمشروبات والعوافي ورزق[13] الباطن العقل والمعرفة والفهم وما ركب فيه من انواع البدائع كالسمع والبصر والشم والذوق واللمس والظن[14] والهمة .

7,1 وقال جعفر بن محمد[15] : « صراط الذين انعمت عليهم » بالعلم بك والفهم عنك .

---

1) Y : سمعت منصورا باسناده عن جعفر || 2) B : — عن الرضا... والارزاق || 3) Y : + بجميع || 4) B : جعفر الصادق || 5) B : نعماه || 6) YB : صنيعه || 7) B : آلائه || 8) Y : فألف || 9) F : سره || 10) B : — ودينه الاسلام || 11) Y : — بن محمد الصادق || 12) YB : الخلق || 13) Y : — ورزق || 14) B : والنطق || 15) B : + الصادق ||

«ولم يشتغل احد منهم بجمع فهم خطابه على لسان اهل الحقيقة الا آيات متفرقة نُسبت الى ابي العباس بن عطاء وآيات ذكر انها عن جعفر بن محمد الصادق رضي الله عنهما عــلى غير ترتيب»

حقائق التفسير للسلمي

1,1 **مقدمة :** حكي عن جعفر بن محمد[1] انه قال : كتاب الله على اربعة اشياء : العبارة والاشارة واللطائف والحقائق . فالعبارة للعوام والاشارة للخواص واللطائف للاولياء والحقائق للانبياء .

1,1 « بسم » . عن جعفر بن محمد[2] قال : الباء بقاؤه والسين اسماؤه والميم ملكه . فايمان المؤمن ذكره ببقائه وخدمة المريد ذكره باسمائه والعارف فناؤه عن المملكة بالمالك لها[3] .

1,1 وقال ايضاً[4] : «بسم» ثلاثة احرف : باء وسين وميم . فالباء باب[5] النبوة والسين سرّ النبوة الذي أسر النبي به الى خواص أمته[6] والميم مملكة الدين الذي يعم الابيض والاسود[7] .

1,1 عن جعفر بن محمد انه سئل عن « بسم الله الرحمن الرحيم » قال : الباء بهاء الله والسين سناؤه والميم مجده . والله إله كل شيء ، الرحمن لجميع خلقه ، الرحيم بالمؤمنين خاصة[8] . عن جعفر[9] انه قال في قوله[10] « الله » : انه اسم تام لانه اربعة احرف : الالف وهو عمود التوحيد واللام الاول لوح الفهم واللام الثاني لوح النبوة والهاء النهاية في الاشارة . والله هو الاسم الفرد[11] المتفرد لا يضاف الى شيء بل تضاف الاشياء كلها اليه وتفسيره المعبود الذي[12] أله الخلق منزه[13] عن كل[14] درك مائيته[15] والاحاطة بكيفيته وهو المستور عن الابصار والاوهام[16] والمحتجب بجلاله عن الادراك .

1) B : عن جعفر الصادق || 2) B : عن علي بن موسى الرضا عن ابيه عن جده || 3) B: له || 4) B : – وقال ايضاً (فبسم) || 5) B : باء || 6) B : لخواصه || 7) B : والميم مملكته الذي يعم ؛ Y : الذي انعم به للابيض والاسود || 8) YB : – عن جعفر... خاصة || 9) B : عن علي... عن جده || 10) B : اسمه || 11) YB : – الفرد || 12) Y : + هو || 13) F : – منزه || 14) YB : – كل || 15) B : ماهيته || 16) Y : والافهام ||

Publisher's note

The following is Paul Nwyia's edited text, as it appears in "Le Tafsīr mystique attibué à Ǧaʿfar Ṣādiq," *Mélanges de l'Universitié Saint-Joseph* 43, 1967 (printed erronously in 1968): 181–230. Note that the Arabic text placed at the end of the book has been arranged to read from right to left and thus ends where the English text ends (at page 225). The publisher wishes to acknowledge Professor Gerhard Böwering of the Department of Religious Studies at Yale University for his kind help in facilitating our acquisition of a clear copy of Nwyia's edition. Also thanks are due to Fr. Salah Aboujaoudé, s.j. of the Centre de recherches et de publications pour l'Orient chrétien at Université Saint-Joseph de Beyrouth, Lebanon, who was kind enough to scan and email these pages.

كلمة الناشر:

هذا النص الكامل لنشرة الاب بولس نويه للتفسير المنسوب لجعفر الصادق ﷺ وقد أُعيد ترتيب صفحات النشرة ليسهل على القاري العربي متابعة النص مع الشكر الخالص لكل من الأبوين چيرهارد بوورينغ وصالح أبو جوده الذين جادو علينا بهذه الصفحات. ونود ان نشير هنا ان هذا جزء من "المتن" المنسوب لجعفر الصادق ﷺ المنقول من حقائق التفسير لمحمد بن الحسين السُلَمي المتوفي عام ٤١٢/١٠٢١.

طبع في مطباع الفريزنس في كنده في نهايه عام ٢٠١١ للميلاد

تفسير جعفر الصادق

حققه

الأب بولس نويا

نقلاً عن "حقائق التفسير" للسلمي